Entity Framework 4.1: Expert's Cookbook

More than 40 recipes for successfully mixing Test Driven Development, Architecture, and Entity Framework Code First

Devlin Liles

Tim Rayburn

BIRMINGHAM - MUMBAI

Entity Framework 4.1: Expert's Cookbook

Copyright © 2012 Packt Publishing

All rights reserved. No part of this book may be reproduced, stored in a retrieval system, or transmitted in any form or by any means, without the prior written permission of the publisher, except in the case of brief quotations embedded in critical articles or reviews.

Every effort has been made in the preparation of this book to ensure the accuracy of the information presented. However, the information contained in this book is sold without warranty, either express or implied. Neither the authors, nor Packt Publishing, and its dealers and distributors will be held liable for any damages caused or alleged to be caused directly or indirectly by this book.

Packt Publishing has endeavored to provide trademark information about all of the companies and products mentioned in this book by the appropriate use of capitals. However, Packt Publishing cannot guarantee the accuracy of this information.

First published: March 2012

Production Reference: 1190312

Published by Packt Publishing Ltd.
Livery Place
35 Livery Street
Birmingham B3 2PB, UK.

ISBN 978-1-84968-446-0

www.packtpub.com

Cover Image by David Gimenez (bilbaorocker@yahoo.co.uk)

Credits

Authors
Devlin Liles
Tim Rayburn

Reviewers
Chandana N. Athauda
Alexandre Brisebois
Jiri Cincura
Barry Forrest
Hajan Selmani
Rob Vettor

Acquisition Editor
Dhwani Devater

Lead Technical Editor
Dayan Hyames

Technical Editors
Ameya Sawant
Lubna Shaikh
Mehreen Shaikh

Project Coordinator
Alka Nayak

Proofreader
Joel Johnson

Copy Editor
Brandt D'Mello

Indexers
Hemangini Bari
Tejal Daruwale

Production Coordinator
Shantanu Zagade

Cover Work
Shantanu Zagade

About the Authors

Devlin Liles is a Principal Consultant at Improving Enterprises and a Data Platform Development MVP. Devlin has been writing software since he first crashed a DOS box back in 1989, and still loves pushing the envelope. Devlin has worked on all sizes of projects from enterprise-wide inventory systems, to single install scheduling applications. He is a regular national presenter at user groups, conferences, and corporate events, speaking on data access practices, techniques, and architecture. He is an active community leader, and helps put on several conferences in Dallas and Houston. Devlin works for Improving Enterprises, a Dallas-based company that has been awesome enough to support him in chasing his dreams, and writing awesome code.

> I would like to thank my loving wife and best friend, Christina, without whom this book would not have happened, and Tim Rayburn—a better friend, mentor, and a geek there never was.

Tim Rayburn is a Principal Consultant with Improving Enterprises, and a Microsoft MVP for Connected Systems Development. He has worked with Microsoft technologies for over 13 years, is the organizer of the Dallas TechFest, the Founder of the Dallas/Fort Worth Connected Systems User Group, and a blogger at `TimRayburn.net`. When he is not pursuing the ever moving technology curve, he is an avid gamer, from consoles to table-top RPGs, and is the host of a podcast called Radio Free Hommlet. He welcomes questions about any of the above to `tim@timrayburn.net`.

About the Reviewers

Chandana N. Athauda (Windows Azure MVP) is currently employed at BAG (Brunei Accenture Group) Networks, Brunei and has been working professionally in the IT industry for more than 11 years. His roles in the IT industry have spanned the entire spectrum from programmer to technical consultant and management. Technology has always been a passion for him and in his spare time, Chandana enjoys watching association football.

If you would like to talk to Chandana about the book or the Microsoft development platform, feel free to write to him at info@inzeek.net or by giving him a tweet @inzeek.

Alexandre Brisebois has been exploring .Net since 2002. A strong believer in clean code and best practices, his passion for new technologies has driven him to work for companies like Pratt & Whitney Canada, Air France, and CGI. After two years in Paris as a .Net consultant, he is now part of RunAtServer working with the latest Microsoft technologies.

RunAtServer (www.runatserver.com) is a team of highly qualified, certified experts specialized in web, touch, and mobile applications using Microsoft technologies.

Jiří Činčura is a long time .NET developer and database enthusiast. He is focused mainly on language features and language designs, multithreading/parallel applications, and databases (programming as well as creating/designing). He also works as a consultant around these topics and he's a speaker at various conferences. He is a developer for ADO.NET, and a data provider for Firebird and his own product ID3 renamer. You can contact him via his company x2develop.com (http://www.x2develop.com) or via his blog http://blog.cincura.net.

Barry Forrest had his first exposure to computers in a lab on campus at Dartmouth College, while visiting relatives, in the early '80s. That was followed by an introduction to BASIC on a TRS-80. He began programming professionally with Perot Systems in 2000 and has worked with Microsoft technologies ever since. In 2010, Barry had an agile awakening and started consulting for Improving Enterprises.

Hajan Selmani is Microsoft MVP in ASP.NET/IIS, MCP, Microsoft community contributor, MKDOT.NET web user group leader, DZone MVB (Most Valuable Blogger), and Microsoft technologies expert and enthusiast. He is a regular speaker in Microsoft technology events such as MS TechDays, MS Vizija, Code Camps, local group events, and many other similar events. Hajan works as a Senior Software Engineer / Team Lead at Seavus Group. He holds an MSc degree in Computer Sciences, Intelligent Systems from SEE University. He has also reviewed the Packt title *ASP.NET jQuery Cookbook*.

www.PacktPub.com

Support files, eBooks, discount offers and more

You might want to visit www.PacktPub.com for support files and downloads related to your book.

Did you know that Packt offers eBook versions of every book published, with PDF and ePub files available? You can upgrade to the eBook version at www.PacktPub.com and as a print book customer, you are entitled to a discount on the eBook copy. Get in touch with us at service@packtpub.com for more details.

At www.PacktPub.com, you can also read a collection of free technical articles, sign up for a range of free newsletters and receive exclusive discounts and offers on Packt books and eBooks.

http://PacktLib.PacktPub.com

Do you need instant solutions to your IT questions? PacktLib is Packt's online digital book library. Here, you can access, read and search across Packt's entire library of books.

Why Subscribe?

- Fully searchable across every book published by Packt
- Copy and paste, print and bookmark content
- On demand and accessible via web browser

Free Access for Packt account holders

If you have an account with Packt at www.PacktPub.com, you can use this to access PacktLib today and view nine entirely free books. Simply use your login credentials for immediate access.

Instant Updates on New Packt Books

Get notified! Find out when new books are published by following @PacktEnterprise on Twitter, or the *Packt Enterprise* Facebook page.

I would like to dedicate this book to my amazing wife, Kate, who is always there to support me in all of my efforts and to my father, Ray Rayburn, who fostered my love for computers from the first time he sat with me in front of a TSR-80 Model 1.

Table of Contents

Preface — 1

Chapter 1: Improving Entity Framework in the Real World — 5
- Introduction — 5
- Improving Entity Framework by using code first — 7
- Creating mock database connections — 11
- Implementing the repository pattern — 14
- Implementing the unit of work pattern — 19
- Testing queries — 28
- Creating databases from code — 33
- Testing queries for performance — 37
- Performing load testing against a database — 40

Chapter 2: Understanding the Fluent Configuration API — 45
- Introduction — 46
- Improving property maps — 46
- Creating one-to-one maps — 52
- Creating one-to-many maps — 58
- Creating many-to-many maps — 64
- Mapping one table to many objects — 71
- Mapping many tables to one object — 76
- Handling inheritance based on database values — 81
- Handling complex key maps — 87

Chapter 3: Handling Validation in Entity Framework — 93
- Introduction — 93
- Validating simple properties — 94
- Validating complex properties — 102
- Validating collection properties — 109
- Creating custom property validation — 116
- Improving MVC UI with entity framework validation — 123

Table of Contents

Chapter 4: Working with Transactions and Stored Procedures — 133
- Introduction — 133
- Using transaction scopes — 134
- Handling multiple context transactions — 142
- Executing stored procedures — 148
- Retrieving entities with stored procedures — 154
- Updating entities with stored procedures — 160

Chapter 5: Improving Entity Framework with Query Libraries — 169
- Introduction — 169
- Creating reusable queries — 170
- Improving entity and library reuse — 175
- Implementing composed queries — 183
- Increasing performance with code access — 191
- Improving query testing — 198

Chapter 6: Improving Complex Query Scenarios — 203
- Introduction — 203
- Grouping at runtime without Lambda — 220
- Handling explicit loading — 227
- Improving complex where clauses — 233
- Implementing the specification pattern — 242

Chapter 7: Using Concurrent and Parallel Processing — 255
- Introduction — 255
- Implementing optimistic concurrency — 256
- Managing parallel contexts — 262
- Handling data retrieval in highly-threaded environments — 268
- Attaching objects with unit of work — 276
- Improving multiple context performance — 284

Chapter 8: Improving Entity Framework with Complex Business Scenarios — 295
- Introduction — 295
- Handling soft delete — 296
- Implementing refreshing data on save — 303
- Capturing the audit data — 308
- Improving MVC 3 applications — 314

Index — 331

Preface

In this book, we attempt to bring together the best practices around using Entity Framework in a test-first manner, focusing on the architectural separation of concerns, and testability at all times. Throughout the book, we focus on ways to ensure the best quality of performance from your data layer, providing you with measurable ways to test performance, to reviewing SQL statements generated by Entity Framework.

What this book covers

Chapter 1, Improving Entity Framework in the Real World, describes how to use code first, establish repository and unit of work patterns, and test your queries.

Chapter 2, Understanding Fluent Configuration API, goes into detail on how to manage configuration mappings between your entities and your database.

Chapter 3, Handling Validation in Entity Framework, discusses validation from the simple to the complex, and how to integrate that with an ASP.NET MVC user interface.

Chapter 4, Working with Transactions and Stored Procedures, provides best practices around using Stored Procedures in your environment while maintaining separation of concerns between the database and Entity Framework.

Chapter 5, Improving Entity Framework with Query Libraries, begins the ground work of separating your queries in a testable, composable manner.

Chapter 6, Improving Complex Queries Scenarios, opens by discussing dynamic sorting and grouping and closes with a complete Specification pattern implementation.

Chapter 7, Using Concurrent and Parallel Processing, describes the challenges faced in highly concurrent applications, and when managing multiple database contexts.

Chapter 8, Improving Entity Framework with Complex Business Scenarios, discusses some of the more difficult business requests, such as handling soft deletes, capturing audit data, and refreshing entities from the database on save.

Preface

What you need for this book

In order to use this book you will need access to Visual Studio 2010, Express Edition or above. There are a small number of recipes that discuss load testing, which require the Ultimate Edition, but those are specifically called out in those recipes.

Who this book is for

This book is intended for professional software developers who advocate, or are interested in, test driven development and Entity Framework. It assumes basic knowledge of a test runner, in this case MS Test, the integrated test runner of Visual Studio 2010.

Conventions

In this book, you will find a number of styles of text that distinguish between different kinds of information. Here are some examples of these styles, and an explanation of their meaning.

Code words in text are shown as follows: "We can include other contexts through the use of the `include` directive."

A block of code is set as follows:

```
{
  [TestClass]
  public class QueryTests
  {

    [TestMethod]
    public void ShouldReturnRecordsFromTheDatabase()
    {
      //Arrange
      var init = new Initializer();
      var context = new
        BlogContext(Settings.Default.BlogConnection);
      init.InitializeDatabase(context);
      IBlogRepository repo = new BlogRepository(context);


      //Act
      var items = repo.Set<Blog>().FilterByBlogName("Test");

      //Assert
      Assert.AreEqual(2, items.Count());
    }
  }
```

When we wish to draw your attention to a particular part of a code block, the relevant lines or items are set in bold:

```
{
  public class Blog
  {
    public int Id { get; set; }
    public DateTime Creationdate { get; set; }
    public string ShortDescription { get; set; }
    public string Title { get; set; }
    public double Rating { get; set; }
  }
}
```

New terms and **important words** are shown in bold. Words that you see on the screen, in menus or dialog boxes for example, appear in the text like this: "Open the **Improving Collection Property Validation** solution in the included source code examples."

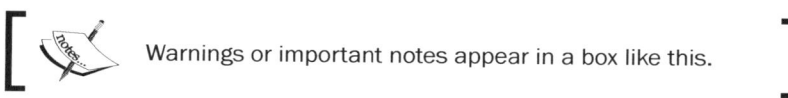
Warnings or important notes appear in a box like this.

Tips and tricks appear like this.

Reader feedback

Feedback from our readers is always welcome. Let us know what you think about this book—what you liked or may have disliked. Reader feedback is important for us to develop titles that you really get the most out of.

To send us general feedback, simply send an e-mail to feedback@packtpub.com, and mention the book title through the subject of your message.

If there is a topic that you have expertise in and you are interested in either writing or contributing to a book, see our author guide on www.packtpub.com/authors.

Customer support

Now that you are the proud owner of a Packt book, we have a number of things to help you to get the most from your purchase.

Downloading the example code

You can download the example code files for all Packt books you have purchased from your account at http://www.packtpub.com. If you purchased this book elsewhere, you can visit http://www.packtpub.com/support and register to have the files e-mailed directly to you.

Errata

Although we have taken every care to ensure the accuracy of our content, mistakes do happen. If you find a mistake in one of our books—maybe a mistake in the text or the code—we would be grateful if you would report this to us. By doing so, you can save other readers from frustration and help us improve subsequent versions of this book. If you find any errata, please report them by visiting http://www.packtpub.com/support, selecting your book, clicking on the **errata submission form** link, and entering the details of your errata. Once your errata are verified, your submission will be accepted and the errata will be uploaded to our website, or added to any list of existing errata, under the Errata section of that title.

Piracy

Piracy of copyright material on the Internet is an ongoing problem across all media. At Packt, we take the protection of our copyright and licenses very seriously. If you come across any illegal copies of our works, in any form, on the Internet, please provide us with the location address or website name immediately so that we can pursue a remedy.

Please contact us at copyright@packtpub.com with a link to the suspected pirated material.

We appreciate your help in protecting our authors, and our ability to bring you valuable content.

Questions

You can contact us at questions@packtpub.com if you are having a problem with any aspect of the book, and we will do our best to address it.

1
Improving Entity Framework in the Real World

In this chapter, we will cover the following topics:

- Improving the Entity Framework by using code first
- Creating mock database connections
- Implementing the repository pattern
- Implementing the unit of work pattern
- Testing queries
- Creating databases from code
- Testing queries for performance
- Performing load testing against a database

Introduction

If we were to buy the materials to build a house, would we buy the bare minimum to get four walls up and a roof, without a kitchen or a bathroom? Or would we buy enough material to build the house with multiple bedrooms, a kitchen, and multiple bathrooms? The problem lies in how we define "bare minimum". The progression of software development has made us realize that there are ways of building software that do not require additional effort, but reap serious rewards. This is the same choice we are faced with when we decide the approach to take with Entity Framework. We could just get it running, and it would work most of the time.

Customizing and adding to it later would be difficult, but doable. There are few things that we would need to give up for this approach. The most important among those is control over how code is written. We have already seen that applications grow, mature, and have features added. The only thing that stays constant is the fact that at some point of time, we will come to push the envelope of almost any tool in some way that we leverage to help us. The other side is that we could go into development, being aware of the value added benefits that cost nothing, and with that knowledge, avoid dealing with unnecessary constraints.

When working with Entity Framework, there are many paths and options presented to us. We can approach the business problem by thinking of the database-first approach, modelling our domain-first approach, or by writing our **POCOs** (**Plain Old CLR Objects**) first. While modelling the domain-first approach, we are not concerned with the implementation of classes, but merely the structure of interactions. In contrast, in POCO or code first, we write the implementation as a way to communicate that design. All of these approaches will solve the problem with varying degrees of code and flexibility. When we are connecting to a database and working with data, there are a couple of areas where the code is almost the same. No matter what our implementation is, these pieces will not change much. However, it can affect their flexibility.

Starting with a database-first approach in Entity Framework means we have an existing database schema and are going to let the schema, along with metadata in the database, determine the structure of our business objects and domain model. The **database-first** approach is normally how most of us start out with Entity Framework, but the tendency is to move towards more flexible solutions as we gain proficiency with the framework. This will drastically reduce the amount of code that we need to write, but will also limit us to working within the structure of the generated code. Business objects, which are generated by default here, are not usable with WCF services and have database logic in them that makes them poor candidates for usage throughout the application. This is not necessarily a bad thing if we have a well-built database schema and a domain model that contains simple structures which will translate well into objects. Such a domain and database combination is a rare exception in the world of code production. Due to the lack of flexibility and the restrictions on the way these objects are used, this solution is viewed as a short-term or small-project solution.

Modelling the domain first allows us to fully visualize the structure of the data in the application, and work in a more object-oriented manner while developing our application. This lends itself to the architect and solution lead developers as a way to define and control the schema which will be used. However, this approach is rarely used due to a lack of adoption, and that it has the same constraints as the generated database-first approach. The main reasons for the lack of adoption have been the lack of support for round trip updates, and the lack of documentation on manipulating the model as to produce the proper database structure. The database is created each time from the data model causing data loss when structural changes are made.

Coding the objects first allows us to work entirely in an object-oriented direction, and not worry about the structuring of the database, without the restrictions that the model-first designer imposes. This abstraction gives us the ability to craft a more logically sound application that focuses on the behavior of the application rather than the data generated by it. The objects that we produce which are capable of being serialized over any service, have "true persistence ignorance", and can be shared as contract objects as they are not specific to the database implementation. This approach is also much more flexible as it is entirely dependent on the code that we write. This allows us to translate our objects into database records without modifying the structure of our application.

Improving Entity Framework by using code first

In this recipe, we start by separating the application into a user interface, a data access layer, and a business logic layer. This will allow us to keep our objects segregated from database-specific implementations. The objects and the implementation of the database context will be a layered approach so we can slot testing and abstraction into the application.

Getting ready

We will be using the NuGet Package Manager to install Entity Framework 4.1 assemblies.

The package installer can be found at `http://www.nuget.org/`. We will also be using a database in order to connect to the data and update it.

Open **Using Code First Solution** from the included source code examples.

Execute the database setup script from the code samples included for this recipe. This can be found in the `DataAccess` project within the `Database` folder.

How to do it...

Let us get connected to the database using the following steps:

1. In the `BusinessLogic` project, add a new C# class named `Blog` with the following code:

    ```csharp
    using System;
    namespace BusinessLogic
    {
      public class Blog
      {
        public int Id { get; set; }
        public string Title { get; set; }
      }
    }
    ```

2. In the `DataAccess` project, create a new C# class named `BlogContext` with the following code:

```
using System.Data.Entity;
using BusinessLogic;
namespace DataAccess
{
  public class BlogContext : DbContext
  {
    public BlogContext(string connectionString) :
      base(connectionString)
    {
    }
    public DbSet<Blog> Blogs { get; set; }
  }
}
```

3. In the `Recipe1UI` project, add a setting `Blog` with the connection string shown in the following screenshot:

Name	Type	Scope	Value
Blog	(Connectio...	Application	Data Source=(local);Initial Catalog=Blog;Integrated Security=True

4. In the `UI` project in the `BlogController.cs`, modify the `Display` method with the following code:

```
using System;
using System.Collections.Generic;
using System.Linq;
using System.Web;
using System.Web.Mvc;
using BusinessLogic;
using DataAccess;
using UI.Properties;
namespace UI.Controllers
{
  public class BlogController : Controller
  {
    private BlogContext _blogContext;
    public BlogController() :this(new
      BlogContext(Settings.Default.BlogConnection)) { }
    public BlogController(BlogContext blogContext)
    {
      _blogContext = blogContext;
```

```
      }
      // GET: /Blog/
      public ActionResult Display()
      {
        Blog blog = _blogContext.Blogs.First();
        return View(blog);
      }
    }
  }
```

How it works...

The blog entity is created but not mapped explicitly to a database structure. This takes advantage of convention over configuration, found in the code first approach, wherein the properties are examined and then table mappings are determined. This is obviously a time saver, but it is fairly limited if you have a non-standard database schema. The other big advantage of this approach is that the entity is "persistence-ignorant". In other words, it has no code or knowledge of how it is to be stored in the database.

The blog context in the `DataAccess` project has a few key elements to understand. The first is to understand that the inheritance from `DbContext`. `DbContext` is the code first version of `ObjectContext`, which runs exposing all connection pooling, entity change tracking, and database interactions. We added a constructor to take in the connection string, but note that this is not the standard connection string used with the database-first and model-first approaches to the embedded Entity Framework metadata connection string. Instead, the connection string is a standard provider connection string. You can also pass the name of an application setting through here, but the recommended approach is to provide the full connection string after it has been retrieved from the application settings store.

We used the standard built-in functionality for the connection string, but this could easily be any application setting store. Larger applications require more flexibility for where the settings are stored so we pass in the connection string on the construction of the `BlogContext`. It enables us to source that connection string from anywhere.

We did need to pass in the `BlogContext` as a parameter of the controller. Doing so allows us to interact with the database. The context here allows us to access the collection of objects that directly translate to database objects at request time.

There's more...

Approaching the use of code first development, we have several overarching themes and industry standards that we need to be aware of. Knowing about them will help us leverage the power of this tool without falling into the pit of using it without understanding.

Convention over configuration

This is a design paradigm that specifies default rules about how each aspect of an application will behave, but allows the developer to override any of the default rules with specific behavior required by the application. This allows us, as programmers, to avoid using a lot of configuration files to specify how we intended something to be used or configured. In our case, Entity Framework allows the most common behaviors to use default conventions that remove the need for a majority of the configurations. When the behavior we wish to create is not supported by the convention, we can easily override the convention and add the required behavior to it without the need to get rid of it everywhere else. This leaves us with a flexible and extendable system to configure the database interaction.

Model-View-Controller

In our example, we use **Microsoft ASP.NET**. We are using **MVC** (**Model-View-Controller**) framework to deliver the User Interface (UI) because it builds a naturally testable model to house our code. You will see that we predominantly used the MVC approach in our examples. The implementations can be ported to any UI, or no UI for that matter at all, if that is your preference. All of our samples use the **MVC 3 Framework** and **Razor view engine** for rendering the UI. We have provided some simple views which will allow us to focus on the solutions and the code without needing to deal with UI design and markup.

Single responsibility principle

One of the solid principles of development, that is, the single responsibility principle, states that every class should have only one reason to change. In this chapter, there are several examples of that in use. For example, the separation of model, view and controller in MVC. However, this important tenant is also why we favor the code first approach to begin with.

Entities in code first have the structure of data as their singular responsibility in memory. This means that only if the structure needs to be changed will we need to modify the entities. By contrast, the code automatically generated by the database-first tools of Entity Framework inherits your entities from base classes within the Entity Framework **Application Programming Interface** (**API**). The process of Microsoft making occasional updates to the base classes of Entity Framework is the one that introduces a second reason to change, thus violating our principle.

Testing

While we did not actively test this recipe, we did layer in the abstractions to do so. All of the other recipes will be executed and presented using test-driven development, as we believe it leads to a better software design, and a much more clear representation of intent.

See also

In this chapter:

- Implementing the unit of work pattern
- Implementing the repository pattern

Creating mock database connections

When working with Entity Framework in a test-driven manner, we need to be able to slip a layer between our last line of code and the framework. This allows us to simulate the database connection without actually hitting the database.

Getting ready

We will be using NuGet Package Manager to install the Entity Framework 4.1 assemblies.

The package installer can be found at http://www.nuget.org/.

We will also be using a database for connecting to the data, and updating it.

Open the **Mocking the Database** solution in the included source code examples.

Execute the database setup script from the code samples included with this recipe. This can be found in the `DataAccess` project within the `Database` folder.

How to do it...

1. In the `BusinessLogic` project, add a new C# interface named `IDbContext` using the following code:

   ```csharp
   using System.Linq;
   namespace BusinessLogic
   {
     public interface IDbContext
     {
       IQueryable<T> Find<T>() where T : class;
     }
   }
   ```

2. Add a new unit test in the `Test` project to test so we can supply false results from a fake database with the following code:

   ```csharp
   using System.Collections.Generic;
   using System.Linq;
   using BusinessLogic;
   using DataAccess;
   ```

```csharp
using Microsoft.VisualStudio.TestTools.UnitTesting;
using Rhino.Mocks;
namespace Test
{
  [TestClass]
  public class QueryTest
  {
    [TestMethod]
    public void ShouldFilterDataProperly()
    {
      //Arrange
      IDbContext mockContext =
        MockRepository.GenerateMock<IDbContext>();
      mockContext.Expect(x => x.Find<Blog>()).Return(new
        List<Blog>()
      {
        new Blog(){Id = 1,Title = "Title"},
        new Blog(){Id=2,Title = "no"}
      }.AsQueryable());
      //Act
      var items = mockContext.Find<Blog>().ToList();
      //Assert
      Assert.AreEqual(2,items.Count());
      Assert.AreEqual("Title",items[0].Title);
      Assert.AreEqual("no",items[1].Title);
    }
  }
}
```

3. In the `DataAccess` project, create a new C# class named `BlogContext` with the following code:

```csharp
using System.Data.Entity;
using BusinessLogic;
namespace DataAccess
{
  public class BlogContext : DbContext, IDbContext
  {
    public BlogContext(string connectionString) :
      base(connectionString)
    {
    }
    public DbSet<Blog> Blogs { get; set; }
    public IQueryable<T> Find<T>() where T : class
    {
      return this.Set<T>();
    }
  }
}
```

4. In the `BusinessLogic` project, add a new C# interface called `IDbContext` with the following code:

```
using System.Linq;
namespace BusinessLogic
{
  public interface IDbContext
  {
    IQueryable<T> Find<T>() where T : class;
  }
}
```

How it works...

The mocking framework that we are using (called **RhinoMocks**) allows us to pass a fake object which can simulate the responses that a database would provide for us without having that connection. This allows us to keep our tests from being dependent on SQL data, and therefore brittle. Now that we have data available from our mock, we can test whether it acts exactly like we coded it to. Knowing the inputs of the data access code, we can test the outputs for validity.

This layering is accomplished by putting our `Find` method as an abstraction between the public framework method of `Set<T>` and our code, so we can change the type to something constructible. This is required due to the constructors of `DbSet<T>` being internal (not callable from any other assembly). By layering this method, we can now control every return from the database in the test scenarios.

This layering also provides for the better separation of concerns, as the `DbSet<T>` in Entity Framework mingles multiple independent concerns, such as connection management and querying, into a single object. We will continue to separate these concerns in future recipes.

There's more...

Testing to the edges of an application requires that we adhere to certain practices which allow us to shrink the untestable sections of the code. This will allow us to unit test more code, and make our integration tests far more specific.

One object under test

An important point to remember while performing unit testing is that we should only be testing a single class. The point of a unit test is to ensure that a single unit, a single class, performs the way we expect it to.

This is why simulating classes that are not under test is so important. We do not want the behavior of these supporting classes to affect the outcomes of unit tests for our class under test.

Integration tests

Often, it is equally important to test the actual combination of your various classes, to ensure they work properly together. These integration tests are valuable, but are almost always more brittle, require more setup, and are run slower than the unit tests. We certainly need integration tests on any project of a reasonable size, but we want unit tests first.

Arrange, act, assert

Most unit tests can be viewed as having three parts: arrange, act, and assert. **Arrange** is where we prepare the environment to perform the test, for instance, mocking of the `IDBContext` and setting up an expectation that `Find<T>` will be called. **Act** is where we perform the action under test and is most often a singular line of code. **Assert** is where we ensure that the proper result was reached. Note the comments in the examples above that call out these sections. We will use them throughout the book to make it clear what the test is trying to do.

Implementing the repository pattern

This recipe is an implementation of the repository pattern which allows us to separate the usage of a database and its data from the act of reading that data.

Getting ready

We will be using NuGet Package Manager to install the Entity Framework 4.1 assemblies.

The package installer can be found at `http://www.nuget.org/`.

We will also be using a database for connecting to and updating data.

Open the **Repository Pattern** solution in the included source code examples.

Execute the database setup script from the code samples included with this recipe. This can be found in the `DataAccess` project within the `Database` folder.

How to do it...

1. In the `DataAccess` project, add a new C# interface name `IBlogRepository` with the following code:

   ```csharp
   using System.Linq;
   namespace DataAccess
   {
     public interface IBlogRepository
     {
       IQueryable<T> Set<T>() where T : class;
     }
   }
   ```

2. In the `DataAccess` project, create a new C# class named `BlogRepository` with the following code:

```csharp
using System.Data.Entity;
using System.Linq;
using BusinessLogic;
namespace DataAccess
{
  public class BlogRepository : IBlogRepository
  {
    private readonly IDbContext _context;
    public BlogRepository(IDbContext context)
    {
      _context = context;
    }
    public IQueryable<T> Set<T>() where T : class
    {
      return _context.Find<T>();
    }
  }
}
```

3. First, we start by adding a new unit test in the `Test` project that defines a test for using repository with the following code:

```csharp
using BusinessLogic;
using DataAccess;
using Microsoft.VisualStudio.TestTools.UnitTesting;
using Rhino.Mocks;
namespace Test
{
  [TestClass]
  public class RepositoryTest
  {
    [TestMethod]
    public void ShouldAllowGettingASetOfObjectsGenerically()
    {
      //Arrange
      IDbContext mockContext =
        MockRepository.GenerateMock<IDbContext>();
      IBlogRepository repository = new
        BlogRepository(mockContext);
      //Act
      var items = repository.Set<Blog>();
      //Assert
      mockContext.AssertWasCalled(x => x.Find<Blog>());
    }
  }
}
```

4. In the `BusinessLogic` project, add a new C# interface name `IBlogRepository` with the following code:

```
using System.Linq;
namespace DataAccess
{
  public interface IBlogRepository
  {
    IQueryable<T> Set<T>() where T : class;
  }
}
```

5. In the `DataAccess` project, create a new C# class named `BlogRepository` with the following code:

```
using System.Data.Entity;
using System.Linq;
using BusinessLogic;
namespace DataAccess
{
  public class BlogRepository : IBlogRepository
  {
    private readonly IDbContext _context;
    public BlogRepository(IDbContext context)
    {
      _context = context;
    }
    public IQueryable<T> Set<T>() where T : class
    {
      return _context.Find<T>();
    }
  }
}
```

6. In the `BlogController` update the usage of `BlogContext` to use `IBlogRepository` with the following code:

```
using System.Linq;
using System.Web.Mvc;
using BusinessLogic;
using DataAccess;
using UI.Properties;
namespace UI.Controllers
{
  public class BlogController : Controller
  {
    private IBlogRepository _blogRepository;
```

```
      public BlogController() : this(new BlogRepository(new
        BlogContext(Settings.Default.BlogConnection))) { }
      public BlogController(IBlogRepository blogRepository)
      {
        _blogRepository = blogRepository;
      }
      //
      // GET: /Blog/
      public ActionResult Display()
      {
        Blog blog = _blogRepository.Set<Blog>().First();
        return View(blog);
      }
    }
  }
```

How it works...

We start off with a test that defines what we hope to accomplish. We use mocking (or verifiable fake objects) to ensure that we get the behavior that we expect. The test states that any `BlogRepository` will communicate with the context to connect for the data. This is what we are hoping to accomplish as doing so allows us to layer tests and extension points into the domain.

The usage of the repository interface is a key part of this flexible implementation as it will allow us to leverage mocks, and test the business layer, while still maintaining an extensible solution. The interface to the context is a straightforward API for all database communication. In this example, we only need to read data from the database, so the interface is very simple.

Even in this simple implementation of the interface, we see that there are opportunities to increase reusabilty. We could have created a method or property that returned the list of blogs, but then we would have had to modify the context and interface for every new entity. Instead, we set up the `Find` method to take a generic type, which allows us to add entities to the usage of the interface without modifying the interface. We will only need to modify the implementation.

Notice that we constrained the interface to accept only the reference types for T, using the where T : class constraint. We did this because value types cannot be stored using entity framework. If you had a base class, you could use it here to constrain the usage of the generic even further. Importantly, not all reference types are valid for T, but the constraint is as close as we can get using C#. Interfaces are not valid because Entity Framework cannot construct them when it needs to create an entity. Instead, it will produce a runtime exception as they are valid reference types.

Improving Entity Framework in the Real World

Once we have the context, we need to wrap it with an abstraction. The `BlogRepository` will allow us to query the data without allowing direct control over the database connection. This is what `BlogRepository` accomplishes for us. We can hide the details of the specific implementation, the actual context object, while surfacing a simplified API for gathering data.

The other interface that we abstracted is the `IDbContext` interface. This abstraction allows us to intercept tests just before they would be sent to the database. This makes the untestable part of the application as thin as possible. We can, and will, test right up to the point of database connection.

There's more...

Keeping the repository implementation clean requires us to leverage some principles and patterns that are at the core of object-oriented programming, but not specific to using Entity Framework. These principles will not only help us to write clean implementations of Entity Framework, but can also be leveraged by other areas of our code.

Dependency inversion principle

Dependency inversion is another solid principle. This states that all of the dependencies of an object should be clearly visible and passed in, or injected, to create the object. The benefit of this is two-fold: the first is exposing all of the dependencies so the effects of using a piece of code are clear to those who will use the class. The second benefit is by injecting these dependencies at construction, they allow us to unit test by passing in mocks of the dependant objects. Granular unit tests require the ability to abstract dependencies, so we can ensure only one object is under test.

Repository and caching

This repository pattern gives us the perfect area for implementing a complex or global caching mechanism. If we want to persist some value into the cache at the point of retrieval, and not retrieve it again, the repository class is the perfect location for such logic. This layer of abstraction allows us to move beyond simple implementations and start thinking about solving business problems quickly, and later extend to handle more complex scenarios as they are warranted by the requirements of the specific project. You can think of repository as a well-tested 80+% solution. Put off anything more until the last responsible moment.

Mocking

The usage of mocks is commonplace in tests because mocks allow us to verify underlying behavior without having more than one object under test. This is a fundamental piece of the puzzle for test-driven development. When you test at a unit level, you want to make sure that the level directly following the one you are testing was called correctly while not actually executing the specific implementation. This is what mocking buys us.

Where constraint

There are times when we need to create complex sets of queries which will be used frequently, but only by one or two objects. When this situation occurs, we want to reuse that code without needing to duplicate it for each object. This is where the "where" constraint helps us. It allows us to limit generically defined behavior to an object or set of objects that share a common interface or base class. The extension possibilities are near limitless.

See also

In this chapter:

- *Implementing the unit of work pattern*
- *Creating mock database connections*

Implementing the unit of work pattern

In the next example, we present an implementation of the unit of work pattern which will allow us to limit our connections to the database, and keep the application in a stable state.

Getting ready

We will be using NuGet Package Manager to install the Entity Framework 4.1 assemblies.

The package installer can be found at `http://www.nuget.org/`.

We will also be using a database for connecting to the data and updating it.

Open the **Unit of Work Pattern** solution in the included source code examples.

Execute the database setup script from the code samples included with this recipe. This can be found in the `DataAccess` Project within the `Database` folder.

How to do it...

1. First, we start by adding a new unit test in the `Test` project to define the tests for using a unit of work pattern with the following code:

    ```
    using System;
    using System.Data.Entity.Infrastructure;
    using System.Text;
    using System.Collections.Generic;
    using System.Linq;
    using BusinessLogic;
    using DataAccess;
    using Microsoft.VisualStudio.TestTools.UnitTesting;
    ```

```csharp
using Rhino.Mocks;
namespace Test
{
  [TestClass]
  public class UnitOfWorkTest
  {
    [TestMethod]
    public void ShouldReadToDatabaseOnRead()
    {
    //Arrange
    IDbContext mockContext =
      MockRepository.GenerateMock<IDbContext>();
    IUnitOfWork unitOfWork = new UnitOfWork(mockContext);
    IBlogRepository repository = new BlogRepository(unitOfWork);
    //Act
    var items = repository.Set<Blog>();
    //Assert
    mockContext.AssertWasCalled(x => x.Find<Blog>());
    }
    [TestMethod]
    public void ShouldNotCommitToDatabaseOnDataChange()
    {
    //Arrange
    IDbContext mockContext =
      MockRepository.GenerateMock<IDbContext>();
    IUnitOfWork unitOfWork = new UnitOfWork(mockContext);
    mockContext.Stub(x => x.Find<Blog>()).Return(new List<Blog>()
      {new Blog() {Id = 1, Title = "Test"}}.AsQueryable());
    IBlogRepository repository = new BlogRepository(unitOfWork);
    var items = repository.Set<Blog>();
    //Act
    items.First().Title = "Not Going to be Written";
    //Assert
    mockContext.AssertWasNotCalled(x => x.SaveChanges());
    }
    [TestMethod]
    public void ShouldPullDatabaseValuesOnARollBack()
    {
      //Arrange
      IDbContext mockContext =
        MockRepository.GenerateMock<IDbContext>();
      IUnitOfWork unitOfWork = new UnitOfWork(mockContext);
      mockContext.Stub(x => x.Find<Blog>()).Return(new
        List<Blog>() { new Blog() { Id = 1, Title = "Test" }
      }.AsQueryable());
      IBlogRepository repository = new BlogRepository(unitOfWork);
```

```csharp
  var items = repository.Set<Blog>();
  items.First().Title = "Not Going to be Written";
  //Act
  repository.RollbackChanges();
  //Assert
  mockContext.AssertWasNotCalled(x=>x.SaveChanges());
  mockContext.AssertWasCalled(x=>x.Rollback());
}
[TestMethod]
public void ShouldCommitToDatabaseOnSaveCall()
{
  //Arrange
  IDbContext mockContext =
    MockRepository.GenerateMock<IDbContext>();
  IUnitOfWork unitOfWork = new UnitOfWork(mockContext);
  mockContext.Stub(x => x.Find<Blog>()).Return(new
  List<Blog>() { new Blog() { Id = 1, Title = "Test" }
}.AsQueryable());
IBlogRepository repository = new BlogRepository(unitOfWork);
var items = repository.Set<Blog>();
items.First().Title = "Going to be Written";
//Act
repository.SaveChanges();
//Assert
mockContext.AssertWasCalled(x=>x.SaveChanges());
}
[TestMethod]
public void ShouldNotCommitOnError()
{
  //Arrange
  IDbContext mockContext =
    MockRepository.GenerateMock<IDbContext>();
  IUnitOfWork unitOfWork = new UnitOfWork(mockContext);
  mockContext.Stub(x => x.Find<Blog>()).Return(new
    List<Blog>() { new Blog() { Id = 1, Title = "Test" }
}.AsQueryable());
mockContext.Stub(x => x.SaveChanges()).Throw(new
  ApplicationException());
IBlogRepository repository = new BlogRepository(unitOfWork);
var items = repository.Set<Blog>();
items.First().Title = "Not Going to be Written";
//Act
try
{
  repository.SaveChanges();
```

```
            }
            catch (Exception)
            {
            }
            //Assert
            mockContext.AssertWasCalled(x => x.Rollback());
        }
    }
}
```

2. In the `DataAccess` project, create a new C# class named `BlogContext` with the following code:

```
using System;
using System.Data.Entity;
using System.Data.Entity.Infrastructure;
using System.Linq;
using BusinessLogic;
namespace DataAccess
{
  public class BlogContext : DbContext, IDbContext
  {
    public BlogContext(string connectionString)
      : base(connectionString)
    {
    }
    public DbSet<Blog> Blogs { get; set; }
    public IQueryable<T> Find<T>() where T : class
    {
       return this.Set<T>();
    }
    public void Rollback()
    {
      this.ChangeTracker.Entries().ToList().ForEach(x=>x.Reload());
    }
  }
}
```

3. In the `DataAccess` project, create a new C# interface called `IDbContext` with the following code:

```
using System.Data.Entity;
using System.Data.Entity.Infrastructure;
using System.Linq;
namespace DataAccess
{
```

```csharp
    public interface IDbContext
    {
      DbChangeTracker ChangeTracker { get; }
      DbSet<T> Set<T>() where T : class;
      IQueryable<T> Find<T>() where T : class;
      DbEntityEntry<T> Entry<T>(T entity) where T : class;
      int SaveChanges();
      void Rollback();
    }
}
```

4. In the DataAccess project, create a new C# interface called IUnitOfWork with the following code:

```csharp
using System;
namespace DataAccess
{
  public interface IUnitOfWork
  {
    void RegisterNew<T>(T entity) where T : class;
    void RegisterUnchanged<T>(T entity) where T : class;
    void RegisterChanged<T>(T entity) where T : class;
    void RegisterDeleted<T>(T entity) where T : class;
    void Refresh();
    void Commit();
    IDbContext Context { get; set; }
  }
}
```

5. In the DataAccess project, add a new C# class named UnitOfWork with the following code:

```csharp
using System.Data;
using System.Linq;
namespace DataAccess
{
  public class UnitOfWork : IUnitOfWork
  {
    public IDbContext Context { get; set; }
    public UnitOfWork(IDbContext context)
    {
      Context = context;
    }
    public void RegisterNew<T>(T entity) where T : class
    {
      Context.Set<T>().Add(entity);
```

```csharp
      }
      public void RegisterUnchanged<T>(T entity) where T : class
      {
         Context.Entry(entity).State = EntityState.Unchanged;
      }
      public void RegisterChanged<T>(T entity) where T : class
      {
         Context.Entry(entity).State = EntityState.Modified;
      }
      public void RegisterDeleted<T>(T entity) where T : class
      {
         Context.Set<T>().Remove(entity);
      }
      public void Refresh()
      {
         Context.Rollback();
      }
      public void Commit()
      {
         Context.SaveChanges();
      }
   }
}
```

6. In the `BusinessLogic` project, add a new C# interface named `IBlogRepository` with the following code:

```csharp
using System.Linq;
namespace DataAccess
{
   public interface IBlogRepository
   {
      IQueryable<T> Set<T>() where T : class;
      void RollbackChanges();
      void SaveChanges();
   }
}
```

7. In the `DataAccess` project, create a new C# class named `BlogRepository` with the following code:

```csharp
using System;
using System.Data.Entity;
using System.Linq;
using BusinessLogic;
namespace DataAccess
```

```csharp
{
  public class BlogRepository : IBlogRepository
  {
    private readonly IUnitOfWork _unitOfWork;
    public BlogRepository(IUnitOfWork unitOfWork)
    {
      _unitOfWork = unitOfWork;
    }
    public IQueryable<T> Set<T>() where T : class
    {
      return _unitOfWork.Context.Find<T>();
    }
    public void RollbackChanges()
    {
      _unitOfWork.Refresh();
    }
    public void SaveChanges()
    {
      try
      {
        _unitOfWork.Commit();
      }
      catch (Exception)
      {
        _unitOfWork.Refresh();
        throw;
      }
    }
  }
}
```

8. In the `BlogController`, update the usage of `BlogContext` to use `IBlogRepository` with the following code:

```csharp
using System.Linq;
using System.Web.Mvc;
using BusinessLogic;
using DataAccess;
using UI.Properties;
namespace UI.Controllers
{
  public class BlogController : Controller
  {
    private IBlogRepository _blogRepository;
```

```
      public BlogController() : this(new BlogRepository(new
        UnitOfWork(new
          BlogContext(Settings.Default.BlogConnection)))) { }
      public BlogController(IBlogRepository blogRepository)
      {
        _blogRepository = blogRepository;
      }
      //
      // GET: /Blog/
      public ActionResult Display()
      {
        Blog blog = _blogRepository.Set<Blog>().First();
        return View(blog);
      }
    }
  }
```

How it works...

The tests set up the scenarios in which we would want to use a unit of work pattern, reading, updating, rolling back, and committing. The key to this is that these are all separate actions, not dependant on anything before or after it. If the application is web-based, this gives you a powerful tool to tie to the HTTP request so any unfinished work is cleaned up, or to ensure that you do not need to call `SaveChanges` since it can happen automatically.

The unit of work was originally created to track the changes made so they could be persisted, and it functions that way now. We are using a more powerful, but less recognized, feature defining the scope of the unit of work. We gave the ability to control both scope and the changes that are committed in the database in this scenario. We also have put in some clean-up which will ensure that even in the event of a failure our unit of work will try to clean up after itself before throwing the error to be handled at a higher level. We do not want to ignore these errors, but we do want to make sure they do not destroy the integrity of our database.

In addition to this tight encapsulation of work against the database, pass in our unit of work to each repository. This enables us in coupling multiple object interactions to a single unit of work. This will allow us to write code, specific to the object, without giving up the shared feature set of the database context. This is an explicit unit of work, but Entity Framework in the context defines it to give you an implicit unit of work. If you want to tie this to the HTTP request, rollback on error, or tie multiple data connections together in new and interesting ways, then you will need to code in an explicit implementation like this one.

This basic pattern will help to streamline data access, and resolve the concurrency issues caused by conflicts in the objects that are affected by a transaction.

There's more...

The unit of work is a concept which is deep at the heart of Entity Framework, and adheres, out of the box, to the principles following it. Knowing these principles, and why they are leveraged, will help us use Entity Framework to it's fullest without running into the walls built in the system on purpose.

Call per change

There is a cost for every connection to the database. If we were to make a call to keep the state in the database in sync with the state in the application, we would have thousands of calls each with connection, security, and network overhead. Limiting the number of times that we hit the database not only allows us to control this overhead, but also allows the database software to handle the larger transactions for which it was built.

Interface segregation principle

Some might be inclined to ask why we should separate unit of work from the repository pattern. Unit of work is definitely a separate responsibility from repository, and as such it is important to not only define separate classes, but also to ensure that we keep small, clear interfaces. The `IDbContext` interface is specific in the area of dealing with database connections through an Entity Framework object context. This allows the mocking of a context to give us testability to the lowest possible level. The `IUnitOfWork` interface deals with the segregation of work, and ensures that the database persistence happens only when we intend it to, ignorant of the layer under it that does the actual commands. The `IRepository` interface deals with selecting objects back from any type of storage, and allows us to remove all thoughts of how the database interaction happens from our dependent code base. These three objects, while related in layers, are separate concerns, and therefore need to be separate interfaces.

Refactor

We have added `IUnitOfWork` to our layered approach to database communication, and if we have seen anything over the hours of coding, it is code changes. We change it for many reasons, but the bottom line is that code changes often, and we need to make it easy to change. The layers of abstraction that we have added to this solution with `IRepository`, `IUnitOfWork`, and `IDbContext`, have all given us a point at which the change would be minimally painful, and we can leverage the interfaces in the same way. This refactoring to add abstraction levels is a core tenant of clean extensible code. Removing the concrete implementation details from related objects, and coding to an interface, forces us to encapsulate behavior and abstract our sections of code.

Improving Entity Framework in the Real World

See also

In this chapter:

- *Testing queries*
- *Implementing the repository pattern*
- *Performing load testing against a database*

Testing queries

One of the questions that you will undoubtedly come across in using Entity Framework is the usage of LINQ statements getting transformed into SQL statements everywhere, and how to output those for testing. These tests are not meant to truly unit test the generated SQL, but rather provide a simple way to inform the development staff, possibly DataBase Administrators (DBAs), as to what SQL is actually being executed for a given LINQ statement.

Getting ready

We will be using NuGet Package Manager to install the Entity Framework 4.1 assemblies.

The package installer can be found at http://www.nuget.org/.

We will also be using a database for connecting to the data and updating it.

Open the **Testing SQL Output** solution in the included source code examples.

Execute the database setup script from the code samples included with this recipe. This can be found in the DataAccess project within the Database folder.

How to do it...

1. First, we start by adding a new unit test in the Test project to extract the SQL statements for us and a test to verify the filters on a given set of data:

    ```
    using System;
    using System.Text;
    using System.Collections.Generic;
    using System.Linq;
    using BusinessLogic;
    using DataAccess;
    using Microsoft.VisualStudio.TestTools.UnitTesting;
    using Rhino.Mocks;
    ```

```csharp
namespace Test
{
  [TestClass]
  public class QueryTest
  {
    [TestMethod]
    public void ShouldFilterDataProperly()
    {
      IUnitOfWork mockContext =
        MockRepository.GenerateMock<IUnitOfWork>();
      mockContext.Expect(x => x.Find<Blog>()).Return(new
        List<Blog>()
      {
        new Blog(){Id = 1,Title = "Title"},
        new Blog(){Id=2,Title = "no"}
      }.AsQueryable());
      IBlogRepository repository = new
        BlogRepository(mockContext);
      var items =
        repository.Set<Blog>().Where(x=>x.Title.Contains("t"));
      mockContext.AssertWasCalled(x => x.Find<Blog>());
      Assert.AreEqual(1,items.Count());
      Assert.AreEqual("Title",items.First().Title);
    }
    [TestMethod]
    public void ShouldAllowSqlStringOutput()
    {
      IBlogRepository repository = new BlogRepository(new
        BlogContext(Settings.Default.BlogConnection));
      var items = repository.Set<Blog>();
      var sql = items.ToString();
      Console.WriteLine(sql);
      Assert.IsTrue(sql.Contains("SELECT"));
    }
  }
}
```

2. In the `Test` project, add a setting for the connection to the database, as shown in the following screenshot:

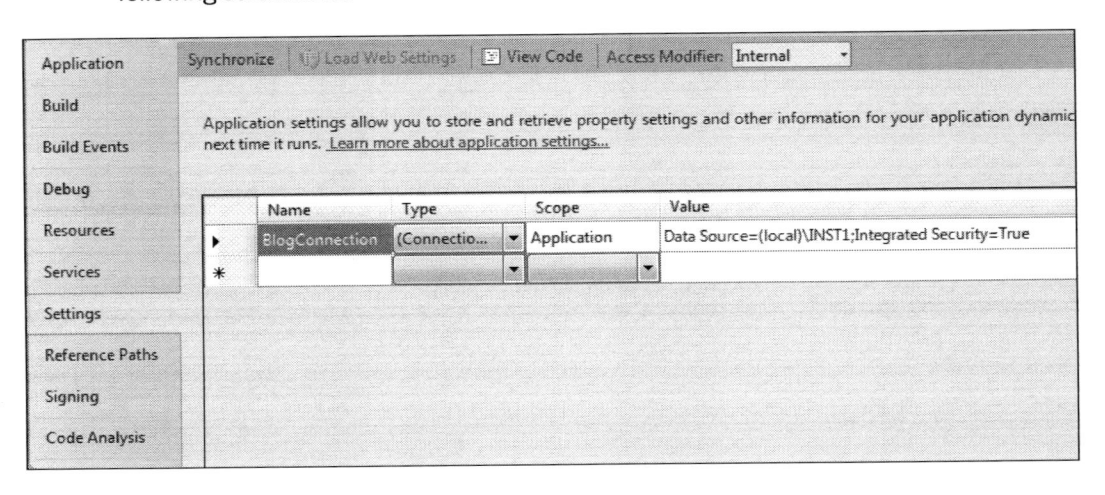

3. In the test results window, we want to right-click and open the View **Test Result Details** for our SQL string test, as shown in the following screenshot:

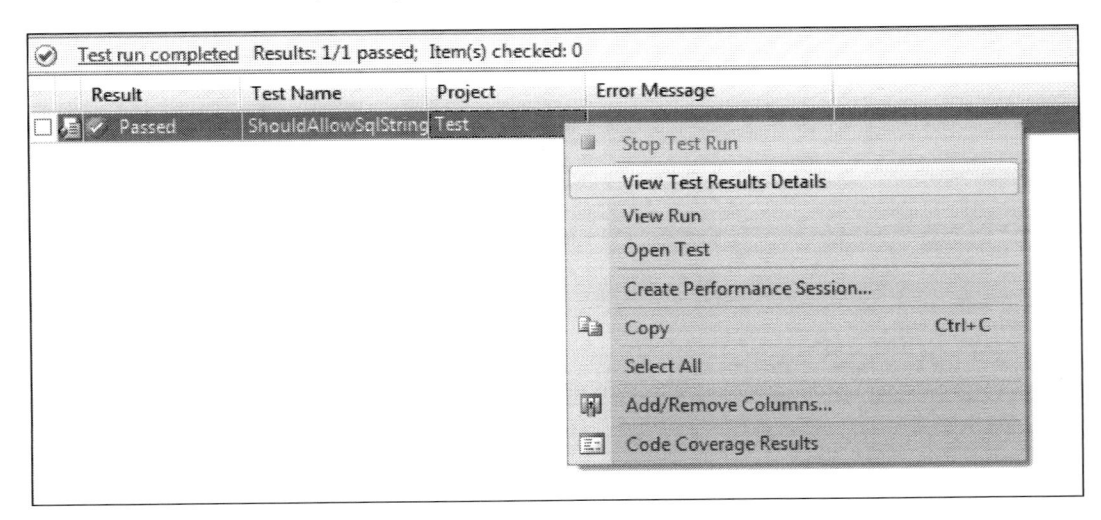

4. Notice the output for SQL console in the following screenshot:

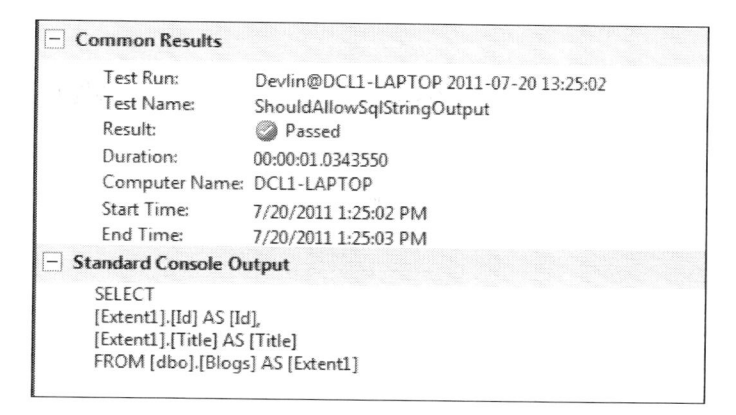

```
Common Results
    Test Run:        Devlin@DCL1-LAPTOP 2011-07-20 13:25:02
    Test Name:       ShouldAllowSqlStringOutput
    Result:          Passed
    Duration:        00:00:01.0343550
    Computer Name:   DCL1-LAPTOP
    Start Time:      7/20/2011 1:25:02 PM
    End Time:        7/20/2011 1:25:03 PM
Standard Console Output
    SELECT
    [Extent1].[Id] AS [Id],
    [Extent1].[Title] AS [Title]
    FROM [dbo].[Blogs] AS [Extent1]
```

How it works...

The first test is to make sure that our LINQ statements are executing the filters that we believe them to be. This will allow us to encapsulate the filters and sorts that we use throughout our application to keep the query footprint small. Entity Framework writes parameterized SQL. The fewer queries we use in structure, the better the performance will be. The query paths for our set of queries will be stored in SQL Server, just like the query plans of stored procedures, which provides us huge performance gains without sacrificing the code base of our application.

With this recipe, we start leveraging the abstraction layers built in the repository and the unit of work patterns that we implemented earlier. We leverage the unit of work to get a false set of data in the first test. This is the set that allows us to verify filters, and if you have a complex data structure, this can be abstracted into a factory so we only need to provide the dummy list at one time, but then can test multiple filters and sorts against it.

The second test requires a fully formed context, which is why we loaded a connection string to the `Test` project. This is not hitting the database for data, but is connecting at the construction of the context to check metadata and schema definition. This is the metadata which the context will use along with the standard convention, and any exceptions that you have configured to translate the LINQ statements into SQL statements.

There's more...

Some of the Entity Framework presentations that we have seen over the last couple of years have implied that we can ignore the database with an object relational mapper such as Entity Framework. This is not entirely true. We can ignore the structure of the database while defining our objects, but we still must be aware of it while querying and mapping our objects.

Query execution plan

As SQL is declarative, there are often many ways to get the same set of results, each of these varying widely in performance. When a query is submitted to the database, it is run through the query optimizer that evaluates some of the possible plans for executing the query, and returns what it considers the best of them. The query optimizer is not perfect, but it is good. The cost of this optimizer is that it takes some overhead on the query. When a query is sent with the parameters, the optimizer evaluates it and returns it, but caches the resulting plan. If the same query is called with different parameters, the optimizer knows the resulting plan will be the same, and uses the cached version. This storage of query plans is what gives Entity Framework an advantage because it uses parameterized SQL statements. If we are able to keep the query footprint (the number of different queries) in our application small, then we will reap the most benefit from this optimization and storage.

Query performance

When looking at using Entity Framework, we all need to consider performance, as we do not control the query directly. Some developers will write LINQ statements without a thought to translating it to SQL at the backend. This can lead to performance problems that are blamed on Entity Framework. The problem rests with the LINQ code that was written. There are several tools on the market which will allow you to analyze the generated SQL, and some even allow you to get a real-time look at the query execution plan.

Here are some of them:

- **IntelliTrace** (built in Visual Studio Ultimate): `http://msdn.microsoft.com/en-us/library/dd264915.aspx`
- **Entity Framework profiler**: `http://efprof.com`
- **Manual tracing**: You can add this by wrapping extension methods to the `IQueryable` interface that use `Debug.WriteLine()` for more information. Try `http://blog.nappisite.com/2011/01/poor-mans-entity-framework-profiler.html`

See also

In this chapter:

- *Implementing the repository pattern*
- *Implementing the unit of work pattern*

In *Chapter 5, Improving Entity Framework with Query Libraries*:

- *Creating reusable queries*

Chapter 1

Creating databases from code

As we start down the code first path, there are a couple of things that could be true. If we already have a database, then we will need to configure our objects to that schema, but what if we do not have one? That is the subject of this recipe, creating a database from the objects we declare.

Getting ready

We will be using NuGet Package Manager to install the Entity Framework 4.1 assemblies.

The package installer can be found at http://www.nuget.org/.

Open the **Creating a Database from Code** solution in the included source code examples.

How to do it...

1. First, we write a test which will set up the context for us to use as a starting point for creating the database with the following code:

```
using System.Data.Entity;
using System.Linq;
using BusinessLogic;
using DataAccess;
using Microsoft.VisualStudio.TestTools.UnitTesting;
using Test.Properties;
namespace Test
{
  [TestClass]
  public class DatabaseCreationTests
  {
    [TestMethod]
    public void ShouldCreateDatabaseOnCreation()
    {
      BlogContext context = new
        BlogContext(Settings.Default.BlogConnection);
      Assert.IsTrue(context.Database.Exists());
      context.Database.Delete();
      Assert.IsFalse(context.Database.Exists());
      context = new BlogContext(Settings.Default.BlogConnection);
      Assert.IsTrue(context.Database.Exists());
    }
    [TestMethod]
    public void ShouldSeedDataToDatabaseOnCreation()
    {
```

```
            System.Data.Entity.Database.SetInitializer<BlogContext>(new
              BlogContextInitializer());
            BlogContext context = new
              BlogContext(Settings.Default.BlogConnection);
            Assert.IsTrue(context.Database.Exists());
            context.Database.Delete();
            Assert.IsFalse(context.Database.Exists());
            context = new BlogContext(Settings.Default.BlogConnection);
            context.Database.Initialize(true);
            Assert.IsTrue(context.Database.Exists());
            DbSet<Blog> blogs = context.Set<Blog>();
            Assert.AreEqual(3,blogs.Count());
        }
    }
}
```

2. We will need to add a connection setting to the `Test` project to our database, and make sure that the database name is populated (the database name needs to be typed as it does not exist yet):

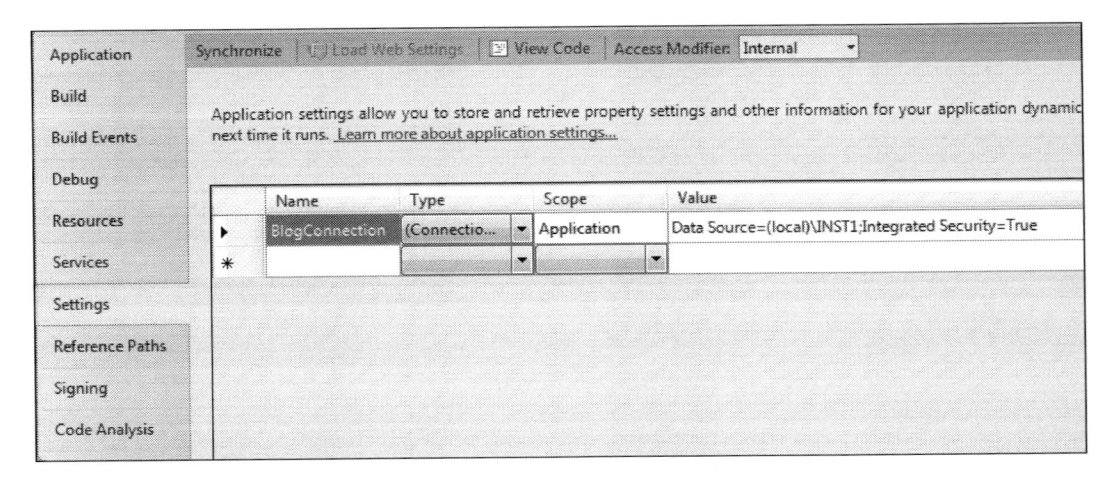

Name	Type	Scope	Value
BlogConnection	(Connectio...	Application	Data Source=(local)\INST1;Integrated Security=True

3. In the `DataAccess` project, create a new C# class named `BlogContext` with the following code:

```
using System.Data.Entity;
using System.Linq;
using BusinessLogic;
namespace DataAccess
{
    public class BlogContext : DbContext
    {
        public BlogContext(string connectionString)
```

```csharp
      : base(connectionString)
    {
      if (this.Database.Exists() &&
        !this.Database.CompatibleWithModel(false))
          this.Database.Delete();
      if (!this.Database.Exists()) this.Database.Create();
    }
    protected override void OnModelCreating(DbModelBuilder
      modelBuilder)
    {
      base.OnModelCreating(modelBuilder);
    }
    public DbSet<Blog> Blogs { get; set; }
  }
}
```

4. In the `DataAccess` project, create a new C# class named `BlogContextInitializer` with the following code:

```csharp
using System;
using System.Collections.Generic;
using System.Data.Entity;
using BusinessLogic;
namespace DataAccess
{
  public class BlogContextInitializer :
    IDatabaseInitializer<BlogContext>
  {
    public void InitializeDatabase(BlogContext context)
    {
      new List<Blog>
      {
        new Blog {Id = 1, Title = "One"},
        new Blog {Id = 2, Title = "Two"},
        new Blog {Id = 3, Title = "Three"}
      }.ForEach(b => context.Blogs.Add(b));
      context.SaveChanges();
    }
  }
}
```

Improving Entity Framework in the Real World

How it works...

On the construction of the context, Entity Framework creates an in-memory version of the expected database model and then tries to connect to that database. If the database is not there, and sufficient rights have been granted to the user, then Entity Framework will create the database. This is done by using the same conventions that the context uses for connecting and retrieving the data. The context defines the metadata schema and then creates the database. There is an additional table that stores the model hash for future comparisons against the model in use.

We are checking for an existing database that is incompatible, and deleting it if found, and then creating one from the objects that we have registered onto the data context with the `DbSet` properties. You can use the model check to keep the application from starting against a malformed database as well.

Notice that we also call the `Initialize` method but pass it as true to force the script to run even if the model has not changed. This is for testing purposes, but in a real scenario you would want this code in the start of the application. This will load whatever data we have defined in the initializer. We have given the database three blog entries to seed for the test data, but you can use this to load many other table records. This also ensures that the database gets created correctly every time.

There are some objects which will be static but configured into the database, for example, reference tables or lookup tables come to the mind. These are normally populated by a manual script that needs to be updated every time data is added to the reference tables, or a new lookup is created. We can code these items to be populated when the database is created so the manual update does not need to be run.

There's more...

When we start a green field project, we have that rush of happiness to be working in a problem domain that no one has touched before. This can be exhilarating and daunting at the same time. The objects we define and the structure of our program come naturally to a programmer, but most of us need to think with a different method to design the database schema. This is where the tools can help to translate our objects and intended structure into the database schema if we leverage some patterns. We can then take full advantage of being object-oriented programmers.

Configuration and creation

If you have added configuration for the schema layout of your database, it will be reflected in the database that gets created. This allows you to set up configurations to match any requirements on the schema without sacrificing the object model internal to your application.

Sample data

Testing the database layer has always been complex, but there are tools and strategies which will make it simpler. First, we layer abstractions to allow for unit testing at each level of the application. This will help us cover most of the applications, but there are still integration tests which will need to verify the whole story. This is where database initializers can help us to set up the test so they are brittle and more repeatable.

Testing queries for performance

While working within the constraints of application development, one of the things that you need to be aware of and work to avoid is performance problems with queries that hit the database. While working with Entity Framework, you have several tools which will help with this.

Getting ready

We will be using NuGet Package Manager to install the Entity Framework 4.1 assemblies.

The package installer can be found at http://www.nuget.org/.

We will also be using a database for connecting to the data and updating it.

Open the **Performance Testing Queries** in the included source code examples.

Execute the database setup script from the code samples included with this recipe. This can be found in the `DataAccess` project within the `Database` folder.

How to do it...

1. First, we start by adding a test class named `PerformanceTests` using the following code:

```
using System;
using System.Collections.Generic;
using System.Data.Entity;
using System.Diagnostics;
using System.Linq;
using BusinessLogic;
using DataAccess;
using Microsoft.VisualStudio.TestTools.UnitTesting;
using Test.Properties;
namespace Test
{
  [TestClass]
  public class PerformanceTests
```

```csharp
{
    private static BlogContext _context;
    [ClassInitialize]
    public static void ClassSetup(TestContext a)
    {
        Database.SetInitializer(new PerformanceTestInitializer());
        _context = new BlogContext(Settings.Default.BlogConnection);
        _context.Database.Delete();
        _context.Database.Create();
        _context.Database.Initialize(true);
    }
    [TestMethod]
    public void
        ShouldReturnInLessThanASecondForTenThousandRecords()
    {
        var watch = Stopwatch.StartNew();
        var items = _context.Set<Blog>();
        watch.Stop();
        Assert.IsTrue(watch.Elapsed < new TimeSpan(1000));
    }
    [TestMethod]
    public void ShouldReturnAFilteredSetInLessThan500Ticks()
    {
        var watch = Stopwatch.StartNew();
        var items = _context.Set<Blog>().Where(x=>x.Id > 500 && x.Id
        < 510);
        watch.Stop();
        Assert.IsTrue(watch.Elapsed < new TimeSpan(500));
    }
  }
}
```

2. Add a new C# class named `PerformanceTestInitializer` to the `Test` project using the following code:

```csharp
public class PerformanceTestInitializer :
    IDatabaseInitializer<BlogContext>
{
 public void InitializeDatabase(BlogContext context)
 {
    long totalElapsed = 0;
    for (int i = 0; i < 10000; i++)
    {
       Stopwatch stopwatch = Stopwatch.StartNew();
```

```
        Blog b = new Blog {Id = i,Title = string.Format("Test
          {0}", i)};
        context.Blogs.Add(b);
        context.SaveChanges();
        stopwatch.Stop();
        totalElapsed += stopwatch.ElapsedTicks;
      }
      Console.WriteLine(totalElapsed / 10000);
    }
  }
```

How it works...

The test initialization calls a new context, and then inserts 10,000 rows of data. This is done once for the test class, and then all of the tests use that data. It is time-intensive, but can be automated for performance. This is not a unit test, but an integration test. These should not be run with every build like unit tests, but should be run at key points in the continuous build and deployment processes. Nightly builds are a great place for testing like this as it will head of costly changes late in the development cycle caused by performance.

This kind of performance testing ensures that the critical pieces of the application meet the expected level of responsiveness for our customers. The only way to elicit these kinds of requirements for us is to sit down with the customer and ask about them. How slow is unacceptable? How long does it currently take? How fast does it need to be to fit into the rhythm of your work?

There's more...

When we shop for a car, we look at the miles per gallon, the engine size, the maintenance, and all of the other performance markers. Writing software should be no different. If we run into resistance to this idea, we can use the following information for help.

Why do performance testing?

Performance testing is a tool used to avoid not meeting expectations. When we release software to a customer, there are certain expectations which come along with that process. Some of these are communicated in requirements and some are not. Most of the time the performance expectations are not communicated, but can sink the success of a project anyway. Performance testing is not about trying to squeeze every millisecond out of an application, it is about making sure that it is good enough to meet the needs of the customer.

Improving Entity Framework in the Real World

See also

In this chapter:

- *Performing load testing against a database*
- *Testing queries*

Performing load testing against a database

When we deploy to a production environment, we want to make sure that it can handle the load that we are going to put on it with the application. We are going to build a load testing suite that allows us to test our data access for this purpose.

Getting ready

For this recipe, you will need the load testing tools from Visual Studio. These are part of the load testing feature pack which is available to the Visual Studio Ultimate users with active MSDN accounts.

We will be using NuGet Package Manager to install the Entity Framework 4.1 assemblies.

The package installer can be found at `http://www.nuget.org/`.

We will also be using a database for connecting to the data and updating it.

Open the **Load Testing against a Database** solution in the included source code examples.

Execute the database setup script from the code samples included with this recipe. This can be found in the `DataAccess` project within the `Database` folder.

How to do it...

1. We are going to take our already prepared performance tests and use them in a new load test by adding a load test to the `Test` project and naming the scenario **BasicDataAccess** in the wizard. Select the **Use normal distribution centered on recorded think times** option, and change the **Think time between iterations** to **1** second, as shown in the following screenshot:

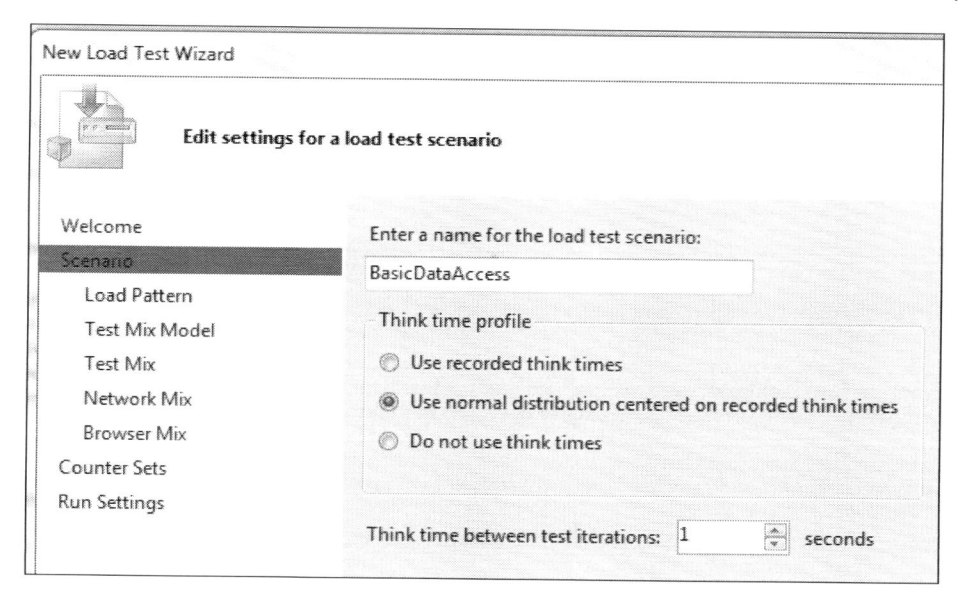

Chapter 1

[Screenshot: New Load Test Wizard — Edit settings for a load test scenario. Scenario pane with "Enter a name for the load test scenario:" set to "BasicDataAccess". Think time profile: "Use normal distribution centered on recorded think times" selected. Think time between test iterations: 1 seconds.]

2. We are going to simulate 25 users, for a constant load, as shown in the following screenshot:

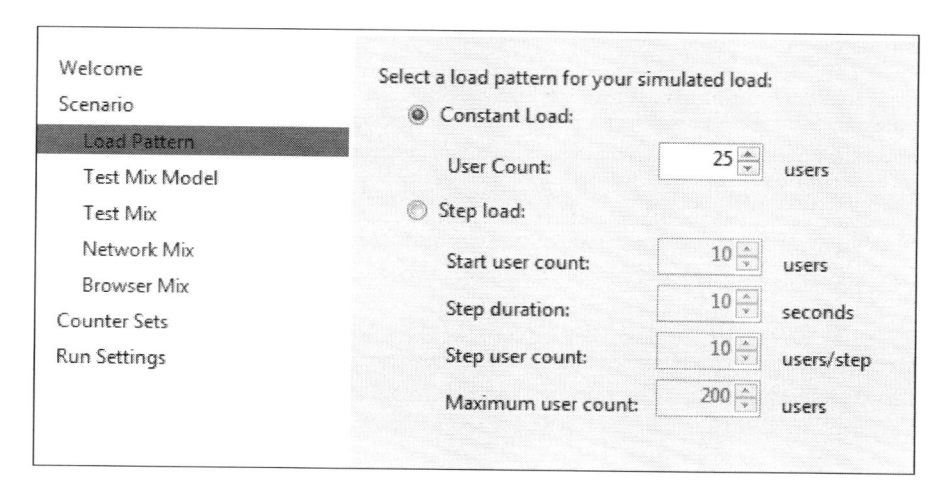

[Screenshot: Load Pattern pane. Select a load pattern for your simulated load: Constant Load selected, User Count: 25 users. Step load: Start user count: 10 users, Step duration: 10 seconds, Step user count: 10 users/step, Maximum user count: 200 users.]

41

Improving Entity Framework in the Real World

3. Set the **Test Mix Model** to **Based on the total number of tests,** as shown in the following screenshot:

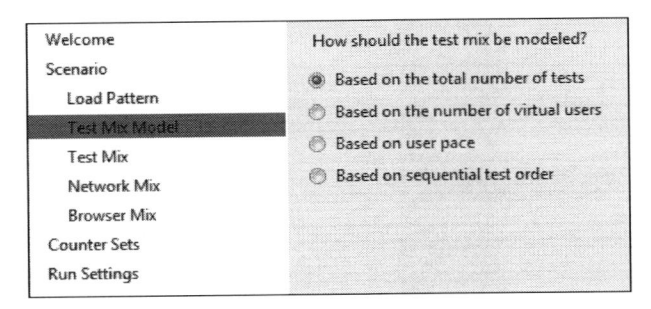

4. Add both existing tests to the **Test Mix** at **50%** of load, as shown in the following screenshot:

5. We skip **Network Mix** and **Counter Sets** for this test, and on **Run Settings,** we set a **10** minute duration for the test run, as shown in the following screenshot:

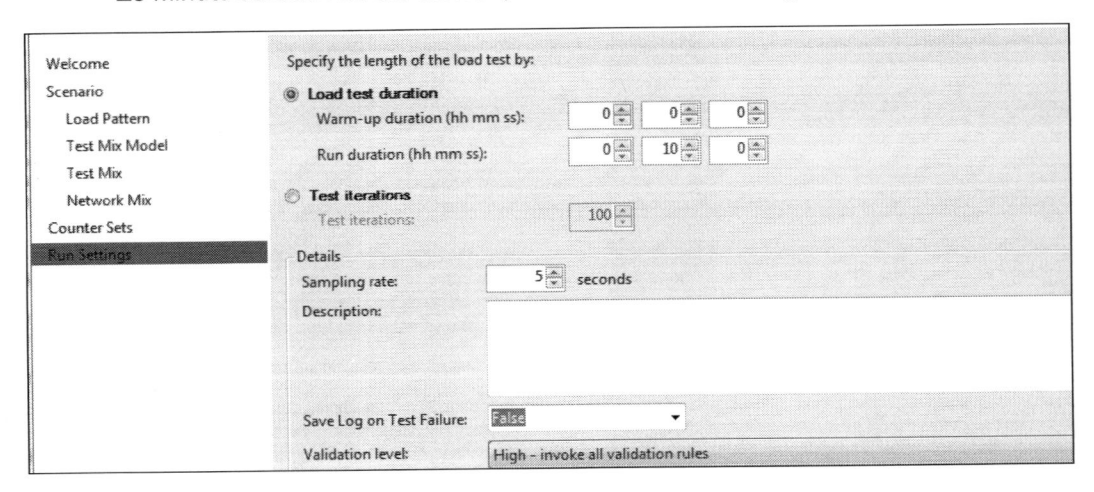

6. Finish the setup, and you should get the following screenshot. Click on the **Run Test** button in the upper left corner as follows:

Chapter 1

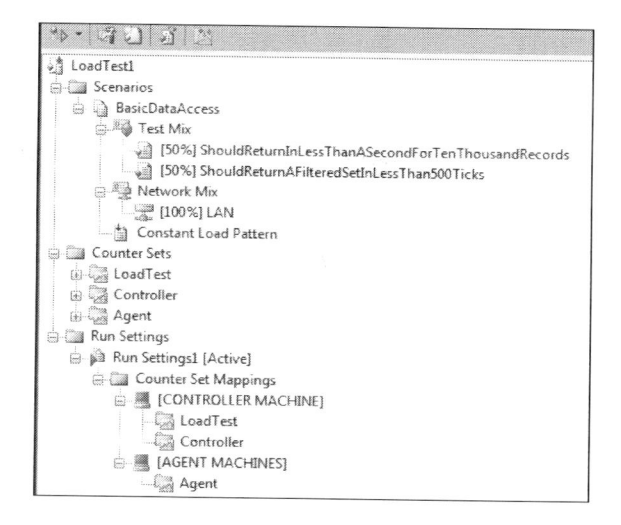

[Screenshot of LoadTest1 tree structure showing Scenarios, BasicDataAccess, Test Mix with [50%] ShouldReturnInLessThanASecondForTenThousandRecords and [50%] ShouldReturnAFilteredSetInLessThan500Ticks, Network Mix [100%] LAN, Constant Load Pattern, Counter Sets (LoadTest, Controller, Agent), Run Settings with Run Settings1 [Active], Counter Set Mappings for [CONTROLLER MACHINE] and [AGENT MACHINES].]

7. When you open the test, you will get a very complex screen. The left panel holds the counters that you can drag onto the graphs to the right to monitor system and test performance. The graphs hold the these values. The table on the bottom right holds the numeric values that drive the graphs, and the list on the bottom left holds the number of run and completed tests. It should take a while for the first test to run due to the setup scripts, but after that it should run pretty fast:

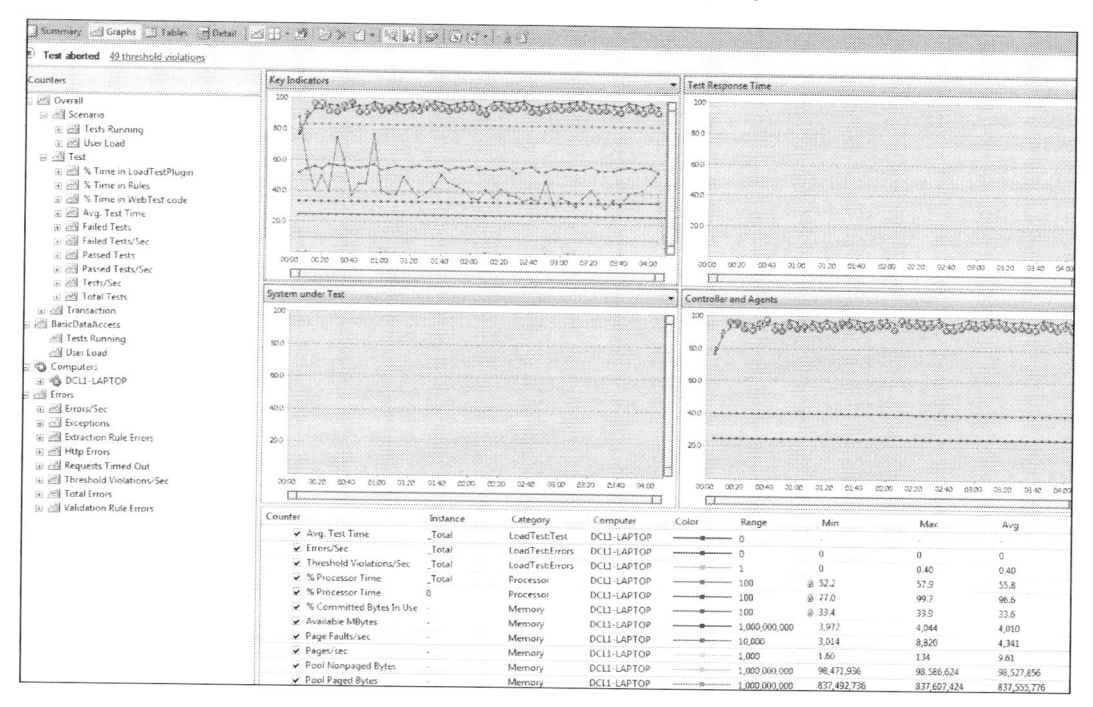

[Screenshot of load test results screen showing Counters panel on left, Key Indicators and Test Response Time graphs at top, System under Test and Controller and Agents graphs in middle, and counter data table at bottom with columns: Counter, Instance, Category, Computer, Color, Range, Min, Max, Avg.]

43

How it works...

This load test spins up threads across as many processors as it can to simulate multiple users hitting the application at the same time. This in turn creates many connections to the database. This flood of connectivity and processing would have been impossible except by full production load in the past, but is now a simple setup to get. We are able to test not only our database connections this way, but also other internal pieces of our application that may come under the load. This allows us to identify bottlenecks and resolve them before they cause a production issue.

There's more...

Load and performance testing are tightly coupled, and should be used in conjunction. The two styles of load testing need to be leveraged on our application in the same combination.

Stress testing

Stress testing is one of the two main ways to load test an application. This is the test in which we slowly increase the amount of load on a system until it fails. This does two very important functions for us. First, it identifies the initial point of failure, or the bottleneck. Second, it allows us to view the pieces of software on the value of their scalability, and work to increase the throughput and handling of those pieces that do not function well. This will help us ward off problems before they bring our boss to our desk at 4:45pm.

Real-world simulation

Real world simulation is the second of the two main ways to load test an application. This puts a slightly higher than expected load on the system to see how the performance and functionality will handle the load. This is an assurance that the system will function day-to-day at an acceptable level. We are not hunting for bottlenecks with this type of testing, but merely making sure we have met the expectations and that we are fully prepared to hand over this software to our customers without the fear of a major performance issue.

See also

In this chapter:

- Testing queries for performance
- Creating mock database connections

2
Understanding the Fluent Configuration API

In this chapter, we will cover the following topics:

- Improving property maps
- Creating one-to-one maps
- Creating one-to-many maps
- Creating many-to-many maps
- Mapping one table to many objects
- Mapping many tables to one object
- Handling inheritance based on database values
- Handling complex key maps

Introduction

Have you ever tried to explain the **unified field theory** to someone that has no understanding of physics? We would have to tell them about the ideas of *Einstein* on how the universe was put together, and how the basic physic particles interact. If they have not fallen asleep by this point, we then have to explain even more things that are the final details. These details are required for the explanation of theory, but not everyone is interested in them. This is much like what the storage schema in a database means to object-oriented programmers. They have to worry about it at some point, but it will never be their focal point in the way that it is for a database administrator. When we say that the two objects are related, we think something completely different from a database administrator who hears the same phrase. When we try to convey our ideas to someone, it often helps to put them into terms that the other person can understand and relate to. This is not so different from storing objects in a database.

Objects at their most basic level are **behavior** and **state**. Objects can be either some kinds of data or the ability to act upon that data, but are often a combination. Storing data is something that our industry has become quite good at over the years, but most of us do not truly understand that it is only half the story.

While the data is within an object, it is hard to store it, as the object is closely tied to the data but not closely tied to the best storage schema. As such, we must recognize that the representation in the database and the representation in the objects should differ sometimes. Converting an object to a record in a table or multiple tables requires separating the data from the object and flattening it out. This process has been accomplished by many **Object Relational Mappers** (**ORMs**) through a variety of different approaches. **Entity Framework** approaches the problem of objects that differ greatly from the relational tables by allowing you to configure the mapping manually where it differs from the standard convention. This will reduce the amount of code that you have to write for the configuration, but it will require the learning of a new and fluent **Application Programming Interface** (**API**), which shows the database layer how to translate the code into SQL statements. This allows us, as the programmers, to completely separate the way data is stored in the database from the way our application packages the same data, allowing us to adhere to both object-oriented principles and best database practices.

Improving property maps

This recipe will allow us to map a property and attach some metadata to it, to guide the connection to the related table and the column in the database.

Getting ready

We will be using **NuGet Package Manager** to install the Entity Framework 4.1 assemblies.

The package installer can be found at `http://nuget.org/`.

We will also be using a database for connecting to the data and updating it.

Open the **Improving Property Maps** solution in the included source code examples.

How to do it...

Let us get connected to the database using the following steps:

1. We start by adding a new unit test named `MappingTest` to the `Test` project. We make a test that connects to the database and retrieves an object. This will test the configuration and ensure that the model matches the database schema, using the following code:

```
using System;
using System.Collections.Generic;
using System.Linq;
using System.Text;
using BusinessLogic;
using DataAccess;
using DataAccess.Database;
using Microsoft.VisualStudio.TestTools.UnitTesting;
using Test.Properties;
using System.Data.Entity;
namespace Test
{
  [TestClass]
  public class MappingTest
  {
    [TestMethod]
    public void ShouldReturnABlogWithAuthorDetails()
    {
      //Arrange
      var init = new Initializer();
      var context = new
        BlogContext(Settings.Default.BlogConnection);
      init.InitializeDatabase(context);
      //Act
      var blog = context.Blogs.FirstOrDefault();
      //Assert
      Assert.IsNotNull(blog);
    }
  }
}
```

Understanding the Fluent Configuration API

2. Add an initializer to the `DataAccess` project in the `Database` folder, with the following code, to set up the data:

```csharp
using System;
using System.Collections.Generic;
using System.Data.Entity;
using BusinessLogic;
namespace DataAccess.Database
{
  public class Initializer : DropCreateDatabaseAlways<BlogContext>
  {
    public Initializer()
    {
    }
    protected override void Seed(BlogContext context)
    {
      context.Set<Blog>().Add(new Blog()
      {
        Creationdate = DateTime.Now,
        ShortDescription = "Testing",
        Title = "Test Blog"
      });
      base.Seed(context);
    }
  }
}
```

3. In the `BusinessLogic` project, add a new C# class named `Blog`, with the following code:

```csharp
using System;
namespace BusinessLogic
{
  public class Blog
  {
    public int Id { get; set; }
    public DateTime Creationdate { get; set; }
    public string ShortDescription { get; set; }
    public string Title { get; set; }
  }
}
```

4. Add a Mapping folder to the DataAccess project, and then add a BlogMapping class to the folder, with the following code:

```csharp
using System.ComponentModel.DataAnnotations;
using System.Data.Entity.ModelConfiguration;
using BusinessLogic;
namespace DataAccess.Mappings
{
  public class BlogMapping : EntityTypeConfiguration<Blog>
  {
    public BlogMapping()
    {
      this.ToTable("Blogs");
      this.HasKey(x => x.Id);
      this.Property(x =>
x.Id).HasDatabaseGeneratedOption(DatabaseGeneratedOption.Identity);
      this.Property(x => x.Title).IsRequired().HasMaxLength(250);
      this.Property(x =>
       x.Creationdate).HasColumnName("CreationDate").IsRequired();
      this.Property(x =>
x.ShortDescription).HasColumnType("Text").IsMaxLength().IsOptional
        ().HasColumnName("Description");
    }
  }
}
```

5. Modify the BlogContext class to contain the new mappings and a DbSet property for Blogs, with the following code:

```csharp
using System;
using System.Data.Entity;
using System.Linq;
using BusinessLogic;
using DataAccess.Mappings;
namespace DataAccess
{
  public class BlogContext : DbContext   {
  public BlogContext(string connectionString)
   : base(connectionString)
  {
  }
  protected override void OnModelCreating(DbModelBuilder
    modelBuilder)
  {
    modelBuilder.Configurations.Add(new BlogMapping());
    base.OnModelCreating(modelBuilder);
```

Understanding the Fluent Configuration API

```
        }
        public DbSet<Blog> Blogs { get; set; }
        public IQueryable<T> Find<T>() where T : class
        {
           return this.Set<T>();
        }
        public void Refresh()
        {
           this.ChangeTracker.Entries().ToList().ForEach(x=>x.Reload());
        }
        public void Commit()
        {
           this.SaveChanges();
        }
    }
```

6. Run our test, and see how it works.

How it works...

Our solution starts with a test, as always, to set up the intended behaviour of mapping the properties to the database correctly. It is pivotal to the structure of our code, as this is how we validate the database schema. This also allows us to set up data for the test.

We create an object with a couple of properties that are similar but not exactly the same as the database object. We then create a mapping class that inherits from the `EntityTypeConfiguration<T>` class. This inheritance gives us the fluent configuration Application Programming Interface (API) that we will leverage. The conventions will cover some of the configuration for us but leave us open to the issues caused by renaming. If we refactor a property name to make the program more concise, it will break the convention and will no longer talk to the database. This seems like a huge vulnerability that we should avoid. We make sure that every property has a `HasColumnName()` configuration. This takes us a bit more time but is worth doing for the trouble it saves us on risk and supportability.

The object needs to know the table in which we would like to save this, and as such, we have the `ToTable()` method that allows us to configure this.

Once the table is configured, the first property that we need to specify is the key. We can use `HasKey()` method to set the property or the properties that will be the key. Once we have that defined, we want to use `Property()` to attach a `HasColumnName()` method to the key, so that we control the name that it gets generated with. Then, we attach the `HasDatabaseGeneratedOption()` method to allow us to configure the identity column, so that we do not try to set this property, and overwrite it in the database. Trying to do it without this setting would throw an error.

The columns as well as each of the properties in our database are marked either nullable or non-nullable. The fluent API gives us this ability through the `IsRequired` and `IsOptional` methods. These two methods not only mark the column as nullable or not nullable in the schema for generation, but also validate this on the program side before sending the bad data to the database for an SQL error.

The `Title` property has a limited length in our database, and we need to communicate it to the configuration. The `HasMaxLength` method not only allows us to set this up, but also gives us the program-side validation.

The `ShortDescription` property is not stored as the default string storage varchar but as a text field that allows for the maximum length of SQL. This can be communicated through the use of the `HasColumnType()` and `IsMaxLength()` methods. The `HasColumnType()` method allows you to specify the type that a property should be stored as. However, if the property cannot be converted to that type, it will show an error and fail.

There's more...

There are several more areas that are less frequently used but definitely need to be mentioned. The following section supplies more detail about why you may want to specify the configuration even while matching the convention, the tools that help to generate these mappings from a database, and the explanation for the approach to storing the mappings.

Mapping storage

There are two main thought processes involved in the storage of mappings. First is the idea that they should be stored in a class in the same file as the domain object. This not only allows for the easy changing of the mappings when the object changes, but also pushes the storage mechanism dependencies into our core layer. If we want to change the storage mechanism at some point, we will have to change our core code too. This does not sit well with us, so we opt for the second option, that is, the storage of the mappings in a folder close to the context declaration. This allows us to keep the implementation specifics in one place, and also keeps our dependencies within Entity Framework out of the core programming logic.

More fluent configurations

The following is a list of the more fluent configurations:

- **ToTable(tableName,schemaName)**: It allows us to connect the objects to the tables and schemas that do not share their naming convention with our objects.
- **HasColumnOrder()**: It specifies the order for the key while using a composite key.
- **IsUnicode()**: It specifies that the text is Unicode-compliant.
- **IsConcurrencyToken()**: It specifies the column to be the token that is used in determining the optimistic concurrency for parallel processings.

Understanding the Fluent Configuration API

Finding tools to help

In 2010, the Entity Framework team announced the community technology preview of Entity Framework Code First Power Toys. This software package is a Visual Studio extension that allows for the generation of true **Plain Old CLR Objects** (**POCOs**) and their mappings, based on an existing database schema. These tools are not aware of the schema at this moment, but are otherwise fairly full-featured. They create a type for each table, so that most of the cases will have to modify the generated code. The generation is not meant for long-term usage, but a one-time help to overcome the overhead of writing hundreds of mapping tables while starting in an existing application.

See also

In this chapter:

- *Creating one-to-one maps*

In *Chapter 1, Improving Entity Framework in the Real World*:

- *Creating databases from the code*

Creating one-to-one maps

This recipe will allow us to map the direct relationships between two objects into the foreign keys that will hold this relationship in the database.

Getting ready

We will be using NuGet Package Manager to install the Entity Framework 4.1 assemblies.

The package installer can be found at http://nuget.org/.

We will also be using a database for connecting to and updating data.

Open the **Improving One-To-One References** solution in the included source code examples.

How to do it...

Let us get connected to the database using the following steps:

1. We start by adding a new unit test named `MappingTest` to the `Test` project. We make a test that connects to the database and retrieves an object. This will test the configuration and ensure that the model matches the database schema. Use the following code:

```csharp
using System;
using System.Collections.Generic;
using System.Linq;
using System.Text;
using BusinessLogic;
using DataAccess;
using DataAccess.Database;
using Microsoft.VisualStudio.TestTools.UnitTesting;
using Test.Properties;
using System.Data.Entity;
namespace Test
{
  [TestClass]
  public class MappingTest
  {
    [TestMethod]
    public void ShouldReturnABlogWithAuthorDetails()
    {
      //Arrange
      var init = new Initializer();
      var context = new
        BlogContext(Settings.Default.BlogConnection);
      init.InitializeDatabase(context);
      //Act
      var blog = context.Blogs.Include(x =>
        x.AuthorDetail).FirstOrDefault();
      //Assert
      Assert.IsNotNull(blog);
      Assert.IsNotNull(blog.AuthorDetail);
    }
  }
}
```

2. Add an initializer to the `DataAccess` project in the `Database` folder, with the following code to set up the data:

```csharp
using System;
using System.Collections.Generic;
using System.Data.Entity;
using BusinessLogic;
namespace DataAccess.Database
{
  public class Initializer : DropCreateDatabaseAlways<BlogContext>
  {
    public Initializer()
    {
    }
    protected override void Seed(BlogContext context)
```

Understanding the Fluent Configuration API

```
        {
          context.Set<Blog>().Add(new Blog()
          {
            AuthorDetail = new AuthorDetail() { Bio = "Test", Email =
              "Email", Name = "Testing" },
            Creationdate = DateTime.Now,
            ShortDescription = "Testing",
            Title = "Test Blog"
          });
          context.SaveChanges();
        }
      }
    }
```

3. In the `BusinessLogic` project, add a new C# class named `Blog` with the following code:

```csharp
using System;
namespace BusinessLogic
{
  public class Blog
  {
    public int Id { get; set; }
    public DateTime Creationdate { get; set; }
    public string ShortDescription { get; set; }
    public string Title { get; set; }
    public AuthorDetail AuthorDetail { get; set; }
  }
}
```

4. In the `Business Logic` project, add a new C# class named `AuthorDetail` with the following code:

```csharp
namespace BusinessLogic
{
  public class AuthorDetail
  {
    public int Id { get; set; }
    public string Name { get; set; }
    public string Email { get; set; }
    public string Bio { get; set; }
  }
}
```

5. Add a `Mapping` folder to the `DataAccess` project, and then add a `BlogMapping` class to the folder with the following code:

```csharp
using System.ComponentModel.DataAnnotations;
using System.Data.Entity.ModelConfiguration;
using BusinessLogic;
namespace DataAccess.Mappings
{
  public class BlogMapping : EntityTypeConfiguration<Blog>
  {
    public BlogMapping()
    {
      this.ToTable("Blogs");
      this.HasKey(x => x.Id);
      this.Property(x => x.Id).HasDatabaseGeneratedOption(DatabaseGeneratedOption.Identity)
        .HasColumnName("BlogId");
      this.Property(x => x.Title).IsRequired().HasMaxLength(250);
      this.Property(x =>
        x.Creationdate).HasColumnName("CreationDate").IsRequired();
      this.Property(x => x.ShortDescription).HasColumnType("Text").IsMaxLength().IsOptional
          ().HasColumnName("Description");
      this.HasRequired(x =>
        x.AuthorDetail).WithOptional().WillCascadeOnDelete();
    }
  }
}
```

6. Add a new C# class named `PostMapping` to the `Mappings` folder with the following code:

```csharp
using System.ComponentModel.DataAnnotations;
using System.Data.Entity.ModelConfiguration;
using BusinessLogic;
namespace DataAccess.Mappings
{
  public class AuthorDetailMapping :
    EntityTypeConfiguration<AuthorDetail>
  {
    public AuthorDetailMapping()
    {
      this.ToTable("AuthorDetails");
      this.HasKey(x => x.Id);
      this.Property(x =>
        x.Id).HasColumnName("AuthorDetailId")
          .HasDatabaseGeneratedOption
```

```
                    (DatabaseGeneratedOption.Identity);
            this.Property(x =>
              x.Bio).HasColumnType("Text").IsMaxLength();
            this.Property(x => x.Email).HasMaxLength(100).IsRequired();
            this.Property(x => x.Name).HasMaxLength(100).IsRequired();
        }
      }
    }
```

7. Modify the `BlogContext` class with the following code to add the collections and mappings for our objects:

```
using System;
using System.Data.Entity;
using System.Linq;
using BusinessLogic;
using DataAccess.Mappings;
namespace DataAccess
{
  public class BlogContext : DbContext
  {
    public BlogContext(string connectionString)
    : base(connectionString)
    {
    }
    protected override void OnModelCreating(DbModelBuilder
       modelBuilder)
    {
      modelBuilder.Configurations.Add(new BlogMapping());
      modelBuilder.Configurations.Add(new AuthorDetailMapping());
      base.OnModelCreating(modelBuilder);
    }
    public DbSet<Blog> Blogs { get; set; }
    public DbSet<AuthorDetail> AuthorDetails { get; set; }
    public IQueryable<T> Find<T>() where T : class
    {
      return this.Set<T>();
    }
    public void Refresh()
    {
     this.ChangeTracker.Entries().ToList().ForEach(x=>x.Reload());
    }

    public void Commit()
    {
      this.SaveChanges();
    }
  }
}
```

8. Run our test, and see how it works.

How it works...

When we map a one-to-one relationship in Entity Framework, we are not only relating the objects but also defining the foreign key. This allows us to set up the relationships, but we have to be careful when we configure the relationship as the configuration determines how the foreign key looks.

The `HasRequired()` method defines the foreign key as a required constraint. If we try to commit an insert without this object, it will fail. This maps to a non-nullable key column on the schema side of the `Blogs` table.

The `WithOptional()` method configures the targeted property type as having a 0:1 relationship to the current type. When we use this in combination with the `HasRequired()` method, this creates a 1 to 0..1 relationship in the database. Configuring the relationship this way allows us to insert `AuthorDetail` without `blog`.

The `WillCascadeOnDelete()` method deletes related `AuthorDetail` when `blog` is deleted. This allows us to clean up the **object graphs** with a single delete statement, and avoid littering the database with orphaned data that holds no reference to any other objects.

There's more...

When we are mapping a one-to-one relationship, there are many options to consider, but the largest concern should be the object graph. When we query these objects, we have to be certain that we get all the related data that we need.

Using more fluent configurations

More fluent configurations are as follows:

- **HasOptional()**: It configures a nullable relationship.
- **Map()**: It allows for the configuration of relationships using columns not exposed in the object model.
- **WithRequiredPrinciple()**: It configures a one-to-one relationship that is required on both the sides, and the object being configured is the principle object.
- **WithRequiredDependant()**: It configures a one-to-one relationship that is required on both the sides, and the object being configured is the dependant object.

Understanding the Fluent Configuration API

Considering eager versus lazy

Entity Framework allows us to either eager load the related objects (to explicitly decide when to load these objects), or to lazy load the objects (allow the framework to load these objects when they are needed). This gives us a choice between having the ability to reduce the total number of calls to the database tightly, while possibly increasing the amount of data retrieved, and performing a larger number of queries overall without worrying about the loading code. In Window forms and small-platform (less than 100 installs) applications, lazy loading may make sense for ease of coding, but for anything that has to be used in a web page, serialized over WCF, or large platform applications, you need the explicit nature of eager loading. The `Include()` method has been expanded to include the usage of lambdas to make this area of Entity Framework less dependent on magic strings.

See also

In this chapter:

- *Creating one-to-many maps*

In *Chapter 5, Improving Entity Framework with Query Libraries*::

- *Implementing composed queries*

Creating one-to-many maps

This recipe will take us through the process of configuring the relationship between one object and many other objects.

Getting ready

We will be using NuGet Package Manager to install the Entity Framework 4.1 assemblies.

The package installer can be found at `http://nuget.org/`.

We will also be using a database for connecting to the data and updating it.

Open the **Improving One-To-Many References** solution in the included source code examples.

How to do it...

Let us get connected to the database using the following steps:

1. We start by adding a new unit test named `MappingTest` to the `Test` project. We make a test that connects to the database and retrieves an object. This will test the configuration and ensure that the model matches the database schema. Use the following code:

```csharp
using System;
using System.Collections.Generic;
using System.Linq;
using System.Text;
using BusinessLogic;
using DataAccess;
using DataAccess.Database;
using Microsoft.VisualStudio.TestTools.UnitTesting;
using Test.Properties;
using System.Data.Entity;
namespace Test
{
  [TestClass]
  public class MappingTest
  {
    [TestMethod]
    public void ShouldReturnABlogWithPosts()
    {
      //Arrange
      Database.SetInitializer(new Initializer());
      var context = new
        BlogContext(Settings.Default.BlogConnection);
      //Act
      var blog = context.Blogs.Include(x =>
        x.Posts).FirstOrDefault();
      //Assert
      Assert.IsNotNull(blog);
      Assert.IsNotNull(blog.Posts);
    }
  }
}
```

2. In the `BusinessLogic` project, add a new C# class named `Blog` to the following code:

```csharp
using System;
using System.Collections.Generic;
using DataAccess;
namespace BusinessLogic
{
  public class Blog
  {
    public int Id { get; set; }
    public DateTime Creationdate { get; set; }
    public string ShortDescription { get; set; }
```

Understanding the Fluent Configuration API

```csharp
            public string Title { get; set; }
            public AuthorDetail AuthorDetail { get; set; }
            public ICollection<Post> Posts { get; set; }
        }
    }
```

3. In the `BusinessLogic` project, add a new C# class named `Post` to the following code:

   ```csharp
   using System;
   namespace BusinessLogic
   {
     public class Post
     {
       public int Id { get; set; }
       public string Title { get; set; }
       public string Content { get; set; }
       public DateTime PostedDate { get; set; }
       public Blog Blog { get; set; }
     }
   }
   ```

4. Add a `Mapping` folder to the `DataAccess` project, and then add a `BlogMapping` class to the folder with the following code:

   ```csharp
   using System.ComponentModel.DataAnnotations;
   using System.Data.Entity.ModelConfiguration;
   using BusinessLogic;
   namespace DataAccess.Mappings
   {
     public class BlogMapping : EntityTypeConfiguration<Blog>
     {
       public BlogMapping()
       {
         this.ToTable("Blogs");
         this.HasKey(x => x.Id);
         this.Property(x =>
   x.Id).HasDatabaseGeneratedOption(DatabaseGeneratedOption.
   Identity);
         this.Property(x => x.Title).IsRequired().HasMaxLength(250);
         this.Property(x =>
          x.Creationdate).HasColumnName("CreationDate").IsRequired();
         this.Property(x =>
   x.ShortDescription).HasColumnType("Text").IsMaxLength().IsOptional
             ().HasColumnName("Description");
         this.HasRequired(x => x.AuthorDetail);
   ```

```
          this.HasMany(x => x.Posts).WithRequired(x =>
            x.Blog).WillCascadeOnDelete();
        }
      }
    }
```

5. Add a new C# class named `PostMapping` to the `Mapping` folder with the following code:

```
using System.ComponentModel.DataAnnotations;
using System.Data.Entity.ModelConfiguration;
using BusinessLogic;
namespace DataAccess.Mappings
{
    public class PostMapping : EntityTypeConfiguration<Post>
    {
        public PostMapping()
        {
        this.ToTable("Posts");
        this.HasKey(x => x.Id);
        this.Property(x =>
x.Id).HasColumnName("PostId").HasDatabaseGeneratedOption(DatabaseG
            eneratedOption.Identity);
        this.Property(x =>
            x.Content).HasColumnName("Body").IsMaxLength();
        this.Property(x => x.PostedDate).HasColumnName("PostedDate");
        this.Property(x =>
            x.Title).HasColumnName("Title").IsMaxLength();
        }
    }
}
```

6. Modify the `BlogContext` class, with the following code, to add the collections and mappings for our objects:

```
using System;
using System.Data.Entity;
using System.Linq;
using BusinessLogic;
using DataAccess.Mappings;
namespace DataAccess
{
    public class BlogContext : DbContext
    {
        public BlogContext(string connectionString)
         : base(connectionString)
        {
```

Understanding the Fluent Configuration API

```
        }
        protected override void OnModelCreating(DbModelBuilder
          modelBuilder)
        {
          modelBuilder.Configurations.Add(new BlogMapping());
          modelBuilder.Configurations.Add(new AuthorDetailMapping());
          modelBuilder.Configurations.Add(new PostMapping());
          base.OnModelCreating(modelBuilder);
        }
        public DbSet<Blog> Blogs { get; set; }
        public DbSet<Post> Posts { get; set; }
        public DbSet<AuthorDetail> AuthorDetails { get; set; }
        public IQueryable<T> Find<T>() where T : class
        {
           return this.Set<T>();
        }
        public void Refresh()
        {
          this.ChangeTracker.Entries().ToList().ForEach(x=>x.Reload());
        }
        public void Commit()
        {
           this.SaveChanges();
        }
      }
    }
```

7. Run our test, and see how it works.

How it works...

We start off with a test that ensures that the `Posts` property does not come back null from the database after initializing data to it. This will allow us to ensure that our code accomplishes the intended behaviour.

The `HasMany()` method is what we are focusing on in this recipe. This method allows us to establish one-to-many relationships in the code. Here, the collection of `Posts` that we added to `Blog` is `ICollection<T>` for usage. All the collections of objects on the "many" side need to be housed this way. This allows Entity Framework to return `DbSet<T>`, but we do not have to spread that Entity Framework-specific type (and the dependencies it has) throughout our code.

The `WithRequired()` method sets up the dependent side of the relationship, and forces the object relationship to exist. This is mapped to a foreign key column in the database that is not null. This will give an update error if an object is not provided, to prevent the attempt to insert bad data.

The `WillCascadeOnDelete()` method allows us to specify that the related objects are in context. When a delete on this object happens, the mapped relationship will be deleted as well. This only applies to objects that are previously loaded by the context and are still in the context tracker. If you need the database side cascades, you must set the property on the foreign key.

There's more...

When dealing with one-to-many relationships, there are many varieties, and configuring them takes several methods and practices.

More fluent configurations

More fluent configurations are as follows:

- **WithOptional()**: This allows for an option named, one-to-many relationship.
- **Map()**: This allows for the configuration of relationships using columns not exposed in the object model.
- **HasForeignKey()**: This allows for the use of a named foreign key (in the database to be used for a relationship), instead of a coded configuration.

More than one way to improve

Often, there is more than one way to work through the configuration in a code, as there is to set up a data structure. This variability will also lead to differing opinions on how to define these configurations. We take the "configuration" approach of consolidating configuration to the central objects in the domain model. This allows more configurations to be viewed from those key maps. This has the added benefit of showing you the object interaction at the hubs of the application. You can define the same one-to-many relationship by using `HasRequired(x=>x.Blog)` with `Many(x=>x.Posts)`, from `PostMapping`. This, however, would start spreading out the configuration and makes it harder to maintain.

See also

In this chapter:

- *Creating many-to-many maps*

Understanding the Fluent Configuration API

Creating many-to-many maps

This recipe allows us to map a set of objects to another set of objects without constraining either side.

Getting ready

We will be using NuGet Package Manager to install the Entity Framework 4.1 assemblies.

The package installer can be found at http://nuget.org/.

We will also be using a database for connecting to the data and updating it.

Open the **Improving Many-To-Many References** solution in the included source code examples.

How to do it...

Let us get connected to the database using the following steps:

1. We start by adding a new unit test named `MappingTest` to the `Test` project. We make a test that connects to the database and retrieves an object. This will test the configuration and ensure that the model matches the database schema, using the following code:

```
using System;
using System.Collections.Generic;
using System.Linq;
using System.Text;
using BusinessLogic;
using DataAccess;
using DataAccess.Database;
using Microsoft.VisualStudio.TestTools.UnitTesting;
using Test.Properties;
using System.Data.Entity;
namespace Test
{
  [TestClass]
  public class MappingTest
  {
    [TestMethod]
    public void ShouldReturnABlogWithAuthors()
    {
      //Arrange
      var init = new Initializer();
```

```
            var context = new
              BlogContext(Settings.Default.BlogConnection);
            init.InitializeDatabase(context);
            //Act
            var post = context.Posts.Include(x =>
              x.Authors).FirstOrDefault();
            //Assert
            Assert.IsNotNull(post);
            Assert.IsTrue(post.Authors.Count == 1);
        }
    }
}
```

2. Add a new C# class named `Initializer` to the `DataAccess` project in the `Database` folder with the following code:

```
using System;
using System.Collections.Generic;
using System.Data.Entity;
using BusinessLogic;
namespace DataAccess.Database
{
  public class Initializer : DropCreateDatabaseAlways<BlogContext>
  {
    public Initializer()
    {
    }
    protected override void Seed(BlogContext context)
    {
      AuthorDetail authorDetail = new AuthorDetail() { Bio =
        "Test", Email = "Email", Name = "Testing" };
      Post item = new Post() { Content = "Test", PostedDate =
        DateTime.Now, Title = "Test", Authors = new
          List<AuthorDetail>{authorDetail} };
      context.Set<Blog>().Add(new Blog()
      {
        Posts = new List<Post>() { item },
        AuthorDetail = authorDetail,
        Creationdate = DateTime.Now,
        ShortDescription = "Testing",
        Title = "Test Blog"
      });
      context.SaveChanges();
    }
  }
}
```

Understanding the Fluent Configuration API

3. Add a new C# class named `Post` to the `BusinessLogic` project with the following code:

```csharp
using System;
using System.Collections.Generic;
namespace BusinessLogic
{
  public class Post
  {
    public int Id { get; set; }
    public string Title { get; set; }
    public string Content { get; set; }
    public DateTime PostedDate { get; set; }
    public ICollection<AuthorDetail> Authors { get; set; }
  }
}
```

4. Add another C# class named `AuthorDetail` to the `BusinessLogic` project with the following code:

```csharp
using System.Collections.Generic;
namespace BusinessLogic
{
  public class AuthorDetail
  {
    public int Id { get; set; }
    public string Name { get; set; }
    public string Email { get; set; }
    public string Bio { get; set; }
    public ICollection<Post> Posts { get; set; }
  }
}
```

5. Add another C# class named `Blog` to the `BusinessLogic` project with the following code:

```csharp
using System;
using System.Collections.Generic;
using DataAccess;
namespace BusinessLogic
{
  public class Blog
  {
    public int Id { get; set; }
    public DateTime Creationdate { get; set; }
    public string ShortDescription { get; set; }
    public string Title { get; set; }
    public AuthorDetail AuthorDetail { get; set; }
    public ICollection<Post> Posts { get; set; }
  }
}
```

6. Now that we have our domain objects, we want to add a `Mapping` folder to the `DataAccess` project and then add a `BlogMapping` class to the folder with the following code:

```csharp
using System.ComponentModel.DataAnnotations;
using System.Data.Entity.ModelConfiguration;
using BusinessLogic;
namespace DataAccess.Mappings
{
    public class BlogMapping : EntityTypeConfiguration<Blog>
    {
        public BlogMapping()
        {
            this.ToTable("Blogs");
            this.HasKey(x => x.Id);
            this.Property(x =>
x.Id).HasDatabaseGeneratedOption(DatabaseGeneratedOption.Identity)
                ;
            this.Property(x => x.Title).IsRequired().HasMaxLength(250);
            this.Property(x =>
             x.Creationdate).HasColumnName("CreationDate").IsRequired();
            this.Property(x =>
x.ShortDescription).HasColumnType("Text").IsMaxLength().IsOptional
                ().HasColumnName("Description");
            this.HasRequired(x => x.AuthorDetail);
            this.HasMany(x => x.Posts).WithRequired(x =>
                x.Blog).WillCascadeOnDelete(false);
        }
    }
}
```

7. Add a new C# class to the `Mapping` folder named `PostMapping` with the following code:

```csharp
using System.ComponentModel.DataAnnotations;
using System.Data.Entity.ModelConfiguration;
using BusinessLogic;
namespace DataAccess.Mappings
{
    public class PostMapping : EntityTypeConfiguration<Post>
    {
        public PostMapping()
        {
            this.ToTable("Posts");
            this.HasKey(x => x.Id);
```

```csharp
            this.Property(x =>
    x.Id).HasColumnName("PostId").HasDatabaseGeneratedOption(DatabaseG
            eneratedOption.Identity);
            this.Property(x =>
               x.Content).HasColumnName("Body").IsMaxLength();
            this.Property(x =>
               x.PostedDate).HasColumnName("PostedDate");
            this.Property(x =>
               x.Title).HasColumnName("Title").IsMaxLength();
            this.HasMany(x => x.Authors).WithMany(x => x.Posts);
         }
      }
   }
```

8. Add another C# class named `AuthorDetailMapping` to the `Mapping` folder with the following code:

```csharp
using System.ComponentModel.DataAnnotations;
using System.Data.Entity.ModelConfiguration;
using BusinessLogic;
namespace DataAccess.Mappings
{
   public class AuthorDetailMapping :
      EntityTypeConfiguration<AuthorDetail>
   {
      public AuthorDetailMapping()
      {
         this.ToTable("AuthorDetails");
         this.HasKey(x => x.Id);
         this.Property(x =>
   x.Id).HasColumnName("AuthorDetailId").HasDatabaseGeneratedOption(D
            atabaseGeneratedOption.Identity);
         this.Property(x =>
            x.Bio).HasColumnType("Text").IsMaxLength();
         this.Property(x =>
            x.Email).HasMaxLength(100).IsRequired();
         this.Property(x => x.Name).HasMaxLength(100).IsRequired();
      }
   }
}
```

9. Modify the `BlogContext` class to include the new mappings and `DbSet<T>` for each type, with the following code:

```csharp
using System;
using System.Data.Entity;
using System.Linq;
```

```csharp
using BusinessLogic;
using DataAccess.Mappings;
namespace DataAccess
{
  public class BlogContext : DbContext, IUnitOfWork
  {
    public BlogContext(string connectionString)
     : base(connectionString)
    {
      if (Database.Exists() &&
         !Database.CompatibleWithModel(false)) Database.Delete();
      if (!Database.Exists()) Database.Create();
    }
    protected override void OnModelCreating(DbModelBuilder
    modelBuilder)
    {
      modelBuilder.Configurations.Add(new BlogMapping());
      modelBuilder.Configurations.Add(new AuthorDetailMapping());
      modelBuilder.Configurations.Add(new PostMapping());
      base.OnModelCreating(modelBuilder);
    }
    public DbSet<Blog> Blogs { get; set; }
    public DbSet<Post> Posts { get; set; }
    public DbSet<AuthorDetail> AuthorDetails { get; set; }
    public IQueryable<T> Find<T>() where T : class
    {
      return this.Set<T>();
    }
    public void Refresh()
    {
     this.ChangeTracker.Entries().ToList().ForEach(x=>x.Reload());
    }
    public void Commit()
    {
      this.SaveChanges();
    }
  }
}
```

10. Run our test, and see how it works.

Understanding the Fluent Configuration API

How it works...

Our solution starts off, as always, with a test that defines the behaviour that we wish to code. We focus on this test at the beginning of each recipe to reaffirm the importance of test-driven code that only accomplishes the goal and nothing more.

Secondly, we set up our domain objects. The simple version is that `Blog` has many posts and `Post` has many `Tags`, but `Tag` also has many posts. This can create some interesting options for the database for reference, but for the objects, it is a very simple task of putting collections into each object.

The `HasMany()` method starts on one side of this many-to-many relationship. It tells the code that it is looking for a related set of objects.

This `WithMany()` method loops back to `Post`, which allows us to find a tag, and then find all the posts that it is used in. This not only creates some power for searching the application, but also creates multiple cascade paths for the cascading deletes. That is why `WillCascadeOnDelete(false)` had to be used in the `Blog` configuration. Any cascaded deletes that hit this will cause errors and, therefore, have to be turned off. Unrelated cascades are fine though.

There's more...

Many-to-many relationships in the database are fairly simple in the configuration. There are very few extras here.

Payload

If you need any kind of payload on many-to-many relationships, you must define an intermediate type. For instance, if you have a menu with tasks and menu items with a sort order in the many-to-many relationship tables, then you must define the relationship table as an entity to use the payload.

More fluent configuration

Map(): This allows you to configure many-to-many relationship with columns not surfaced in the object model.

See also

In this chapter:

- *Creating one-to-one maps*
- *Creating one-to-many maps*

Mapping one table to many objects

This allows us to map multiple objects from a single table, which will separate large load situations and allow for better performance.

Getting ready

We will be using NuGet Package Manager to install the Entity Framework 4.1 assemblies.

The package installer can be found at http://nuget.org/.

We will also be using a database to connect to the data and update it.

Open the **Improving Single Table To Multiple Object Maps** solution in the included source code examples.

How to do it...

Let us get connected to the database using the following steps:

1. We start by adding a new unit test named `MappingTest` to the `Test` project. We make a test that connects to the database and retrieves an object. This will test the configuration and ensure that the model matches the database schema using the following code:

```
using System;
using System.Collections.Generic;
using System.Linq;
using System.Text;
using BusinessLogic;
using DataAccess;
using DataAccess.Database;
using Microsoft.VisualStudio.TestTools.UnitTesting;
using Test.Properties;
using System.Data.Entity;
namespace Test
{
  [TestClass]
  public class MappingTest
  {
    [TestMethod]
    public void ShouldReturnABlogWithLogo()
    {
      //Arrange
      var init = new Initializer();
```

Understanding the Fluent Configuration API

```csharp
            var context = new
               BlogContext(Settings.Default.BlogConnection);
            init.InitializeDatabase(context);
            //Act
            var post = context.Blogs.FirstOrDefault();
            //Assert
            Assert.IsNotNull(post);
            Assert.IsNotNull(post.BlogLogo);
        }
    }
}
```

2. Add a new C# class named `Initializer` to the `DataAccess` project in the `Database` folder, with the following code:

```csharp
using System;
using System.Collections.Generic;
using System.Data.Entity;
using BusinessLogic;
namespace DataAccess.Database
{
   public class Initializer : DropCreateDatabaseAlways<BlogContext>
   {
      public Initializer()
      {
      }
      protected override void Seed(BlogContext context)
      {
         context.Set<Blog>().Add(new Blog()
         {
            Creationdate = DateTime.Now,
            ShortDescription = "Testing",
            Title = "Test Blog",
            BlogLogo = new BlogLogo(){Logo = new byte[0]}
         });
         context.SaveChanges();
      }
   }
}
```

3. Add a new C# class named `Blog` to the `BusinessLogic` project, with the following code:

```csharp
using System;
using System.Collections.Generic;
using DataAccess;
```

```csharp
namespace BusinessLogic
{
  public class Blog
  {
    public int Id { get; set; }
    public DateTime Creationdate { get; set; }
    public string ShortDescription { get; set; }
    public string Title { get; set; }
    public virtual BlogLogo BlogLogo { get; set; }
  }
}
```

4. Add another C# class named `BlogLogo` to the `BusinessLogic` project, with the following code:

```csharp
namespace BusinessLogic
{
  public class BlogLogo
  {
    public int Id { get; set; }
    public byte[] Logo { get; set; }
  }
}
```

5. Now that we have our domain objects, we want to add a `Mapping` folder to the `DataAccess` project and then add a `BlogMapping` class to the folder, with the following code:

```csharp
using System.ComponentModel.DataAnnotations;
using System.Data.Entity.ModelConfiguration;
using BusinessLogic;
namespace DataAccess.Mappings
{
  public class BlogMapping : EntityTypeConfiguration<Blog>
  {
    public BlogMapping()
    {
      this.ToTable("Blogs");
      this.HasKey(x => x.Id);
      this.Property(x => x.Id)
       .HasDatabaseGeneratedOption(DatabaseGeneratedOption.Identity)
        .HasColumnName("BlogId");
      this.Property(x => x.Title).HasMaxLength(175);
      this.HasRequired(x => x.BlogLogo).WithRequiredPrincipal();
    }
  }
}
```

Understanding the Fluent Configuration API

6. Add another C# class named `BlogLogoMapping` to the `Mapping` folder, with the following code:

```
using System.ComponentModel.DataAnnotations;
using System.Data.Entity.ModelConfiguration;
using BusinessLogic;
namespace DataAccess.Mappings
{
  public class BlogLogoMapping : EntityTypeConfiguration<BlogLogo>
  {
    public BlogLogoMapping()
    {
      this.ToTable("Blogs");
      this.HasKey(x => x.Id);
      this.Property(x => x.Id)
       .HasDatabaseGeneratedOption(DatabaseGeneratedOption.Identity)
       .HasColumnName("BlogId");
    }
  }
}
```

7. Modify `BlogContext` to include `Blog DbSet<>`, and the new configurations, with the following code:

```
using System;
using System.Data.Entity;
using System.Linq;
using BusinessLogic;
using DataAccess.Mappings;
namespace DataAccess
{
  public class BlogContext : DbContext, IUnitOfWork
  {
    public BlogContext(string connectionString)
    : base(connectionString)
    {
    }
    protected override void OnModelCreating(DbModelBuilder
      modelBuilder)
    {
      modelBuilder.Configurations.Add(new BlogMapping());
      modelBuilder.Configurations.Add(new BlogLogoMapping());
      base.OnModelCreating(modelBuilder);
    }
    public DbSet<Blog> Blogs { get; set; }
    public IQueryable<T> Find<T>() where T : class
```

```
      {
        return this.Set<T>();
      }
      public void Refresh()
      {
        this.ChangeTracker.Entries().ToList().ForEach(x=>x.Reload());
      }
      public void Commit()
      {
        this.SaveChanges();
      }
    }
  }
```

8. Run our test, and see how it works.

How it works...

We start this solution with a test to make sure that we are accomplishing the goals and nothing more. For this solution, the goal is to split a table into multiple objects, so that we can load each of them independently, as needed, without a large data pull. This is often used to separate large images stored in SQL from the data that they are normally stored with.

We added our blog and the logo of our blog to give a representation of this scenario. `BlogLogo` is a `varbinary(max)` in the database, and could take sizable time to load. The key point to note, in the domain objects, is that the virtual keyword is on `BlogLogo`, which will allow for the lazy loading of the logo when needed, but not before.

The mappings that allow for the splitting of a table are fairly straightforward. It requires a one-to-one relationship, of which the blog is the principal. The logo has no navigation property to get to the blog that holds it, as it was not needed in our code. This leads us to the `HasRequired()` and `WithRequiredPrinciple()` methods for the navigation property.

Also, note how the key is configured the same on both the objects, that is, `this` and `ToTable()`; this splits the table into separate objects. The required one-to-one relationship is to enforce that no one tries to insert `BlogLogo` without a blog attached to it. If you are just dealing with objects whose needs may be uncertain to you, you might not know until the context throws an exception to let you know.

There's more...

With splitting tables, you need to make sure that the need is there only for the sake of performance, and not just idle architecting.

Understanding the Fluent Configuration API

The cost
The additional overhead of creating this type of mapping, and the knowledge that we force the future developers to have, is a major concern. We have forced developers to know that `BlogLogo` is related to the `Blog` class, and must be created with one, but that restriction does not exist in our code. This native knowledge is one of the main reasons that the onboarding process for legacy systems is so long. While writing new applications, there are other ways to solve this, such as a **shared primary key association**.

Shared primary key association
Sharing a table through one-to-one relationships that hit it is a fairly simple scenario and can serve to dissect tables. If we pulled `BlogLogo` into a separate table, and marked it as a one-to-one relationship that is required from `Blog` but is optional from `BlogLogo`, we would create a scenario in which we could query directly for `BlogLogo`. This would allow us to reuse that data without the need to query only parts of `BlogTable`.

See also
In this chapter:

- *Creating one-to-one maps*

Mapping many tables to one object

This allows us to map many normalized tables to one object to bring together a cohesive object model without propagating the data structure into our code.

Getting ready

We will be using NuGet Package Manager to install the Entity Framework 4.1 assemblies.

The package installer can be found at `http://nuget.org/`.

We will also be using a database for connecting the data and updating it.

Open the **Improving Many Tables To One Object Maps** solution in the included source code examples.

How to do it...

Let us get connected to the database using the following steps:

1. We start by adding a new unit test named `MappingTest` to the `Test` project. We make a test that connects to the database, and retrieves an object. This will test the configuration and ensure that the model matches the database schema, using the following code:

```csharp
using System;
using System.Collections.Generic;
using System.Linq;
using System.Text;
using BusinessLogic;
using DataAccess;
using DataAccess.Database;
using Microsoft.VisualStudio.TestTools.UnitTesting;
using Test.Properties;
using System.Data.Entity;
namespace Test
{
  [TestClass]
  public class MappingTest
  {
    [TestMethod]
    public void ShouldReturnABlogWithAuthorDetails()
    {
      //Arrange
      var init = new Initializer();
      var context = new
        BlogContext(Settings.Default.BlogConnection);
      init.InitializeDatabase(context);
      //Act
      var post = context.Blogs.FirstOrDefault();
      //Assert
      Assert.IsNotNull(post);
      Assert.IsNotNull(post.AboutTheAuthor);
    }
  }
}
```

2. Add a new C# class named `Initializer` to the `DataAccess` project in the `Database` folder, with the following code:

```csharp
using System;
using System.Collections.Generic;
using System.Data.Entity;
using BusinessLogic;
namespace DataAccess.Database
{
  public class Initializer : DropCreateDatabaseAlways<BlogContext>
  {
    public Initializer()
    {
```

Understanding the Fluent Configuration API

```csharp
      }
      protected override void Seed(BlogContext context)
      {
        context.Set<Blog>().Add(new Blog()
        {
          Creationdate = DateTime.Now,
          ShortDescription = "Testing",
          Title = "Test Blog",
          Description = "Long Test",
          AboutTheAuthor = "Me me me"
        });
        context.SaveChanges();
      }
    }
  }
```

3. Add a new C# class named `Blog` to the `BusinessLogic` project, with the following code:

```csharp
using System;
using System.Collections.Generic;
using DataAccess;
namespace BusinessLogic
{
  public class Blog
  {
    public int Id { get; set; }
    public DateTime Creationdate { get; set; }
    public string ShortDescription { get; set; }
    public string Title { get; set; }
    public string Description { get; set; }
    public string AboutTheAuthor { get; set; }
  }
}
```

4. Now that we have our domain objects, we want to add a `Mapping` folder to the `DataAccess` project and then add a `BlogMapping` class to the folder, with the following code:

```csharp
using System.ComponentModel.DataAnnotations;
using System.Data.Entity.ModelConfiguration;
using BusinessLogic;
namespace DataAccess.Mappings
{
  public class BlogMapping : EntityTypeConfiguration<Blog>
  {
```

```
      public BlogMapping()
      {
        this.Map(m =>
        {
          m.Properties(t => new {t.Id, t.Title,t.ShortDescription});
          m.ToTable("Blog");
        })
        .Map(m =>
        {
          m.Properties(t => new {t.Description, t.Creationdate,
          t.AboutTheAuthor});
          m.ToTable("BlogDetails");
        });
        this.HasKey(x => x.Id);
        this.Property(x => x.Id)
        .HasDatabaseGeneratedOption(DatabaseGeneratedOption.Identity)
        .HasColumnName("BlogId");
      }
    }
}
```

5. Modify `BlogContext` to include `Blog DbSet<>`, and the new configurations, with the following code:

```
using System;
using System.Data.Entity;
using System.Linq;
using BusinessLogic;
using DataAccess.Mappings;
namespace DataAccess
{
  public class BlogContext : DbContext, IUnitOfWork
  {
    public BlogContext(string connectionString)
    : base(connectionString)
    {
    }
    protected override void OnModelCreating(DbModelBuilder
      modelBuilder)
    {
      modelBuilder.Configurations.Add(new BlogMapping());
      base.OnModelCreating(modelBuilder);
    }
    public DbSet<Blog> Blogs { get; set; }
    public IQueryable<T> Find<T>() where T : class
```

Understanding the Fluent Configuration API

```
        {
            return this.Set<T>();
        }
        public void Refresh()
        {
            this.ChangeTracker.Entries().ToList().ForEach(x=>x.Reload());
        }
        public void Commit()
        {
            this.SaveChanges();
        }
    }
}
```

6. Run our test, and see how it works.

How it works...

Our solution starts with a test that defines our intent. This process is intended to map two tables into a single object, for the sake of ease of use and readability. This process can be helpful to solidify a normalized database schema into a cohesive object graph.

The `Map()` method allows us to define mapping fragments that we then use to set up two distinct sets of configuration. This can be almost any number of fragments that we would need to be combined into one object. This technique is normally reserved for mapping to legacy databases that have had large amounts of normalization, due to which they would not translate well into objects.

The `Properties()` method allows us to define new anonymous objects that contain the properties that belong to each table. Each of these fragments will be combined into overall class mapping that will span tables and even schemas.

The `ToTable()` method functions as it always has, mapping to a table on the server. This will allow us to tie the properties together from multiple tables.

There's more...

Mapping more than one table to a single object is a fairly rare scenario, but when we need to handle this kind of database schema, there are several things to keep in mind.

When to combine tables

It is ideal to combine tables when the table structure does not translate properly to the objects, and also when querying performance is not a major concern. The queries that are generated by this are not the fastest out there and will get slower as you combine more tables.

Security concerns

Security concerns may arise while bridging the tables and schemas. Here, you must be aware that if the user has access to both schemas and tables that are bridged, this can cause runtime errors that cripple your application, if not handled properly.

See also

In this chapter:

- *Mapping one table to many objects*

Handling inheritance based on database values

In this recipe, we map a set of related objects to a single table, and map ourselves to the values in the database, to determine the type of object to load.

Getting ready

We will be using NuGet Package Manager to install the Entity Framework 4.1 assemblies.

The package installer can be found at `http://nuget.org/`.

We will also be using a database to connect to the data and update it.

Open the **Improving Inheritance Based On Database Values** solution in the included source code examples.

How to do it...

Let us get connected to the database using the following steps:

1. We start by adding a new unit test named `MappingTest` to the `Test` project. We will make a test that connects to the database and retrieves an object. This will test the configuration, and ensure that the model matches the database schema, using the following code:

    ```
    using System;
    using System.Collections.Generic;
    using System.Linq;
    using System.Text;
    using BusinessLogic;
    using DataAccess;
    using DataAccess.Database;
    ```

Understanding the Fluent Configuration API

```csharp
using Microsoft.VisualStudio.TestTools.UnitTesting;
using Test.Properties;
using System.Data.Entity;
namespace Test
{
  [TestClass]
  public class MappingTest
  {
    [TestMethod]
    public void ShouldReturnABlogWithTypeSafety()
    {
      //Arrange
      var init = new Initializer();
      var context = new
        BlogContext(Settings.Default.BlogConnection);
      init.InitializeDatabase(context);
      //Act
      var pictureBlog =
        context.Set<PictureBlog>().FirstOrDefault();
      var videoBlog = context.Set<VideoBlog>().FirstOrDefault();
      //Assert
      Assert.IsNotNull(pictureBlog);
      Assert.IsNotNull(videoBlog);
    }
  }
}
```

2. Add a new C# class, named `Initializer`, to the `DataAccess` project in the `Database` folder, with the following code:

```csharp
using System;
using System.Collections.Generic;
using System.Data.Entity;
using BusinessLogic;
namespace DataAccess.Database
{
  public class Initializer : DropCreateDatabaseAlways<BlogContext>
  {
    public Initializer()
    {
    }
    protected override void Seed(BlogContext context)
    {
      context.Set<PictureBlog>().Add(new PictureBlog()
      {
```

```csharp
            Creationdate = DateTime.Now,
            ShortDescription = "Testing",
            Title = "Test Blog",
            Description = "Long Test",
            AboutTheAuthor = "Me me me"
          });
          context.Set<VideoBlog>().Add(new VideoBlog()
          {
            Creationdate = DateTime.Now,
            ShortDescription = "Testing",
            Title = "Test Blog",
            Description = "Long Test",
            AboutTheAuthor = "Me me me"
          });
          context.SaveChanges();
        }
      }
    }
```

3. Add a new C# class named `Blog` to the `BusinessLogic` project, with the following code:

```csharp
using System;
using System.Collections.Generic;
using DataAccess;
namespace BusinessLogic
{
  public class Blog
  {
    public int Id { get; set; }
    public DateTime Creationdate { get; set; }
    public string ShortDescription { get; set; }
    public string Title { get; set; }
    public string Description { get; set; }
    public string AboutTheAuthor { get; set; }
  }
  public class PictureBlog : Blog
  {
  }
  public class VideoBlog : Blog
  {
  }
}
```

Understanding the Fluent Configuration API

4. Now that we have our domain objects, we want to add a `Mapping` folder to the `DataAccess` project and then add a `BlogMapping` class to the folder, with the following code:

```csharp
using System.ComponentModel.DataAnnotations;
using System.Data.Entity.ModelConfiguration;
using BusinessLogic;
namespace DataAccess.Mappings
{
  public class BlogMapping : EntityTypeConfiguration<Blog>
  {
    public BlogMapping()
    {
      this.ToTable("Blogs");
      this.HasKey(x => x.Id);
      this.Property(x => x.Id)
       .HasDatabaseGeneratedOption(DatabaseGeneratedOption.Identity)
       .HasColumnName("BlogId");
      this.Property(x => x.Title).HasMaxLength(175);
    }
  }
  public class VideoBlogMapping :
    EntityTypeConfiguration<VideoBlog>
  {
    public VideoBlogMapping()
    {
      this.Map(x =>
      {
        x.MapInheritedProperties();
        x.Requires("BlogType").HasValue("Video");
      });
    }
  }
  public class PictureBlogMapping :
    EntityTypeConfiguration<PictureBlog>
  {
    public PictureBlogMapping()
    {
      this.Map(x =>
      {
        x.MapInheritedProperties();
        x.Requires("BlogType").HasValue("Picture");
      });
    }
  }
}
```

5. Modify `BlogContext` to include `Blog DbSet<>` and the new configurations, with the following code:

```
using System;
using System.Data.Entity;
using System.Linq;
using BusinessLogic;
using DataAccess.Mappings;
namespace DataAccess
{
  public class BlogContext : DbContext, IUnitOfWork
  {
    public BlogContext(string connectionString)
    : base(connectionString)
    {
    }
    protected override void OnModelCreating(DbModelBuilder
      modelBuilder)
    {
      modelBuilder.Configurations.Add(new BlogMapping());
      modelBuilder.Configurations.Add(new PictureBlogMapping());
      modelBuilder.Configurations.Add(new VideoBlogMapping());
      base.OnModelCreating(modelBuilder);
    }
    public DbSet<Blog> Blogs { get; set; }
    public IQueryable<T> Find<T>() where T : class
    {
      return this.Set<T>();
    }
    public void Refresh()
    {
     this.ChangeTracker.Entries().ToList().ForEach(x=>x.Reload());
    }
    public void Commit()
    {
      this.SaveChanges();
    }
  }
}
```

6. Run our test, and see how it works.

Understanding the Fluent Configuration API

How it works...

We start with a test that conveys our intent to store several types of objects in a single table. This allows us to implement the **table per hierarchy** pattern and set a discriminator column that tells Entity Framework which object is to be created, when it loads the data from the database.

Note that we do not map the property for the discriminator column. If we want to use a nullable column for the discriminator, we would map it and then use it with the `HasValue()` method, without parameters. We are looking for a specific value, so we use the string version of `Requires(string).HasValue(string)`. This allows us to map more than one type to a single discriminator column.

There's more...

When we map this kind of table structure, there are several major patterns that come into play.

Table per hierarchy

This defines a pattern by which each class structure (also called the base class), and all the derived classes, get a single table. The framework uses a discriminator column, in the table, that allows it to distinguish between the objects and the load. This will keep the data structure consistent, but makes direct dealing with the data, without the framework, slightly more difficult. If you do not specify the custom configuration of the table structure, this table per hierarchy is the strategy that you will get by default.

Database administrators would likely point out that this model violates the third normal form, and they are right. This model places dependencies on columns that are not keys, but it is much more efficient in handling polymorphic queries than either of the other two options. There are times while attaining efficiency in querying, it is important to break the third normal form, and if you make robust use of polymorphic queries, then this should be one of them.

Table per type

This defines a pattern by which each class gets a table in the database. This is the most straightforward approach, and it will normally get you through most situations. This is where objects are translated directly by convention. If you attempt to map inheritance this way, all the derived relationships will be mapped to one-to-one relationships.

Table per concrete type

This defines a pattern by which each non-abstract class gets a table; the properties that are defined on the base abstract class are mapped and replicated to each table so that there is no sharing between the objects. This kind of denormalization is normally discouraged by our database administrators, as it duplicates columns and the structure that holds the same data.

See also

In this chapter:

- *Mapping many tables to one object*

Handling complex key maps

In this recipe, we use complex keys to map objects that cannot be keyed with a single property.

Getting ready

We will be using NuGet Package Manager to install the Entity Framework 4.1 assemblies as follows:

The package installer can be found at http://nuget.org/.

We will also be using a database for connecting to the data and updating it.

Open the **Improving Complex Key Maps** solution in the included source code examples.

How to do it...

Let us get connected to the database using the following steps:

1. We start by adding a new unit test named `MappingTest` to the `Test` project. We will make a test that connects to the database, and retrieves an object. This will test the configuration and ensure that the model matches the database schema. Use the following code:

    ```
    using System;
    using System.Collections.Generic;
    using System.Linq;
    using System.Text;
    using BusinessLogic;
    using DataAccess;
    using DataAccess.Database;
    using Microsoft.VisualStudio.TestTools.UnitTesting;
    using Test.Properties;
    using System.Data.Entity;
    namespace Test
    {
      [TestClass]
      public class MappingTest
      {
    ```

```csharp
[TestMethod]
public void ShouldReturnABlogWithAuthorDetails()
{
  //Arrange
  var init = new Initializer();
  var context = new
    BlogContext(Settings.Default.BlogConnection);
  init.InitializeDatabase(context);
  //Act
  var blog = context.Set<Blog>().FirstOrDefault();
  //Assert
  Assert.IsNotNull(blog);
   }
  }
}
```

2. Add a new C# class named `Initializer` to the `DataAccess` project in the `Database` folder, with the following code:

```csharp
using System;
using System.Collections.Generic;
using System.Data.Entity;
using BusinessLogic;
namespace DataAccess.Database
{
  public class Initializer : DropCreateDatabaseAlways<BlogContext>
  {
    public Initializer()
    {
    }
    protected override void Seed(BlogContext context)
    {
      context.Set<Blog>().Add(new Blog
      {
        Creationdate = DateTime.Now,
        ShortDescription = "Testing",
        Title = "Test Blog"
      });
      context.SaveChanges();
    }
  }
}
```

3. Add a new C# class named `Blog` to the `BusinessLogic` project, with the following code:

   ```
   using System;
   namespace BusinessLogic
   {
     public class Blog
     {
       public DateTime Creationdate { get; set; }
       public string ShortDescription { get; set; }
       public string Title { get; set; }
     }
   }
   ```

4. Now that we have our domain objects, we want to add a `Mapping` folder to the `DataAccess` project and then add a `BlogMapping` class to the folder, with the following code:

   ```
   using System.ComponentModel.DataAnnotations;
   using System.Data.Entity.ModelConfiguration;
   using BusinessLogic;
   namespace DataAccess.Mappings
   {
     public class BlogMapping : EntityTypeConfiguration<Blog>
     {
       public BlogMapping()
       {
         this.HasKey(x => new{x.Creationdate,x.Title});
         this.Property(x =>
            x.Title).IsRequired().HasMaxLength(250).HasColumnOrder(1);
         this.Property(x =>
   x.Creationdate).HasColumnName("CreationDate").IsRequired().HasColu
           mnOrder(0);
              this.Property(x => x.ShortDescription).
   HasColumnType("Text").IsMaxLength().IsOptional().
   HasColumnName("Description");
       }
     }
   }
   ```

5. Modify `BlogContext` to include `Blog DbSet<>` and the new configurations, with the following code:

   ```
   using System;
   using System.Data.Entity;
   using System.Linq;
   using BusinessLogic;
   using DataAccess.Mappings;
   ```

```
namespace DataAccess
{
  public class BlogContext : DbContext    {
  public BlogContext(string connectionString)
  : base(connectionString)
  {
  }
  protected override void OnModelCreating(DbModelBuilder
    modelBuilder)
  {
    modelBuilder.Configurations.Add(new BlogMapping());
    base.OnModelCreating(modelBuilder);
  }
  public DbSet<Blog> Blogs { get; set; }
  public IQueryable<T> Find<T>() where T : class
  {
    return this.Set<T>();
  }
  public void Refresh()
  {
    this.ChangeTracker.Entries().ToList().ForEach(x=>x.Reload());
  }
  public void Commit()
  {
    this.SaveChanges();
  }
}
```

6. Run our test, and see how it works.

How it works...

We start by defining a test that retrieves the blog object. This will be testing the key mapping for us.

The `HasKey()` method accepts a lambda that allows us to map multiple properties to the key of the table. This creates a composite key that is ordered in the order that we type in the lambda. If we want to adjust this order, we can use the `HasColumnIOrder()` method.

This defines a unique combination of multiple columns that make up the unique identification of a record This is normally reserved for more legacy database mappings, but we can have scenarios where we would want to create this for new databases as well.

There's more...

Keys are used for relationships

While using a complex or composite key, be aware that it is going to be used for your related objects as well, and you will need to use the `Map()` method on one-to-many and many-to-many collections, to define that constraint.

See also

In this chapter:

- *Creating one-to-many maps*
- *Creating many-to-many maps*

3
Handling Validation in Entity Framework

In this chapter, we will cover the following recipes:

- Validating simple properties
- Validating complex properties
- Validating collection properties
- Creating custom property validation
- Improving MVC UI with entity framework validation

Introduction

When we sell a car, do we just take it on faith that the stack of bills we were given show the correct amount, or do we count them to validate it? Often, this validation has little to no effect on the storage system. There are two levels of validation in this scenario. When we count the money, we are doing **content validation** to ensure that it meets the requirements. When we put it in our wallet, we are doing **structure validation**. Is it the right size and shape to meet the storage requirements? This is no different than the approach to data validation that we should take when working with the **Entity Framework**. We can enforce certain restrictions on the content of the data objects, and we can specify different restrictions on the structure of the data in configuration.

The content restrictions are more subjective, and often conditional. We want these rules to be enforced at the same time as the structure restrictions, so our validation is executed together and before any database calls have been made. All of these restrictions will specify some kind of business rule, but will not be tied directly to the structure of the code. These are the topics that this chapter will cover.

Handling Validation in Entity Framework

Validating simple properties

In this recipe, we are going to specify simple validation rules that can be applied to a property value to enforce business rules.

Getting ready

We will be using the `NuGet` Package Manager to install the Entity Framework 4.1 assemblies.

The package installer can be found at `http://nuget.org`.

We will also be using a database for connecting to the data and updating it.

Open the **Improving Single Property Validation** solution in the included source code examples.

How to do it...

Let's get connected to the database using the following steps:

1. We start by adding a new unit test named `ValidationTests` to the test project. We make a test that connects to the database and adds an object. This will test whether the configuration and our validation code are separate concerns, by using the following code:

```
using System;
using System.Collections.Generic;
using System.Data.Entity.Validation;
using System.Linq;
using System.Text;
using System.Text.RegularExpressions;
using BusinessLogic;
using DataAccess;
using DataAccess.Database;
using Microsoft.VisualStudio.TestTools.UnitTesting;
using Test.Properties;
using System.Data.Entity;

namespace Test
{
  [TestClass]
  public class ValidationTest
  {

    [TestMethod]
    [ExpectedException(typeof(DbEntityValidationException))]
```

```csharp
public void ShouldErrorOnTitleToLong()
{
  //Arrange
  var init = new Initializer();
  var context = new
    BlogContext(Settings.Default.BlogConnection);
  init.InitializeDatabase(context);
  StringBuilder builder = new StringBuilder();
  for (int i = 0; i < 20; i++)
  {
    builder.Append("This is going to be repeated");
  }
  var blog = new Blog()
  {
    Creationdate = DateTime.Now,
    ShortDescription = "Test",
    Title = builder.ToString()
  };

  //Act
  context.Set<Blog>().Add(blog);
  context.SaveChanges();

  //Assert
  Assert.Fail("Didn't Error");
}

[TestMethod]
[ExpectedException(typeof(DbEntityValidationException))]
public void ShouldErrorOnDescriptionRequired()
{
  //Arrange
  var init = new Initializer();
  var context = new
    BlogContext(Settings.Default.BlogConnection);
  init.InitializeDatabase(context);
  StringBuilder builder = new StringBuilder();
  var blog = new Blog()
  {
    Creationdate = DateTime.Now,
    ShortDescription = null,
    Title = "Test"
  };
```

```csharp
    //Act
    context.Set<Blog>().Add(blog);
    context.SaveChanges();

    //Assert
    Assert.Fail("Didn't Error");
}

[TestMethod]
[ExpectedException(typeof(DbEntityValidationException))]
public void ShouldErrorOnDateOutsideAcceptableRange()
{
  //Arrange
  var init = new Initializer();
  var context = new
    BlogContext(Settings.Default.BlogConnection);
  init.InitializeDatabase(context);
  StringBuilder builder = new StringBuilder();
  var blog = new Blog()
  {
    Creationdate = new DateTime(1890,1,1),
    ShortDescription = "Test",
    Title = "Test"
  };

  //Act
  context.Set<Blog>().Add(blog);
  context.SaveChanges();

  //Assert
  Assert.Fail("Didn't Error");
}

[TestMethod]
[ExpectedException(typeof(DbEntityValidationException))]
public void ShouldErrorOnRatingOutOfRange()
{
  var init = new Initializer();
  var context = new
    BlogContext(Settings.Default.BlogConnection);
  init.InitializeDatabase(context);
  var blog = new Blog()
  {
    Creationdate = DateTime.Now,
```

```
            ShortDescription = "Test",
            Title = "Test",
            Rating = 6.0
          };

          //Act
          context.Set<Blog>().Add(blog);
          context.SaveChanges();

          //Assert
          Assert.Fail("Didn't Error");

        }

      }

    }
```

2. Add an initializer to the `DataAccess` project in the `Database` folder with the following code to set up the data:

```
using System;
using System.Data.Entity;
using BusinessLogic;

namespace DataAccess.Database
{

  public class Initializer : DropCreateDatabaseAlways<BlogContext>
  {
    public Initializer()
    {

    }
    protected override void Seed(BlogContext context)
    {
      context.Set<Blog>().Add(new Blog()
      {
        Creationdate = DateTime.Now,
        ShortDescription = "Testing",
        Title = "Test Blog"
      });
      context.SaveChanges();
    }
  }
}
```

Handling Validation in Entity Framework

3. In the `BusinessLogic` project, add a new C# class named `Blog` with the following code:

   ```
   using System;
   using System.ComponentModel.DataAnnotations;
   using System.Text.RegularExpressions;

   namespace BusinessLogic
   {
     public class Blog
     {
       private const string DateBetween1900And2100Pattern =
         @"^(19|20)\d\d[- /.](0[1-9]|1[012])[- /.](0[1-9]|
         [12][0-9]|3[01])$";

       public int Id { get; set; }

       [RegularExpression(pattern:
         DateBetween1900And2100Pattern, ErrorMessage =
         "Date is not valid between 1900 and 2100")]
       public DateTime Creationdate { get; set; }

       [Required]
       public string ShortDescription { get; set; }

       [Required]
       [StringLength(120, ErrorMessage = "Title is To Long")]
       public string Title { get; set; }

       [Range(0.0,5.0, ErrorMessage =
         "Invalid Range, must be between 0 and 5")]
       public double Rating { get; set; }
     }
   }
   ```

4. Add a `Mapping` folder to the `DataAccess` project, and add a `BlogMapping` class to the folder with the following code:

   ```
   using System.ComponentModel.DataAnnotations;
   using System.Data.Entity.ModelConfiguration;
   using BusinessLogic;

   namespace DataAccess.Mappings
   {
     public class BlogMapping : EntityTypeConfiguration<Blog>
   ```

```
    {
      public BlogMapping()
      {
        this.ToTable("Blogs");
        this.HasKey(x => x.Id);
        this.Property(x => x.Id)
          .HasDatabaseGeneratedOption(
          DatabaseGeneratedOption.Identity)
          .HasColumnName("BlogId");

        this.Property(x => x.Title).IsRequired().HasMaxLength(250);
        this.Property(x => x.Creationdate).
          HasColumnName("CreationDate").IsRequired();

        this.Property(x => x.ShortDescription).
          HasColumnType("Text").IsMaxLength()
          .IsOptional().HasColumnName("Description");
      }

    }
  }
```

5. Modify the `BlogContext` class to the following code:

```
using System;
using System.Data.Entity;
using System.Linq;
using BusinessLogic;
using DataAccess.Mappings;

namespace DataAccess
{
  public class BlogContext : DbContext, IUnitOfWork
  {
    public BlogContext(string connectionString) :
      base(connectionString)
    {

    }

    protected override void OnModelCreating(DbModelBuilder
      modelBuilder)
    {
      modelBuilder.Configurations.Add(new BlogMapping());
      base.OnModelCreating(modelBuilder);
    }
```

Handling Validation in Entity Framework

```
        public IQueryable<T> Find<T>() where T : class
        {
          return this.Set<T>();
        }

        public void Refresh()
        {
          this.ChangeTracker.Entries().ToList()
            .ForEach(x=>x.Reload());
        }

        public void Commit()
        {
          this.SaveChanges();
        }
      }
    }
```

6. Run our test, and see how it works.

How it works...

We start, as always, with a few tests that specify our intent, and validate that the work we will do meets the requirements of the customer. We have specified that the creation date must be between January 1st, 1900 and December 31st, 2099. The title must be less than 120 characters, the short description must not be null, and rating must be between 0 and 5.

We move to initializing our database with a piece of test data just to set up the structure, and give a `not null` result set for any `get` statement. This will give us a sample set of data.

The next piece is the magic. The `Blog` object looks similar to the objects that we have used throughout the book, but it varies in one important way. We have added attributes that specify the restrictions on our object. These range from simple required attributes to more advanced regular expressions. These attributes are specified directly on the object, so that they can be used to send this data to a database across a service connection, or into a user interface. These validation restrictions are not specific to the Entity Framework, but the Entity Framework does leverage them in a fashion that allows us to keep the database clean.

The database mappings that we notice are contradictory to the specified restrictions. In this case, it operates both sets. The object in its current state must be able to pass both the sets of validation. Structure-based and content-based validation, both, have a place in our code base and exist together, not in a vacuum.

There's more...

Simple properties can hide very complex business logic that restricts what values can be in them, or that means more than they seem. If there are business rules such as this, around an object, then they should be codified in the code and enforced before an object that violates them is created.

Deciding between configuration and attributes

Often, there are questions about when the configuration for structure restriction should be used, or when the attributes for content restriction should be used. The answer to this is fairly simple - when it is a database storage concern, use configuration, and when it has to deal with the values in the object without concern for how it is stored, then use data annotations. There are some content rules, such as discriminator columns, which are storage concerns, and should be specified in configuration. If it is a business rule, then most likely it will be an attribute. Think about the object; if we can say *When X has a Y it means Z*, then we have a good candidate for attribute enforcement.

Sharing validation

One thing for us to be aware of is that if we put the attribute validation into the object, then every place where we use this object, it will be a subject to that validation. This can gain us some great benefits from the standpoint that other code bases, and even user interfaces will be able to handle these rules for us, but it will also mean that we do not want to put anything in an attribute validation that might be different, based on how you use the object.

Delaying validation

This validation is not real-time when used to instantiate the objects. It must be invoked, depending on when you use it, and the framework you are using it in will determine when it is called. The entity framework invokes the validation before saving an object into the context.

Displaying error messages

Each of the validation attributes that we are using allows for the setting of a hardcoded error message, or the setting of a resource type and a resource name that it can look up from the value. This will allow us to develop centralized validation logic and off-load the message delivery to a culture-specific resource file.

See also

In this chapter:

- *Validating complex properties*
- *Improving MVC UI with entity framework validation*

Validating complex properties

In this recipe, we will be creating complex business rule validators that allow us to evaluate more than one property at a time, and the contents of a property.

Getting ready

We will be using the `NuGet` Package Manager to install the entity framework 4.1 assemblies.

The package installer can be found at http://nuget.org.

We will also be using a database for connecting to the data and updating it.

Open the **Improving Complex Property Validation** solution in the included source code examples.

How to do it...

Let's get connected to the database using the following steps:

1. We start by adding a new unit test named `ValidationTests` to the test project. We make a test that connects to the database and adds an object. This will test whether the configuration and our validation code are properly separated:

    ```
    using System;
    using System.Collections.Generic;
    using System.Data.Entity.Validation;
    using System.Linq;
    using System.Text;
    using System.Text.RegularExpressions;
    using BusinessLogic;
    using DataAccess;
    using DataAccess.Database;
    using Microsoft.VisualStudio.TestTools.UnitTesting;
    using Test.Properties;
    using System.Data.Entity;

    namespace Test
    {
      [TestClass]
      public class ValidationTest
      {

        [TestMethod]
        [ExpectedException(typeof (DbEntityValidationException))]
    ```

```csharp
public void ShouldErrorOnTitleLongerThanDescription()
{
  //Arrange
  var init = new Initializer();
  var context = new
    BlogContext(Settings.Default.BlogConnection);
  init.InitializeDatabase(context);

  var blog = new Blog()
  {
    Creationdate = DateTime.Now,
    ShortDescription = "Test",
    Title = "This is a lot longer"
  };

  //Act
  context.Set<Blog>().Add(blog);
  context.SaveChanges();

  //Assert
  Assert.Fail("Didn't Error");
}

[TestMethod]
[ExpectedException(typeof(DbEntityValidationException))]
public void ShouldErrorOnTitleContainsAt()
{
  //Arrange
  var init = new Initializer();
  var context = new
    BlogContext(Settings.Default.BlogConnection);
  init.InitializeDatabase(context);

  var blog = new Blog()
  {
    Creationdate = DateTime.Now,
    ShortDescription = "Test",
    Title = "That"
  };

  //Act
  context.Set<Blog>().Add(blog);
  context.SaveChanges();
```

```csharp
      //Assert
      Assert.Fail("Didn't Error");
   }

   [TestMethod]
   [ExpectedException(typeof(DbEntityValidationException))]
   public void ShouldErrorOnTitleAndDescriptionLengthIs15()
   {
      //Arrange
      var init = new Initializer();
      var context = new
         BlogContext(Settings.Default.BlogConnection);
      init.InitializeDatabase(context);

      var blog = new Blog()
      {
         Creationdate = DateTime.Now,
         ShortDescription = "Testing",
         Title = "Somethin"
      };

      //Act
      context.Set<Blog>().Add(blog);
      context.SaveChanges();

      //Assert
      Assert.Fail("Didn't Error");
   }
  }
}
```

2. Add an initializer to the `DataAccess` project in the `Database` folder with the following code to set up the data:

```csharp
using System;
using System.Data.Entity;
using BusinessLogic;

namespace DataAccess.Database
{

   public class Initializer : DropCreateDatabaseAlways<BlogContext>
   {
     public Initializer()
     {
```

```
      }
      protected override void Seed(BlogContext context)
      {
        context.Set<Blog>().Add(new Blog()
        {
          Creationdate = DateTime.Now,
          ShortDescription = "Testing",
          Title = "Test Blog"
        });
        context.SaveChanges();
      }
    }
  }
```

3. In the `BusinessLogic` project, add a new C# class named `Blog` with the following code:

```
using System;
using System.Collections.Generic;
using System.ComponentModel.DataAnnotations;
using System.Text.RegularExpressions;

namespace BusinessLogic
{
  public class Blog : IValidatableObject
  {
    public int Id { get; set; }

    public DateTime Creationdate { get; set; }

    public string ShortDescription { get; set; }

    public string Title { get; set; }

    public double Rating { get; set; }

    public IEnumerable<ValidationResult>
      Validate(ValidationContext validationContext)
    {
      List<ValidationResult> results = new
        List<ValidationResult>();
      var target = ((Blog)validationContext.ObjectInstance);

      if (target.Title.Length > target.ShortDescription.Length)
        results.Add(new ValidationResult("Description cannot be
          shorter than the title"));
```

```csharp
            if(target.Title.Contains("at"))
               results.Add(new ValidationResult("WE hate the word at!"));

            if(target.Title.Length +
               target.ShortDescription.Length == 15)
               results.Add(new ValidationResult("No adding to 15!!!"));

            return results;
         }
      }
   }
```

4. Add a `Mapping` folder to the `DataAccess` project, and add a `BlogMapping` class to the folder with the following code:

```csharp
using System.ComponentModel.DataAnnotations;
using System.Data.Entity.ModelConfiguration;
using BusinessLogic;

namespace DataAccess.Mappings
{
   public class BlogMapping : EntityTypeConfiguration<Blog>
   {
      public BlogMapping()
      {
         this.ToTable("Blogs");
         this.HasKey(x => x.Id);

         this.Property(x => x.Id).HasDatabaseGeneratedOption(
            DatabaseGeneratedOption.Identity).HasColumnName("BlogId");

         this.Property(x => x.Title).IsRequired().HasMaxLength(250);

         this.Property(x => x.Creationdate).HasColumnName(
            "CreationDate").IsRequired();

         this.Property(x => x.ShortDescription)
            .HasColumnType("Text").IsMaxLength()
            .IsOptional().HasColumnName("Description");

      }

   }
}
```

5. Modify the `BlogContext` class to contain the new mappings with the following code:

```
using System;
using System.Data.Entity;
using System.Linq;
using BusinessLogic;
using DataAccess.Mappings;

namespace DataAccess
{
  public class BlogContext : DbContext, IUnitOfWork
  {
    public BlogContext(string connectionString) :
      base(connectionString)
    {

    }

    protected override void OnModelCreating(DbModelBuilder
      modelBuilder)
    {
      modelBuilder.Configurations.Add(new BlogMapping());
      base.OnModelCreating(modelBuilder);
    }

    public IQueryable<T> Find<T>() where T : class
    {
      return this.Set<T>();
    }

    public void Refresh()
    {
      this.ChangeTracker.Entries().ToList()
      .ForEach(x=>x.Reload());
    }

    public void Commit()
    {
      this.SaveChanges();
    }
  }
}
```

6. Run our test, and see how it works.

Handling Validation in Entity Framework

How it works...

We start off by creating some tests that explain our intent, and will serve to validate that our solutions work. These tests specify that the title and the description, when combined, cannot be exactly 15 characters. The title cannot be longer than the short description, and the title must not contain the letters `at` in order. These are a couple scenarios that will be evaluated at the same time.

The `Blog` object is a normal object, but it implements the `IValidatableObject` interface which will allow us to evaluate the entire object. This interface forces us to implement the `Validate` method. The validation context allows us to look at the properties by casting the object instance to the type for the validator.

The mappings that we have set up have no knowledge of the previously enforced validation rules, but will still be enforced of their own right, once wired into the `Blog` context. These are a standard that we will see often, when dealing with validation.

There's more...

As we proceed, we will observe that the more complex the business rules get, the more we will have to tend toward using this solution. However,, there are several options that will allow us to build reusable validation.

Reusing the base class logic

When dealing with the shared validation logic across many related types, you can put the validation interface implementation on the base class. The validation context allows us to access the values by using the key value pairs by the property name. The preferred method is to deal with the object directly so as to avoid magic strings. The only issue is, if we want to define a generic and non-type specific validation, then we would have to use the key value pairs.

Performing all at once validation

Validation done in an **all at once** fashion is a validation on the object, and each property is not evaluated individually. This loses some of the granularity of the results, but gives us the flexibility to evaluate more complex scenarios that could not be handled in a simple validation solution.

See also

In this chapter:

- *Validating simple properties*
- *Creating custom property validation*

Chapter 3

Validating collection properties

In this recipe, we will learn to define restrictions on the number of related objects that are defined.

Getting ready

We will be using the `NuGet` Package Manager to install the Entity Framework 4.1 assemblies.

The package installer can be found at `http://nuget.org`.

We will also be using a database for connecting to the data and updating it.

Open the **Improving Collection Property Validation** solution in the included source code examples.

How to do it...

Let's get connected to the database using the following steps:

1. We start by adding a new unit test named `ValidationTests` to the test project. We make a test that connects to the database and adds an object. This will test whether the configuration and our validation code are properly separated:

   ```
   using System;
   using System.Collections.Generic;
   using System.Data.Entity.Validation;
   using System.Linq;
   using System.Text;
   using System.Text.RegularExpressions;
   using BusinessLogic;
   using DataAccess;
   using DataAccess.Database;
   using Microsoft.VisualStudio.TestTools.UnitTesting;
   using Test.Properties;
   using System.Data.Entity;

   namespace Test
   {
     [TestClass]
     public class ValidationTest
     {

       [TestMethod]
       [ExpectedException(typeof(DbEntityValidationException))]
   ```

109

Handling Validation in Entity Framework

```csharp
public void ShouldErrorOnBelowMinimumPosts()
{
  //Arrange
  var init = new Initializer();
  var context = new
    BlogContext(Settings.Default.BlogConnection);
  init.InitializeDatabase(context);
  var blog = new Blog()
  {
    Creationdate = DateTime.Now,
    ShortDescription = "Test",
    Title = "Test",
    Posts = new List<Post>()
    {
      new Post()
    }.ToArray()
  };

  //Act
  context.Set<Blog>().Add(blog);
  context.SaveChanges();

  //Assert
  Assert.Fail("Didn't Error");
}

[TestMethod]
[ExpectedException(typeof(DbEntityValidationException))]
public void ShouldErrorOnAboveMaximumPosts()
{
  //Arrange
  var init = new Initializer();
  var context = new
    BlogContext(Settings.Default.BlogConnection);
  init.InitializeDatabase(context);
  var blog = new Blog()
  {
    Creationdate = DateTime.Now,
    ShortDescription = "Test",
    Title = "Test",
    Posts = new List<Post>()
    {
      new Post(),
      new Post(),
```

```
            new Post(),
            new Post()
          }.ToArray()
        };

        //Act
        context.Set<Blog>().Add(blog);
        context.SaveChanges();

        //Assert
        Assert.Fail("Didn't Error");
      }

    }

  }
```

2. Add an initializer to the `DataAccess` project in the `Database` folder with the following code to set up the data:

```
using System;
using System.Data.Entity;
using BusinessLogic;

namespace DataAccess.Database
{

  public class Initializer : DropCreateDatabaseAlways<BlogContext>
  {
    public Initializer()
    {

    }
    protected override void Seed(BlogContext context)
    {
      context.Set<Blog>().Add(new Blog()
      {
        Creationdate = DateTime.Now,
        ShortDescription = "Testing",
        Title = "Test Blog",
        Posts = new Post[]{new Post()}
      });
      context.SaveChanges();
    }
  }
}
```

Handling Validation in Entity Framework

3. In the `BusinessLogic` project, add a new C# class named `Blog` with the following code:

   ```
   using System;
   using System.Collections.Generic;
   using System.ComponentModel.DataAnnotations;
   using System.Text.RegularExpressions;

   namespace BusinessLogic
   {
     public class Blog
     {
       public int Id { get; set; }

       public DateTime Creationdate { get; set; }

       public string ShortDescription { get; set; }

       public string Title { get; set; }

       public double Rating { get; set; }

       [MaxLength(3, ErrorMessage = "Cannot have more than 3 posts"),
          MinLength(2, ErrorMessage = "Must Have at least 2 posts")]
       public Post[] Posts { get; set; }
     }
   }
   ```

4. Add another C# class named `Post` to the `BusinessLogic` project with the following code:

   ```
   namespace BusinessLogic
   {
     public class Post
     {
       public int Id { get; set; }
     }
   }
   ```

5. Add a `Mapping` folder to the `DataAccess` project, and add a `BlogMapping` class to the folder with the following code:

   ```
   using System.ComponentModel.DataAnnotations;
   using System.Data.Entity.ModelConfiguration;
   using BusinessLogic;
   ```

```
namespace DataAccess.Mappings
{
  public class BlogMapping : EntityTypeConfiguration<Blog>
  {
    public BlogMapping()
    {
      this.ToTable("Blogs");
      this.HasKey(x => x.Id);

      this.Property(x => x.Id)
        .HasDatabaseGeneratedOption(
        DatabaseGeneratedOption.Identity).HasColumnName("BlogId");

      this.Property(x => x.Title).IsRequired().HasMaxLength(250);

      this.Property(x => x.Creationdate).HasColumnName
        ("CreationDate").IsRequired();

      this.Property(x => x.ShortDescription).HasColumnType("Text")
        .IsMaxLength().IsOptional().HasColumnName("Description");
    }

  }
}
```

6. Add another mapping C# class named `PostMapping` to the folder with the following code:

```
using System.ComponentModel.DataAnnotations;
using System.Data.Entity.ModelConfiguration;
using BusinessLogic;

namespace DataAccess.Mappings
{
  public class PostMapping : EntityTypeConfiguration<Post>
  {
    public PostMapping()
    {
      this.HasKey(x => x.Id);

      this.Property(x => x.Id).HasDatabaseGeneratedOption
        (DatabaseGeneratedOption.Identity);

    }
  }
}
```

Handling Validation in Entity Framework

7. Modify the `BlogContext` class to contain the new mappings with the following code:

```
using System;
using System.Data.Entity;
using System.Linq;
using BusinessLogic;
using DataAccess.Mappings;

namespace DataAccess
{
  public class BlogContext : DbContext, IUnitOfWork
  {
    public BlogContext(string connectionString) :
      base(connectionString)
    {

    }

    protected override void OnModelCreating(DbModelBuilder
      modelBuilder)
    {
      modelBuilder.Configurations.Add(new BlogMapping());
      modelBuilder.Configurations.Add(new PostMapping());
      base.OnModelCreating(modelBuilder);
    }

    public IQueryable<T> Find<T>() where T : class
    {
      return this.Set<T>();
    }

    public void Refresh()
    {
      this.ChangeTracker.Entries().ToList()
        .ForEach(x=>x.Reload());
    }

    public void Commit()
    {
      this.SaveChanges();
    }
  }
}
```

8. Run our test, and see how it works.

How it works...

We start by defining a test that codifies our intent to limit the maximum number of posts to 3, and the minimum number to 2. This will allow us to test our implementation for completeness, and will make sure that we only write the code required to accomplish the goals.

The `Blog` object has a collection of `Post` objects that is restricted by the `MaxLength` and `MinLength` attributes. This shows that we can layer on validation attributes, and they will both get enforced. This enables us to compose a complex set of restrictions that are simple yet powerful when used in combination.

The mapping and blog context allow us to specify the structure restrictions through the mappings, and wire them into the blog context for communication.

There's more...

When business rules require that certain sets of data have relationships with x number of minimum or maximum objects. Here are some best practices:

Limiting reusability

If we specify the restriction that all blogs must have at least two, but no more than three posts, then we have limited our reusability of the blog. If anyone wants to use this object outside our environment, then we need to spend some design time thinking about how our data validation will affect them, whether positively and negatively.

Validating the internal structure

The length specification does not verify the internal structure of the post, and does not cover any of the post validation. It only restricts the number of objects contained. This will be of limited use, but is powerful.

See also

In this chapter:

- *Creating custom property validation*

Creating custom property validation

In this recipe, we will define our own attribute for validation, so we can validate more advanced scenarios.

Getting ready

We will be using the `NuGet` Package Manager to install the Entity Framework 4.1 assemblies.

The package installer can be found at http://nuget.codeplex.com/.

We will also be using a database for connecting to the data and updating it.

Open the **Improving Custom Property Validation** solution in the included source code examples.

How to do it...

Let's get connected to the database using the following steps:

1. We start by adding a new unit test named `ValidationTests` to the test project. We make a test that connects to the database, and adds an object. This will test whether the configuration and our validation code are separate concerns, by using the following code:

```
using System;
using System.Collections.Generic;
using System.Data.Entity.Validation;
using System.Linq;
using System.Text;
using System.Text.RegularExpressions;
using BusinessLogic;
using DataAccess;
using DataAccess.Database;
using Microsoft.VisualStudio.TestTools.UnitTesting;
using Test.Properties;
using System.Data.Entity;

namespace Test
{
    [TestClass]
    public class ValidationTest
    {

        [TestMethod]
```

Chapter 3

```csharp
      [ExpectedException(typeof (DbEntityValidationException))]
      public void ShouldErrorOnEmailNotHavingAnAtSign()
      {
        //Arrange
        var init = new Initializer();
        var context = new
          BlogContext(Settings.Default.BlogConnection);
        init.InitializeDatabase(context);

        var blog = new Blog()
        {
          Creationdate = DateTime.Now,
          ShortDescription = "Test",
          Title = "This is a lot longer",
          AuthorDetail = new AuthorDetail(){Email = "Test",Name =
            "Test"}
        };

        //Act
        context.Set<Blog>().Add(blog);
        context.SaveChanges();

        //Assert
        Assert.Fail("Didn't Error");
      }

  }
}
```

2. Add an initializer to the `DataAccess` project in the `Database` folder with the following code to set up the data:

```csharp
using System;
using System.Data.Entity;
using BusinessLogic;

namespace DataAccess.Database
{

  public class Initializer : DropCreateDatabaseAlways<BlogContext>
  {
    public Initializer()
    {

    }
```

Handling Validation in Entity Framework

```csharp
            protected override void Seed(BlogContext context)
            {
              context.Set<Blog>().Add(new Blog()
              {
                Creationdate = DateTime.Now,
                ShortDescription = "Testing",
                Title = "Test Blog",
                AuthorDetail = new AuthorDetail(){Email = "Test@test.com",
                  Name = "Test"}
              });
              context.SaveChanges();
            }
          }
        }
```

3. In the `BusinessLogic` project, add a new C# class named `Blog` with the following code:

```csharp
using System;
using System.Collections.Generic;
using System.Text.RegularExpressions;

namespace BusinessLogic
{
  public class Blog
  {
    private const string DateBetween1900And2100Pattern =
      @"^(19|20)\d\d[- /.](0[1-9]|1[012])[- /.]
      (0[1-9]|[12][0-9]|3[01])$";

    public int Id { get; set; }

    public DateTime Creationdate { get; set; }

    public string ShortDescription { get; set; }

    public string Title { get; set; }

    public double Rating { get; set; }

    [AuthorDetailValidator]
    public AuthorDetail AuthorDetail { get; set; }
  }
}
```

4. Add another C# class named `AuthorDetailValidatorAttribute` with the following code:

```csharp
using System.ComponentModel.DataAnnotations;

namespace BusinessLogic
{
  public class AuthorDetailValidatorAttribute :
    ValidationAttribute
  {
    public override string FormatErrorMessage(string name)
    {
      return string.Format(ErrorMessageString, name);
    }

    protected override ValidationResult IsValid(object value,
      ValidationContext validationContext)
    {
      var detail = value as AuthorDetail;

      if (detail != null)
      {
        if (!detail.Email.Contains("@"))
        {
          return new ValidationResult(FormatErrorMessage
            (validationContext.DisplayName));
        }
      }

      return ValidationResult.Success;
    }
  }
}
```

5. Add a `Mapping` folder to the `DataAccess` project, and add a `BlogMapping` class to the folder with the following code:

```csharp
using System.ComponentModel.DataAnnotations;
using System.Data.Entity.ModelConfiguration;
using BusinessLogic;

namespace DataAccess.Mappings
{
  public class BlogMapping : EntityTypeConfiguration<Blog>
  {
    public BlogMapping()
```

```csharp
{
    this.ToTable("Blogs");
    this.HasKey(x => x.Id);

    this.Property(x => x.Id).HasDatabaseGeneratedOption
        (DatabaseGeneratedOption.Identity)
        .HasColumnName("BlogId");

    this.Property(x => x.Title).IsRequired().HasMaxLength(250);

    this.Property(x => x.Creationdate).HasColumnName
        ("CreationDate").IsRequired();

    this.Property(x => x.ShortDescription).HasColumnType("Text")
        .IsMaxLength().IsOptional().HasColumnName("Description");
    }

  }
}
```

6. Add another mapping C# class named `AuthorDetailMapping` to the folder with the following code:

```csharp
using System.ComponentModel.DataAnnotations;
using System.Data.Entity.ModelConfiguration;
using BusinessLogic;

namespace DataAccess.Mappings
{
  public class AuthorDetailMapping :
    EntityTypeConfiguration<AuthorDetail>
  {
    public AuthorDetailMapping()
    {
      this.HasKey(x => x.Id);

      this.Property(x => x.Id).HasDatabaseGeneratedOption
         (DatabaseGeneratedOption.Identity);
    }
  }
}
```

7. Modify the `BlogContext` class to contain the new mappings with the following code:

```
using System;
using System.Data.Entity;
using System.Linq;
using BusinessLogic;
using DataAccess.Mappings;

namespace DataAccess
{
  public class BlogContext : DbContext, IUnitOfWork
  {
    public BlogContext(string connectionString) :
      base(connectionString)
    {

    }

    protected override void OnModelCreating(DbModelBuilder
      modelBuilder)
    {
      modelBuilder.Configurations.Add(new BlogMapping());
      modelBuilder.Configurations.Add(new AuthorDetailMapping());
      base.OnModelCreating(modelBuilder);
    }

    public IQueryable<T> Find<T>() where T : class
    {
      return this.Set<T>();
    }

    public void Refresh()
    {
      this.ChangeTracker.Entries().ToList()
        .ForEach(x=>x.Reload());
    }

    public void Commit()
    {
      this.SaveChanges();
    }
  }
}
```

8. Run our test, and see how it works.

How it works...

We start off by defining a test that will validate our solution, and verify that we have done just enough to accomplish the goals. This step is critical to succeeding with the entity framework, as it will ensure that we do not get hit by a mapping error, or an object graph issue at runtime.

We define an attribute that inherits from `ValidationAttribute`, so that we have overrides for the `validate` method. This override gives us the object (property) that we attributed, and the validation context that allows us to evaluate complex scenarios, by pulling other property values out of the key-value pair collection. This implementation does not only gives us the property-specific validation ability, but also allows for more complex validation.

The mappings defined further restrict the structure of the objects that are tied to the context. This structure exists fully-independent from the business-level validation that we have defined in our new attribute, but will still be enforced before any save operation on the database.

There's more...

We have the power through this kind of customization to define even the most complex scenarios, but there are some things that we need to keep in mind.

Coupling

We have the ability to evaluate many properties and values to make our determination, but the more things that the validation looks at, the more tightly coupled it gets to the class that it is validating. This can increase your support load, if that type has to change drastically.

Avoiding complexity

Beware of adding too much complexity and traversing to many collections that could be lazy loaded or you will drastically affect performance and the memory footprint. If you have to have those levels of complexity in the validator make sure that you eager load the properties that you need and keep performance in mind.

See also

Chapter 1, Improving Entity Framework in the Real World:

- *Testing queries for performance*

Chapter 3

Improving MVC UI with entity framework validation

In this recipe, we will leverage the data annotations to provide real-time feedback to the user, while those same annotations will validate objects before allowing them to be saved to the database.

Getting ready

We will be using the `NuGet` Package Manager to install the Entity Framework 4.1 assemblies.

The package installer can be found at `http://nuget.codeplex.com/`.

We will also be using a database for connecting to the data and updating it.

Open the **Improving Custom Property Validation** solution in the included source code examples.

How to do it...

Let's get connected to the database using the following steps:

1. This is a recipe that deals specifically with the UI interaction, and therefore cannot be wrapped in testing. However, we can verify that the UI responds manually to the same responses that we get programmatically. So, we add the following test:

    ```
    using System;
    using System.Collections.Generic;
    using System.Data.Entity.Validation;
    using System.Linq;
    using System.Text;
    using System.Text.RegularExpressions;
    using BusinessLogic;
    using DataAccess;
    using DataAccess.Database;
    using Microsoft.VisualStudio.TestTools.UnitTesting;
    using Test.Properties;
    using System.Data.Entity;

    namespace Test
    {
      [TestClass]
      public class ValidationTest
      {
    ```

```csharp
[TestMethod]
[ExpectedException(typeof(DbEntityValidationException))]
public void ShouldErrorOnTitleToLong()
{
  //Arrange
  var init = new Initializer();
  var context = new
    BlogContext(Settings.Default.BlogConnection);
  init.InitializeDatabase(context);
  StringBuilder builder = new StringBuilder();
  for (int i = 0; i < 20; i++)
  {
    builder.Append("This is going to be repeated");
  }
  var blog = new Blog()
  {
    Creationdate = DateTime.Now,
    ShortDescription = "Test",
    Title = builder.ToString()
  };

  //Act
  context.Set<Blog>().Add(blog);
  context.SaveChanges();

  //Assert
  Assert.Fail("Didn't Error");
}

[TestMethod]
[ExpectedException(typeof(DbEntityValidationException))]
public void ShouldErrorOnDescriptionRequired()
{
  //Arrange
  var init = new Initializer();
  var context = new
    BlogContext(Settings.Default.BlogConnection);
  init.InitializeDatabase(context);
  StringBuilder builder = new StringBuilder();
  var blog = new Blog()
  {
    Creationdate = DateTime.Now,
    ShortDescription = null,
    Title = "Test"
```

```csharp
  };

  //Act
  context.Set<Blog>().Add(blog);
  context.SaveChanges();

  //Assert
  Assert.Fail("Didn't Error");
}

[TestMethod]
[ExpectedException(typeof(DbEntityValidationException))]
public void ShouldErrorOnDateOutsideAcceptableRange()
{
  //Arrange
  var init = new Initializer();
  var context = new
    BlogContext(Settings.Default.BlogConnection);
  init.InitializeDatabase(context);
  StringBuilder builder = new StringBuilder();
  var blog = new Blog()
  {
    Creationdate = new DateTime(1890,1,1),
    ShortDescription = "Test",
    Title = "Test"
  };

  //Act
  context.Set<Blog>().Add(blog);
  context.SaveChanges();

  //Assert
  Assert.Fail("Didn't Error");
}

[TestMethod]
[ExpectedException(typeof(DbEntityValidationException))]
public void ShouldErrorOnRatingOutOfRange()
{
  var init = new Initializer();
  var context = new
    BlogContext(Settings.Default.BlogConnection);
  init.InitializeDatabase(context);
  var blog = new Blog()
```

Handling Validation in Entity Framework

```csharp
        {
            Creationdate = DateTime.Now,
            ShortDescription = "Test",
            Title = "Test",
            Rating = 6.0
        };

        //Act
        context.Set<Blog>().Add(blog);
        context.SaveChanges();

        //Assert
        Assert.Fail("Didn't Error");

        }

    }

}
```

2. Add an initializer to the `DataAccess` project in the `Database` folder with the following code to set up the data:

```csharp
using System;
using System.Data.Entity;
using BusinessLogic;

namespace DataAccess.Database
{
    public class Initializer : DropCreateDatabaseAlways<BlogContext>
    {
        public Initializer()
        {

        }
        protected override void Seed(BlogContext context)
        {
            context.Set<Blog>().Add(new Blog()
            {
                Creationdate = DateTime.Now,
                ShortDescription = "Testing",
                Title = "Test Blog"
            });
            context.SaveChanges();
        }
    }
}
```

Chapter 3

3. In the `BusinessLogic` project, add a new C# class named `Blog` with the following code:

```csharp
using System;
using System.ComponentModel.DataAnnotations;
using System.Text.RegularExpressions;

namespace BusinessLogic
{
  public class Blog
  {
    private const string DateBetween1900And2100Pattern =
      @"^(19|20)\d\d[- /.](0[1-9]|1[012])[- /.]
      (0[1-9]|[12][0-9]|3[01])$";

    public int Id { get; set; }

    [RegularExpression(pattern:
      DateBetween1900And2100Pattern, ErrorMessage =
      "Date is not valid between 1900 and 2100")]
    public DateTime Creationdate { get; set; }

    [Required]
    public string ShortDescription { get; set; }

    [Required]
    [StringLength(120, ErrorMessage = "Title is To Long")]
    public string Title { get; set; }

    [Range(0.0, 5.0, ErrorMessage = "Invalid Range, must be
      between 0 and 5")]
    public double Rating { get; set; }
  }
}
```

4. Add a `Mapping` folder to the `DataAccess` project, and add a `BlogMapping` class to the folder with the following code:

```csharp
using System.ComponentModel.DataAnnotations;
using System.Data.Entity.ModelConfiguration;
using BusinessLogic;

namespace DataAccess.Mappings
{
  public class BlogMapping : EntityTypeConfiguration<Blog>
```

```csharp
    {
      public BlogMapping()
      {
        this.ToTable("Blogs");
        this.HasKey(x => x.Id);

        this.Property(x => x.Id).HasDatabaseGeneratedOption(
           DatabaseGeneratedOption.Identity).HasColumnName("BlogId");

        this.Property(x => x.Title).IsRequired().HasMaxLength(250);

        this.Property(x => x.Creationdate)
           .HasColumnName("CreationDate").IsRequired();

        this.Property(x => x.ShortDescription).HasColumnType("Text")
           .IsMaxLength().IsOptional().HasColumnName("Description");
      }

    }
}
```

5. Modify the `BlogContext` class to contain the new mappings, and a `DbSet` property for `Blog` with the following code:

```csharp
using System;
using System.Data.Entity;
using System.Linq;
using BusinessLogic;
using DataAccess.Mappings;

namespace DataAccess
{
    public class BlogContext : DbContext, IUnitOfWork
    {
        public BlogContext(string connectionString) :
          base(connectionString)
        {

        }

        protected override void OnModelCreating(DbModelBuilder
          modelBuilder)
        {
          modelBuilder.Configurations.Add(new BlogMapping());
          base.OnModelCreating(modelBuilder);
        }
```

```csharp
      public IQueryable<T> Find<T>() where T : class
      {
        return this.Set<T>();
      }

      public void Refresh()
      {
        this.ChangeTracker.Entries().ToList()
          .ForEach(x=>x.Reload());
      }

      public void Commit()
      {
        this.SaveChanges();
      }
    }
  }
```

6. Run our test, and see how it works.
7. Modify the `BlogController` with the following code:

```csharp
using System;
using System.Data.Entity.Validation;
using System.Linq;
using System.Web.Mvc;
using BusinessLogic;
using DataAccess;
using UI.Properties;

namespace UI.Controllers
{
  public class BlogController : Controller
  {
    private IBlogRepository _blogRepository;

    public BlogController() : this(new BlogRepository(new
      BlogContext(Settings.Default.BlogConnection))) { }

    public BlogController(IBlogRepository blogRepository)
    {
      _blogRepository = blogRepository;
    }

    // GET: /Blog/
```

```csharp
public ActionResult Display()
{
  Blog blog = _blogRepository.Set<Blog>().First();
  return View(blog);
}

public ActionResult Create()
{
  return View(new Blog());
}

[AcceptVerbs(HttpVerbs.Post)]
public ActionResult Create([Bind(Exclude = "Id")]Blog blog)
{
  if (!ModelState.IsValid) return View();
  return RedirectToAction("Display");
}
  }
}
```

8. Run the application, and we should get some verification on the UI from the same validation that executes from the entity framework side.

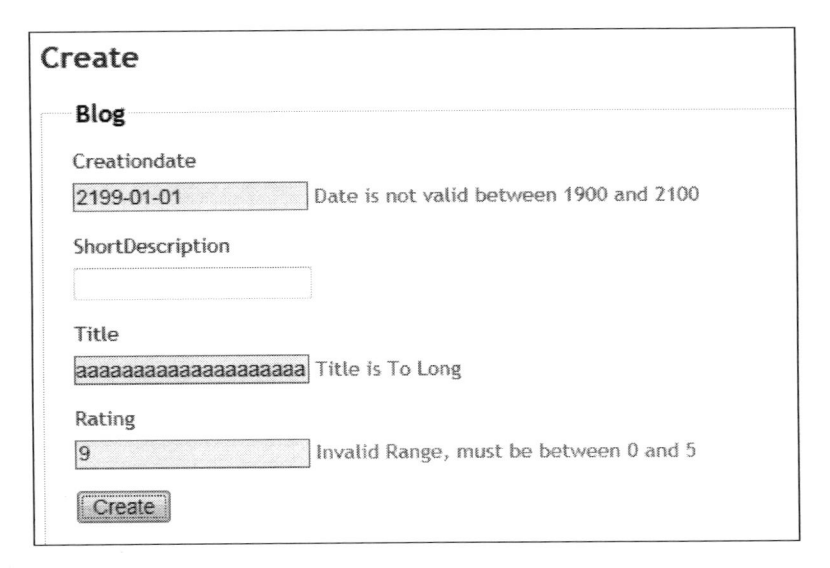

Create

Blog

Creationdate

`2199-01-01`   Date is not valid between 1900 and 2100

ShortDescription

Title

`aaaaaaaaaaaaaaaaaaaa` Title is To Long

Rating

`9`   Invalid Range, must be between 0 and 5

[Create]

How it works...

We start off by specifying a test that will validate the data annotations on the database side. In this example, we will also have to validate the client-side feedback manually to ensure that we have met our intent.

The `Blog` object is restricted with several simple validations that will give some error messages to the MVC View when the user changes inputs and the validation runs. The details of these restrictions, for our example, are not drastically important, but they give us a framework to test against.

We have added a couple `Create` methods to the `BlogController`, so we can add a `Create view` method that is strongly tied to `Blog`, and use the `Create template` method. This will present the UI, and set up the validation message handlers.

The MVC framework will use the `validation` attributes to put messages on the screen as an instant feedback to the user.

There's more...

Validations like these are generated amazingly simply in an MVC user experience, but we need to understand how that is accomplished.

Understanding the HTML helper

The **HTML helper** that enables our validation message to be displayed for a property, must be used to display the message from our attribute. The editor for the helper will not display on its own. This also requires sending the business objects to the UI in strongly-typed views. One of the key features of **Code First** is that we can use the objects throughout our code base, because they are not tied to our database structure.

4
Working with Transactions and Stored Procedures

In this chapter, we will cover the following recipes:

- Using transaction scopes
- Handling multiple context transactions
- Executing stored procedures
- Retrieving entities with stored procedures
- Updating entities with stored procedures

Introduction

We have all been in the situation of having to work on heavily transactional code bases, and we have needed to use stored procedures to retrieve the data. These two usages are normally ignored in the first discussions for the code, but they can be accomplished with fairly little effort.

In code first, the usage of stored procedures is an edge case, but when we have to do it, there are pieces that we can leverage. The idea that stored procedures are a better place for holding some data-centric business logic, or using them to control the access to our database has been widely held for years. This means that we have a very high chance of needing to connect to and communicate with legacy database schemas that use stored procedures to return scalar data about the database, or even use them to populate entities.

Working with Transactions and Stored Procedures

The usage of transactions is a fundamental idea for the Entity Framework as a whole. The context that we use to communicate to the database leverages transactions internally, without any extra code from the user. This allows us to write less code, and think of the larger picture. If we do need multiple contexts or to manually extend transactions beyond the simple call to save changes, then we can take advantage of these features without much effort.

Using transaction scopes

In this recipe, we will create a transaction scope that will allow multiple save operations on a single context to be handled as a single transaction, committing or rolling back, as needed.

Getting ready

We will be using the `NuGet` Package Manager to install the Entity Framework 4.1 assemblies.

The package installer can be found at http://nuget.org.

We will also be using a database for connecting to the data and updating it.

Open the **Improving Transaction Scope** solution in the included source code examples.

How to do it...

1. We start by adding a new unit test named `TransactionTests` to the test project. We make a test that connects to the database and adds an object within several transaction usages by using the following code:

   ```
   using System;
   using System.Collections.Generic;
   using System.Data.Entity.Validation;
   using System.Linq;
   using System.Text;
   using System.Text.RegularExpressions;
   using System.Transactions;
   using BusinessLogic;
   using DataAccess;
   using DataAccess.Database;
   using Microsoft.VisualStudio.TestTools.UnitTesting;
   using Test.Properties;
   using System.Data.Entity;

   namespace Test
   {
     [TestClass]
   ```

```csharp
public class TransactionTests
{

  [TestMethod]
  public void ShouldRollBackMultipleSaveContextCalls()
  {
    //Arrange
    var init = new Initializer();
    var context = new
      BlogContext(Settings.Default.BlogConnection);
    init.InitializeDatabase(context);

    var blog = new Blog()
    {
      Creationdate = DateTime.Now,
      ShortDescription = "Test",
      Title = "Testing"
    };

    var badBlog = new Blog()
    {
      Creationdate = DateTime.Now,
      Title = null,
      ShortDescription = null,
      Rating = 1.0
    };

    //Act
    var scope = new
      TransactionScope(TransactionScopeOption.RequiresNew,
      new TransactionOptions()
    {
      IsolationLevel = IsolationLevel.ReadUncommitted
    });

    try
    {
      using (scope)
      {
        context.Set<Blog>().Add(blog);
        context.SaveChanges();

        context.Set<Blog>().Add(badBlog);
        context.SaveChanges();
```

```
      }
    }
    catch (Exception)
    {

    }

    //Assert
    Assert.AreEqual(0, context.Find<Blog>().Count(x => x.Title
       == "Test"));
}

[TestMethod]
public void ShouldRollbackMultipleObjectsOnSingleBadSave()
{
    //Arrange
    var init = new Initializer();
    var context = new
       BlogContext(Settings.Default.BlogConnection);
    init.InitializeDatabase(context);

    var blog = new Blog()
    {
      Creationdate = DateTime.Now,
      ShortDescription = "Test",
      Title = "Testing"
    };

    var badBlog = new Blog()
    {
      Creationdate = DateTime.Now,
      Title = null,
      ShortDescription = null,
      Rating = 1.0
    };

    //Act
    try
    {
      var set = context.Set<Blog>();
      set.Add(blog);
      set.Add(badBlog);
      context.SaveChanges();
```

```csharp
      }
      catch
      {

      }

      //Assert
      Assert.AreEqual(0, context.Find<Blog>().Count(x => x.Title
        == "Test"));
    }

    [TestMethod]
    public void ShouldAllowImplicitTransactionsForRollback()
    {
      //Arrange
      var init = new Initializer();
      var context = new
        BlogContext(Settings.Default.BlogConnection);
      init.InitializeDatabase(context);

      var blog = new Blog()
      {
        Creationdate = DateTime.Now,
        ShortDescription = "Test",
        Title = "Testing"
      };

      //Act
      using (var scope = new
        TransactionScope(TransactionScopeOption.Required,
        new TransactionOptions(){IsolationLevel =
        IsolationLevel.ReadCommitted}))
      {
        context.Set<Blog>().Add(blog);
        context.SaveChanges();
        //Not calling scope.Complete() here causes a rollback.
      }

      //Assert
      Assert.AreEqual(0,context.Find<Blog>().Count(x=>x.Title ==
        "Test"));
    }
  }

}
```

2. Add an initializer to the `DataAccess` project in the `Database` folder with the following code to set up the data:

```
using System;
using System.Data.Entity;
using BusinessLogic;

namespace DataAccess.Database
{
  public class Initializer : DropCreateDatabaseAlways<BlogContext>
  {
    public Initializer()
    {

    }
    protected override void Seed(BlogContext context)
    {
      context.Set<Blog>().Add(new Blog()
      {
        Creationdate = DateTime.Now,
        ShortDescription = "Testing",
        Title = "Test Blog"
      });
      context.SaveChanges();
    }
  }
}
```

3. In the `BusinessLogic`, project add a new C# class named `Blog`, with the following code:

```
using System;
using System.ComponentModel.DataAnnotations;
using System.Text.RegularExpressions;

namespace BusinessLogic
{
  public class Blog
  {
    public int Id { get; set; }
    public DateTime Creationdate { get; set; }
    public string ShortDescription { get; set; }
    public string Title { get; set; }
    public double Rating { get; set; }
  }
}
```

4. Add a `Mapping` folder to the `DataAccess` project, and add a `BlogMapping` class to the folder with the following code:

   ```
   using System.ComponentModel.DataAnnotations;
   using System.Data.Entity.ModelConfiguration;
   using BusinessLogic;

   namespace DataAccess.Mappings
   {
     public class BlogMapping : EntityTypeConfiguration<Blog>
     {
       public BlogMapping()
       {
         this.ToTable("Blogs");
         this.HasKey(x => x.Id);
         this.Property(x => x.Id)
           .HasDatabaseGeneratedOption(
           DatabaseGeneratedOption.Identity)
           .HasColumnName("BlogId");

         this.Property(x => x.Title).IsRequired().HasMaxLength(250);
         this.Property(x => x.Creationdate)
           .HasColumnName("CreationDate").IsRequired();
         this.Property(x => x.ShortDescription)
           .HasColumnType("Text").IsMaxLength().IsOptional()
           .HasColumnName("Description");
       }

     }
   }
   ```

5. Modify the `BlogContext` class to contain the new mappings, and a `DbSet` property for `Blog` with the following code:

   ```
   using System;
   using System.Data.Entity;
   using System.Linq;
   using BusinessLogic;
   using DataAccess.Mappings;

   namespace DataAccess
   {
     public class BlogContext : DbContext, IUnitOfWork
     {
       public BlogContext(string connectionString) :
         base(connectionString)
       {
   ```

```
    }

    protected override void OnModelCreating(DbModelBuilder
      modelBuilder)
    {
      modelBuilder.Configurations.Add(new BlogMapping());
      base.OnModelCreating(modelBuilder);
    }

    public IQueryable<T> Find<T>() where T : class
    {
      return this.Set<T>();
    }

    public void Refresh()
    {
      this.ChangeTracker.Entries().ToList()
        .ForEach(x=>x.Reload());
    }

    public void Commit()
    {
      this.SaveChanges();
    }
  }
}
```

6. Run our test and see how it works.

How it works...

By creating our tests for transaction support, we accomplish two goals. First we demonstrate in a very clear code what functionality the context has and should have for verification. Second we demonstrate the usage code for a transaction scope.

This usage translates into a transaction scope in the SQL statement, so even outside our code, it is enforced to be a single transaction. Using transaction scope in this context makes for a very clear bundle of work headed for the database. The `DbContext` does this on a small-scale every time it saves to the database, which allows us to ignore the transaction scope most of the time. If you need everything from a single save call to be wrapped in a transaction, then you need not write any addition code as that is the default behavior of the `DbContext`.

We are using the standard transactions for interacting with the Entity Framework, which will also allow us to write in other data access code, if we had to, without modifying our transaction code.

There's more...

There are some key tenants that we will want to adhere to when talking about and working with transactions. These will save us from making very small mistakes with very large effects.

Ensuring read/update separation

When we are write a transaction, we want to make sure that only our updated code is covered by the transaction, our reads should not be, if at all, possible. This will allow for smaller and faster transactions. Keeping a transaction small allows us to avoid many of the locking concerns that could plague our application, otherwise.

Triggering – careful now

We have to be very careful when updating a table with a trigger in a transaction, because when we do this, the trigger is also included in the transaction scope. If the trigger fails, it will roll back the entire transaction. The transaction includes the trigger as soon as the trigger is fired.

Remembering that size matters

We have to read as few rows as possible in the transaction, and try to avoid stringing many operations together within a single transaction. This keeps our transaction scope in control. If we ignore this, then our transactions will bloat to the point of adversely effecting performance, and user experience.

See also

In this chapter:

- *Handling multiple context transactions*

Working with Transactions and Stored Procedures

Handling multiple context transactions

In this recipe, we are going to be using transactions to tightly control the communication of multiple contexts to a database.

Getting ready

We will be using the `NuGet` Package Manager to install the Entity Framework 4.1 assemblies.

The package installer can be found at `http://nuget.org`.

We will also be using a database for connecting data and updating it.

Open the **Improving Multiple Context Transactions** solution in the included source code examples.

How to do it...

1. We start by adding a new unit test named `TransactionTests` to the test project. We make a test that connects to the database and adds an object within several transaction usages by using the following code:

    ```
    using System;
    using System.Collections.Generic;
    using System.Data.Entity.Validation;
    using System.Linq;
    using System.Text;
    using System.Text.RegularExpressions;
    using System.Transactions;
    using BusinessLogic;
    using DataAccess;
    using DataAccess.Database;
    using Microsoft.VisualStudio.TestTools.UnitTesting;
    using Test.Properties;
    using System.Data.Entity;

    namespace Test
    {
      [TestClass]
      public class TransactionTests
      {

        [TestMethod]
        public void ShouldRollBackMultipleContextSaveCalls()
    ```

```csharp
{
    //Arrange
    var init = new Initializer();
    var context = new
        BlogContext(Settings.Default.BlogConnection);
    init.InitializeDatabase(context);
    var context2 = new
        BlogContext(Settings.Default.BlogConnection);

    var blog = new Blog()
    {
        Creationdate = DateTime.Now,
        ShortDescription = "Test",
        Title = "Testing"
    };

    var badBlog = new Blog()
    {
        Creationdate = DateTime.Now,
        Title = null,
        ShortDescription = null,
        Rating = 1.0
    };

    //Act
    var scope = new
        TransactionScope(TransactionScopeOption.RequiresNew,
        new TransactionOptions()
    {
        IsolationLevel = IsolationLevel.ReadUncommitted
    });

    try
    {
        using (scope)
        {
            context.Set<Blog>().Add(blog);
            context.SaveChanges();

            context2.Set<Blog>().Add(badBlog);
            context2.SaveChanges();
        }

    }
    catch (Exception)
```

```csharp
    {

    }

    //Assert
    Assert.AreEqual(0, context.Find<Blog>().Count(x => x.Title
       == "Test"));
}

[TestMethod]
public void ShouldAllowImplicitTransactionsForRollback()
{
  //Arrange
  var init = new Initializer();
  var context = new
    BlogContext(Settings.Default.BlogConnection);
  var context2 = new
    BlogContext(Settings.Default.BlogConnection);
  init.InitializeDatabase(context);

  var blog = new Blog()
  {
    Creationdate = DateTime.Now,
    ShortDescription = "Test",
    Title = "Testing"
  };

  //Act
  using (var scope = new
    TransactionScope(TransactionScopeOption.Required,
    new TransactionOptions(){IsolationLevel =
    IsolationLevel.ReadCommitted}))
  {
    context.Set<Blog>().Add(blog);
    context2.Set<Blog>().Add(blog);
    //Not calling scope.Complete() here causes a rollback.
  }

  //Assert
  Assert.AreEqual(0,context.Find<Blog>().Count(x=>x.Title ==
     "Test"));
  Assert.AreEqual(0, context2.Find<Blog>().Count(x => x.Title
     == "Test"));
  }
 }

}
```

Chapter 4

2. Add an initializer to the `DataAccess` project in the `Database` folder with the following code to set up the data:

```
using System;
using System.Data.Entity;
using BusinessLogic;

namespace DataAccess.Database
{

  public class Initializer : DropCreateDatabaseAlways<BlogContext>
  {
    public Initializer()
    {

    }
    protected override void Seed(BlogContext context)
    {
      context.Set<Blog>().Add(new Blog()
      {
        Creationdate = DateTime.Now,
        ShortDescription = "Testing",
        Title = "Test Blog"
      });
      context.SaveChanges();
    }
  }
}
```

3. In the `BusinessLogic` project, add a new C# class named `Blog` with the following code:

```
using System;
using System.ComponentModel.DataAnnotations;
using System.Text.RegularExpressions;

namespace BusinessLogic
{
  public class Blog
  {
    public int Id { get; set; }
    public DateTime Creationdate { get; set; }
    public string ShortDescription { get; set; }
    public string Title { get; set; }
    public double Rating { get; set; }
  }
}
```

Working with Transactions and Stored Procedures

4. Add a `Mapping` folder to the `DataAccess` project, and add a `BlogMapping` class to the folder with the following code:

```
using System.ComponentModel.DataAnnotations;
using System.Data.Entity.ModelConfiguration;
using BusinessLogic;

namespace DataAccess.Mappings
{
  public class BlogMapping : EntityTypeConfiguration<Blog>
  {
    public BlogMapping()
    {
      this.ToTable("Blogs");
      this.HasKey(x => x.Id);
      this.Property(x => x.Id)
        .HasDatabaseGeneratedOption(
          DatabaseGeneratedOption.Identity)
        .HasColumnName("BlogId");

      this.Property(x => x.Title).IsRequired().HasMaxLength(250);
      this.Property(x => x.Creationdate)
        .HasColumnName("CreationDate").IsRequired();
      this.Property(x => x.ShortDescription).HasColumnType("Text")
        .IsMaxLength().IsOptional().HasColumnName("Description");
    }

  }
}
```

5. Modify the `BlogContext` class to contain the new mappings and a `DbSet` property for `Blog` with the following code:

```
using System;
using System.Data.Entity;
using System.Linq;
using BusinessLogic;
using DataAccess.Mappings;

namespace DataAccess
{
  public class BlogContext : DbContext, IUnitOfWork
  {
    public BlogContext(string connectionString) :
      base(connectionString)
    {
```

```
        }

        protected override void OnModelCreating(DbModelBuilder
          modelBuilder)
        {
          modelBuilder.Configurations.Add(new BlogMapping());
          base.OnModelCreating(modelBuilder);
        }

        public IQueryable<T> Find<T>() where T : class
        {
          return this.Set<T>();
        }

        public void Refresh()
        {
          this.ChangeTracker.Entries().ToList()
            .ForEach(x=>x.Reload());
        }

        public void Commit()
        {
          this.SaveChanges();
        }
      }
    }
```

6. Run our test, and see how it works.

How it works...

We start our solution, as always, by creating a set of tests that communicate our intent, and allow us to verify our results. In this case, we are testing that two separate connections to the databases can be managed by a single transaction.

The system that allows this is compatible with Entity Framework, because of how Entity Framework was built. This structure of **ADO.NET** connections and generated SQL commands allows us to use the **Distributed Transaction Coordinator** (**DTC**). This is a feature of modern versions of Windows, and therefore is restricted to a Windows platform.

This communication not only sets up a transaction on both the database communications, but also wraps the resources (in this case, our `DbContexts`) in a large OS-level transaction. The execution of these statements depends on the program completing the transaction scope. This gives us fine-grain control over these multi-context transactions.

Working with Transactions and Stored Procedures

There's more...

When dealing with distributed transactions, we want to leverage them in a way that makes use of the **ACID** principles.

Atomic

The execution of any transaction should either have the full-intended effect or no effect at all. The results should be either complete (`commit`), or nothing should happen (`abort`).

Consistent

Any transaction is a transition of state in an application, and therefore should preserve a consistent version of the application. For example, when updating a many-to-many relationship, both the foreign key and the reference table relationship should be updated.

Isolation

Each transaction should be isolated from all other incomplete transactions. Due to the transactions being in the state of transition, they are not consistent, and therefore should be removed from affecting the transaction that is currently executing.

Durability

System failures should not cause a committed transaction that fails to persist its effects. If we rename something, but the SQL server crashes in the middle of the `commit` operation, on recovery the transaction should still be fully committed. (This normally involves another call to the database to execute the `commit` operation again, but it is handled by the **DTC**.)

Executing stored procedures

Stored procedures sometimes get a bad rap from developers, given their long history. But we need to remember that, often, they are the most effective way to coalesce complex queries. Just don't let them store business logic.

Getting ready

We will be using the `NuGet` Package Manager to install the Entity Framework 4.1 assemblies.

The package installer can be found at `http://nuget.org`.

We will also be using a database for connecting the data and updating it.

Open the **Improving Stored Procedures** solution in the included source code examples.

How to do it...

1. We start by adding a new unit test named `TransactionTests` to the test project. We make a test that connects to the database, adds an object, and then retrieves a count with a stored procedure, by using the following code:

```csharp
using DataAccess;
using DataAccess.Database;
using DataAccess.Queries;
using Microsoft.VisualStudio.TestTools.UnitTesting;
using Test.Properties;

namespace Test
{
  [TestClass]
  public class StoredProcedureTests
  {

    [TestMethod]
    public void
      ShouldAllowCallingStoredProcedureAndGettingResult()
    {
      //Arrange
      var init = new Initializer();
      var context = new
          BlogContext(Settings.Default.BlogConnection);
      init.InitializeDatabase(context);
      var repo = new BlogRepository(context);

      //Act
      var count = repo.GetBlogCount();

      //Assert
      Assert.AreEqual(1, count);
    }
  }

}
```

Working with Transactions and Stored Procedures

2. Add an initializer to the `DataAccess` project in the `Database` folder with the following code to set up the data:

```csharp
using System;
using System.Data.Entity;
using BusinessLogic;

namespace DataAccess.Database
{
  public class Initializer : DropCreateDatabaseAlways<BlogContext>
  {
    public Initializer()
    {

    }
    protected override void Seed(BlogContext context)
    {
      context.Database.ExecuteSqlCommand(
        StoredProcedureDefinitions.GetBlogCountDefinition);
      context.Set<Blog>().Add(new Blog()
      {
        CreationDate = DateTime.Now,
        ShortDescription = "Testing",
        Title = "Test Blog"
      });
      context.SaveChanges();
    }
  }
}
```

3. In the `DataAccess` project, we add a new C# class named `StoredProcedureDefinitions` with the following code, so we recreate our stored procedures with each database creation:

```csharp
namespace DataAccess.Database
{
  public static class StoredProcedureDefinitions
  {
    public static string GetBlogCountDefinition = @"CREATE
      PROCEDURE [dbo].[GetBlogCount]
      AS
      BEGIN
        SET NOCOUNT ON;
        SELECT Count(*) FROM dbo.Blogs
      END
      ";
  }
}
```

Chapter 4

4. In the `BusinessLogic` project, add a new C# class named `Blog` with the following code:

```csharp
using System;

namespace BusinessLogic
{
  public class Blog
  {
    public int Id { get; set; }
    public DateTime Creationdate { get; set; }
    public string ShortDescription { get; set; }
    public string Title { get; set; }
    public double Rating { get; set; }
  }
}
```

5. Add a `Mapping` folder to the `DataAccess` project, and add a `BlogMapping` class to the folder with the following code:

```csharp
using System.ComponentModel.DataAnnotations;
using System.Data.Entity.ModelConfiguration;
using BusinessLogic;

namespace DataAccess.Mappings
{
  public class BlogMapping : EntityTypeConfiguration<Blog>
  {
    public BlogMapping()
    {
      this.ToTable("Blogs");
      this.HasKey(x => x.Id);
      this.Property(x => x.Id).
        HasDatabaseGeneratedOption(
        DatabaseGeneratedOption.Identity)
        .HasColumnName("BlogId");

      this.Property(x => x.Title).IsRequired().HasMaxLength(250);
      this.Property(x => x.Creationdate)
        .HasColumnName("CreationDate").IsRequired();
      this.Property(x => x.ShortDescription)
        .HasColumnType("Text").IsMaxLength().IsOptional()
        .HasColumnName("Description");
    }

  }
}
```

Working with Transactions and Stored Procedures

6. Modify the `BlogContext` class to contain the new mappings and a `DbSet` property for `Blog` with the following code:

```
using System;
using System.Data.Entity;
using System.Linq;
using BusinessLogic;
using DataAccess.Mappings;

namespace DataAccess
{
  public class BlogContext : DbContext, IUnitOfWork
  {
    public BlogContext(string connectionString) :
      base(connectionString)
    {

    }

    protected override void OnModelCreating(DbModelBuilder
      modelBuilder)
    {
      modelBuilder.Configurations.Add(new BlogMapping());
      base.OnModelCreating(modelBuilder);
    }

    public IQueryable<T> Find<T>() where T : class
    {
      return this.Set<T>();
    }

    public void Refresh()
    {
      this.ChangeTracker.Entries().ToList()
        .ForEach(x=>x.Reload());
    }

    public void Commit()
    {
      this.SaveChanges();
    }
  }
}
```

7. In the `DataAccess` project, we add a new folder named `Queries` with a new C# class named `StoredProcedures`, with the following code:

    ```
    using System.Linq;

    namespace DataAccess.Queries
    {
      public static class StoredProcedures
      {
        public static int GetBlogCount(this IBlogRepository
          repository)
        {
          var items = repository.UnitOfWork.Context.Database
            .SqlQuery<int>(@"GetBlogCount");
          var count = items.FirstOrDefault();
          return count;
        }
      }
    }
    ```

8. Run our test, and see how it works.

How it works...

We start-off our solution, as always, with a test that ensures that our features are properly implemented, and that we have demonstrated the functionality required.

In this example, for clarity alone, we have put the definition of the stored procedure into our code. This is not a requirement, and we could have easily let the stored procedure be defined in an embedded SQL file, or have it already exist in the database.

Once the stored procedure is created, we put an `extension` method on the repository that allows us to invoke the SQL statement from the `Database` object on the `DbContext`. We have to drill through a couple of layers, but this is preferable to surfacing a raw `DbContext`. We want that layered abstraction in this case.

Entity Framework takes the SQL query, executes it, and then tries to map the `return` operation into the type that we have given it. In this case, we told it that the `return` parameter is of the integer type.

There's more...

When dealing with stored procedures in the Entity Framework code first model, we have to be aware of several things that could hamstring us, and cause runtime errors throughout our application.

Working with Transactions and Stored Procedures

Handling return type mapping
If the type that is returned cannot be parsed into the type that it is expecting, we will get a runtime error. This error will bubble from the framework and will need to be guarded against at the point that we call the stored procedure.

Remembering access rules
If we are calling a stored procedure, we need to make sure that we schema qualify any stored procedure name that is outside of the `dbo` schema. We will also need to make sure that we have `execute` permissions to that stored procedure, just as we would if we were calling it directly from ADO.NET.

See also

In this chapter:

- *Retrieving entities with stored procedures*

Retrieving entities with stored procedures

Sometimes, we need a stored procedure to not only return data, but also to return actual and change-tracked entities. To make certain that happens, we need to do just a little bit more.

Getting ready

We will be using the `NuGet` Package Manager to install the Entity Framework 4.1 assemblies.

The package installer can be found at `http://nuget.org`.

We will also be using a database for connecting to the data and updating it.

Open the **Improving Entities with Stored Procedures** solution in the included source code examples.

How to do it...

1. We start by adding a new unit test named `TransactionTests` to the test project. We make a test that connects to the database, adds an object, and then retrieves an entity with a stored procedure, by using the following code:

    ```
    using DataAccess;
    using DataAccess.Database;
    using DataAccess.Queries;
    using Microsoft.VisualStudio.TestTools.UnitTesting;
    using Test.Properties;
    ```

Chapter 4

```csharp
namespace Test
{
  [TestClass]
  public class StoredProcedureTests
  {
    [TestMethod]
    public void
      ShouldAllowReturnOfATrackedEntityFromStoredProcedure()
    {
      //Arrange
      var init = new Initializer();
      var context = new
        BlogContext(Settings.Default.BlogConnection);
      init.InitializeDatabase(context);
      var repo = new BlogRepository(context);

      //Act
      var blog = repo.GetBlog(1);

      //Assert
      Assert.AreEqual(1, blog.Id);
    }
  }

}
```

2. Add an initializer to the `DataAccess` project in the `Database` folder with the following code to set up the data:

```csharp
using System;
using System.Data.Entity;
using BusinessLogic;

namespace DataAccess.Database
{

  public class Initializer : DropCreateDatabaseAlways<BlogContext>
  {
    public Initializer()
    {

    }
    protected override void Seed(BlogContext context)
    {
      context.Database.ExecuteSqlCommand(
        StoredProcedureDefinitions.GetBlogDefinition);
```

Working with Transactions and Stored Procedures

```csharp
          context.Set<Blog>().Add(new Blog()
          {
            CreationDate = DateTime.Now,
            ShortDescription = "Testing",
            Title = "Test Blog"
          });
          context.SaveChanges();
        }
      }
    }
```

3. In the `DataAccess` project, we add a new C# class named `StoredProcedureDefinitions` with the following code, so we can recreate our stored procedures with each database creation:

```csharp
namespace DataAccess.Database
{
  public static class StoredProcedureDefinitions
  {
    public static string GetBlogDefinition = @"CREATE PROCEDURE
      [dbo].[GetBlog]
      @BlogId int
      AS
      BEGIN
        SET NOCOUNT ON;
        SELECT b.BlogId as Id, b.Description as ShortDescription,
          b.Title, b.Rating, b.CreationDate  FROM dbo.Blogs b
      END
      ";
  }
}
```

4. In the `BusinessLogic` project, add a new C# class named `Blog` with the following code:

```csharp
using System;

namespace BusinessLogic
{
  public class Blog
  {
    public int Id { get; set; }
    public DateTime CreationDate { get; set; }
    public string ShortDescription { get; set; }
    public string Title { get; set; }
    public double Rating { get; set; }
  }
}
```

Chapter 4

5. Add a `Mapping` folder to the `DataAccess` project and add a `BlogMapping` class to the folder with the following code:

   ```
   using System.ComponentModel.DataAnnotations;
   using System.Data.Entity.ModelConfiguration;
   using BusinessLogic;

   namespace DataAccess.Mappings
   {
     public class BlogMapping : EntityTypeConfiguration<Blog>
     {
       public BlogMapping()
       {
         this.ToTable("Blogs");
         this.HasKey(x => x.Id);
         this.Property(x => x.Id)
           .HasDatabaseGeneratedOption(
           DatabaseGeneratedOption.Identity)
           .HasColumnName("BlogId");

         this.Property(x => x.Title).IsRequired().HasMaxLength(250);
         this.Property(x => x.Creationdate)
           .HasColumnName("CreationDate").IsRequired();
         this.Property(x => x.ShortDescription).HasColumnType("Text")
           .IsMaxLength().IsOptional().HasColumnName("Description");
       }

     }
   }
   ```

6. Modify the `BlogContext` class to contain the new mappings, and a `DbSet` property for `Blog` with the following code:

   ```
   using System;
   using System.Data.Entity;
   using System.Linq;
   using BusinessLogic;
   using DataAccess.Mappings;

   namespace DataAccess
   {
     public class BlogContext : DbContext, IUnitOfWork
     {
       public BlogContext(string connectionString) :
         base(connectionString)
       {
   ```

```
        }

        protected override void OnModelCreating(DbModelBuilder
          modelBuilder)
        {
          modelBuilder.Configurations.Add(new BlogMapping());
          base.OnModelCreating(modelBuilder);
        }

        public IQueryable<T> Find<T>() where T : class
        {
          return this.Set<T>();
        }

        public void Refresh()
        {
          this.ChangeTracker.Entries().ToList()
            .ForEach(x=>x.Reload());
        }

        public void Commit()
        {
          this.SaveChanges();
        }
      }
    }
```

7. In the `DataAccess` project, we add a new folder named `Queries` with a new C# class named `StoredProcedures` with the following code:

```
using System.Data.Entity;
using System.Data.SqlClient;
using System.Linq;
using BusinessLogic;

namespace DataAccess.Queries
{
  public static class StoredProcedures
  {
    public static Blog GetBlog(this IBlogRepository repository,
      int blogId)
    {
      var items = repository.UnitOfWork.Context.Database
        .SqlQuery<Blog>(@"GetBlog @BlogId", new
        SqlParameter("BlogId",blogId) );
      var blog = items.FirstOrDefault();
```

```
            if (blog != null &&
              repository.UnitOfWork.Context.Entry(blog) == null)
              repository.UnitOfWork.Context.Set<Blog>().Attach(blog);
            return blog;
        }
    }
}
```

8. Run our test and see how it works.

How it works...

We start, as always, with a test that calls our stored procedure and returns a tracked entity, so we can ensure that we have accomplished the goal that we set forth.

We also make sure that the stored procedure is returning columns that match the names of the properties that we have in our entity. This is because there is no mapping between the stored procedure's return operation and the entity instantiation. This lack of mapping causes the framework to use reflection to try and directly correlate columns to properties, and we will need to make sure that correlation can happen seamlessly.

The stored procedure is called from the repository, but notice that it drills down to fire on the `Database` object on `DbContext`. This allows us to map anything from a simple integer return to an object, which are not tracked by default. So, we have to manually attach the object to the context. This will allow us to leverage stored procedures to load objects, but still have generated change statements and tracking on the object.

There's more...

Loading the entity from a stored procedure is complex in the conventions that it relies on, and some runtime errors can occur if we do not prepare against them.

Column Mapping

If a column name doesn't have a matching property, or vice versa, it will cause a runtime error. This is part of the magic making this happen. We have to make sure that our columns from the stored procedure are one-to-one with our objects. If this is not the case, then we will have to define a **Data Transfer Object** (**DTO**) that holds the result and then is parsed into the objects and attached.

See also

In this chapter:

> *Updating entities with stored procedures*

Working with Transactions and Stored Procedures

Updating entities with stored procedures

Sometimes, the policies of a given enterprise require the use of stored procedures for handling insert and update opeartions to the database. While we don't necessarily recommend this practice, this recipe shows how to ensure that Entity Framework complies with such a policy.

Getting ready

We will be using the `NuGet` Package Manager to install the Entity Framework 4.1 assemblies.

The package installer can be found at `http://nuget.org`.

We will also be using a database for connecting to the data and updating it.

Open the **Improving Updating Entities with Stored Procedures** solution in the included source code examples.

How to do it...

1. We start by adding a new unit test named `TransactionTests` to the test project. We make a test that connects to the database, adds an object, and then retrieves an entity with a stored procedure, by using the following code:

```
using System;
using System.Linq;
using BusinessLogic;
using DataAccess;
using DataAccess.Database;
using DataAccess.Queries;
using Microsoft.VisualStudio.TestTools.UnitTesting;
using Test.Properties;

namespace Test
{
  [TestClass]
  public class StoredProcedureTests
  {
    [TestMethod]
    public void ShouldAllowEditsThroughUpsert()
    {
      //Arrange
      var init = new Initializer();
      var context = new
        BlogContext(Settings.Default.BlogConnection);
```

```csharp
      init.InitializeDatabase(context);
      context.Set<Blog>().Add(new Blog
      {
        CreationDate = DateTime.Today.AddDays(-1),
        Rating = 0,
        ShortDescription = "Dummy",
        Title = "Dummy"
      });
      context.SaveChanges();

      //Act
      var blog = context.Set<Blog>().FirstOrDefault();
      blog.Title = "TestingSP";
      context.SaveChanges();

      //Assert
      Assert.IsTrue(context.Set<Blog>().Any(x => x.Title ==
        "TestingSP"));
    }

    [TestMethod]
    public void ShouldAllowInsertsThroughUpsert()
    {
      //Arrange
      var init = new Initializer();
      var context = new
        BlogContext(Settings.Default.BlogConnection);
      init.InitializeDatabase(context);

      //Act
      context.Set<Blog>().Add(new Blog()
      {
        CreationDate = DateTime.Now,
        Rating = 1.5,
        ShortDescription = "Testing",
        Title = "SPInsert"
      });
      context.SaveChanges();

      //Assert
      Assert.IsTrue(context.Set<Blog>().Any(x => x.Title ==
        "SPInsert"));
    }
  }
}
```

Working with Transactions and Stored Procedures

2. Add an initializer to the `DataAccess` project in the `Database` folder with the following code to set up the data:

```csharp
using System;
using System.Data.Entity;
using BusinessLogic;

namespace DataAccess.Database
{
  public class Initializer : DropCreateDatabaseAlways<BlogContext>
  {
    public Initializer()
    {

    }
    protected override void Seed(BlogContext context)
    {
      context.Database.ExecuteSqlCommand(
        StoredProcedureDefinitions.UpsertBlogDefinition);
      context.SaveChanges();
    }
  }
}
```

3. In the `DataAccess` project, we add a new C# class named `StoredProcedureDefinitions` with the following code, so we recreate our stored procedures with each database creation:

```csharp
namespace DataAccess.Database
{
  public static class StoredProcedureDefinitions
  {
    public static string UpsertBlogDefinition = @"CREATE PROCEDURE
      UpsertBlog
      @Id int = 0,
      @CreationDate date,
      @Description text,
      @Title nvarchar(250),
      @Rating float
    AS
      BEGIN
        SET NOCOUNT ON;
        DECLARE @return_status int;
        IF EXISTS (SELECT * FROM BLOGS WHERE BlogId = @Id)
          BEGIN
```

Chapter 4

```sql
              UPDATE [EFCookbook].[dbo].[Blogs]
              SET [Description] = @Description,
                [Title] = @Title,
                [Rating] = @Rating
              WHERE BlogId = @Id
              SET @return_status = @Id
            END
          Else
          BEGIN
            INSERT INTO [EFCookbook].[dbo].[Blogs]
               ([CreationDate]
               ,[Description]
               ,[Title]
               ,[Rating])
            VALUES
               (@CreationDate,
               @Description,
               @Title,
               @Rating)
            SET @return_status = SCOPE_IDENTITY()
              END
              Select 'Return Status' = @return_status;
          END
```
```
    ";
  }
}
```

4. In the `BusinessLogic` project, add a new C# class named `Blog` with the following code:

    ```csharp
    using System;

    namespace BusinessLogic
    {
      public class Blog
      {
        public int Id { get; set; }
        public DateTime CreationDate { get; set; }
        public string ShortDescription { get; set; }
        public string Title { get; set; }
        public double Rating { get; set; }
      }
    }
    ```

Working with Transactions and Stored Procedures

5. Add a `Mapping` folder to the `DataAccess` project, and add a `BlogMapping` class to the folder with the following code:

```
using System.ComponentModel.DataAnnotations;
using System.Data.Entity.ModelConfiguration;
using BusinessLogic;

namespace DataAccess.Mappings
{
  public class BlogMapping : EntityTypeConfiguration<Blog>
  {
    public BlogMapping()
    {
      this.ToTable("Blogs");
      this.HasKey(x => x.Id);
      this.Property(x => x.Id)
        .HasDatabaseGeneratedOption(
        DatabaseGeneratedOption.Identity)
        .HasColumnName("BlogId");

      this.Property(x => x.Title).IsRequired().HasMaxLength(250);
      this.Property(x => x.Creationdate)
        .HasColumnName("CreationDate").IsRequired();
      this.Property(x => x.ShortDescription).HasColumnType("Text")
        .IsMaxLength().IsOptional().HasColumnName("Description");
    }

  }
}
```

6. Modify the `BlogContext` class to contain the new mappings and a `DbSet` property for `Blog` with the following code. Notice the override on the `SaveChanges` utilizes the stored procedure `upsert`:

```
using System.Data;
using System.Data.Entity;
using System.Data.Entity.Infrastructure;
using System.Linq;
using BusinessLogic;
using DataAccess.Mappings;
using DataAccess.Queries;

namespace DataAccess
{
  public class BlogContext : DbContext, IUnitOfWork
  {
```

```csharp
public BlogContext(string connectionString) :
  base(connectionString)
{

}

protected override void OnModelCreating(DbModelBuilder
  modelBuilder)
{
  modelBuilder.Configurations.Add(new BlogMapping());
  base.OnModelCreating(modelBuilder);
}

public IQueryable<T> Find<T>() where T : class
{
  return this.Set<T>();
}

public void Refresh()
{
  this.ChangeTracker.Entries().ToList()
    .ForEach(x=>x.Reload());
}

public void Commit()
{
  this.SaveChanges();
}

public override int SaveChanges()
{
  int storedProcChanges = 0;
  var changeSet = ChangeTracker.Entries<Blog>();

  if (changeSet != null)
  {
    foreach (DbEntityEntry<Blog> entry in changeSet)
    {
      switch (entry.State)
      {
        case EntityState.Added:
        case EntityState.Modified:
        {
          var id = this.UpsertBlog(entry.Entity);
```

Working with Transactions and Stored Procedures

```
                    entry.State = EntityState.Detached;
                    if(id != -1) entry.Entity.Id = id;
                    this.Set<Blog>().Attach(entry.Entity);
                    storedProcChanges++;
                }
                break;
            }
        }
    }

    return base.SaveChanges() + storedProcChanges;
}
public DbContext Context { get { return this; } }
public void Add<T>(T item) where T : class
{
    this.Set<T>().Add(item);
}
    }
}
```

7. In the `DataAccess` project, we add a new folder named `Queries` with a new C# class named `StoredProcedures` with the following code:

```
using System.Data.Entity;
using System.Data.SqlClient;
using System.Linq;
using BusinessLogic;
using DataAccess.Database;

namespace DataAccess.Queries
{
  public static class StoredProcedures
  {
    private static string _upsertQuery = @"
      DECLARE @return_value int

      EXEC @return_value = [dbo].[UpsertBlog]
        @Id,
        @CreationDate,
        @Description,
        @Title,
        @Rating

      SELECT 'Return Value' = @return_value
    ";
```

```csharp
public static Blog GetBlog(this IBlogRepository repository,
    int blogId)
{
  var items = repository.UnitOfWork.Context.Database
    .SqlQuery<Blog>(@"GetBlog @BlogId", new
    SqlParameter("BlogId",blogId) );

  var blog = items.FirstOrDefault();
  if (blog != null &&
    repository.UnitOfWork.Context.Entry(blog) == null)
    repository.UnitOfWork.Context.Set<Blog>().Attach(blog);
  return blog;
}
public static int UpsertBlog(this DbContext context, Blog
    blog)
{
  return context.Database.SqlQuery<int>(_upsertQuery,
    new object[]
    {
      new SqlParameter("Id",blog.Id),
      new SqlParameter("CreationDate",blog.CreationDate),
      new SqlParameter("Description",blog.ShortDescription),
      new SqlParameter("Title",blog.Title),
      new SqlParameter("Rating",blog.Rating)
    }).First();
}
    }
  }
```

8. Run our test, and see how it works.

How it works...

We start-off our solution with a couple of tests that ensure we have achieved the goal, which, in this case, is to insert or update an entity without the use of generated SQL statements, but instead by using an update and insert stored procedure.

We move to setting up an initializer that will create the stored procedure for us every time our test database is dropped and recreated. We also provide a class to centralize these definitions in case of changes. This can load from .txt or .sql files just as easily. This ensures that the stored procedure will be there when we call it.

We then move to defining the blog and the blog mapping for our context. These will not be used by our context for SQL generation on update and insert, but will be used for selections and deletes. These two pieces can, over course, be changed as well, but would be overkill for this recipe.

Working with Transactions and Stored Procedures

The `BlogContext` is where we are able to modify the `save` behavior, by overriding the `SaveChanges` method. We are able to pull all of the `Blog` object state entries from the change tracker. This give us the ability to check for added or modified blog objects, execute our `upsert` stored procedure, and then clear the object modified state, so that the generated SQL doesn't pick up those changes. Notice how we detach the objects before modifying the ID. The reason for that is, the context will return an error if you try to change the key of an attached object.

There's more...

When we are forced to deal with stored procedures, we want to make sure that we avoid some serious runtime errors with the following suggestions and support:

Manually changing states

We have to be very careful with this, as the runtime error chances increase drastically. The following are a few of the common error scenarios to avoid:

- Adding an object with the same key as one already tracked
- Trying to modify a tracked object's key
- Trying to modify the state of an added object without first detaching and changing its ID

Abstract usage

If we are planning to use the stored procedure updates for more than one object type, then we should abstract the query string and the parameter collection behind a factory, so that the `SqlQuery<>` usage in the context can be as clean and generic as possible.

Extensions for stored procedure support

There are several open source libraries that make this easier to accomplish, here are a couple of them:

http://www.codeproject.com/KB/database/CodeFirstStoredProcedures.aspx

http://archive.msdn.microsoft.com/EFExtensions

See also

In this chapter:

- *Retrieving entities with stored procedures*

5
Improving Entity Framework with Query Libraries

In this chapter, we will cover:

- Creating reusable queries
- Improving entity and library reuse
- Implementing composed queries
- Increasing performance with code access
- Improving query testing

Introduction

Have you ever looked for the type of oil a car requires or calculated the expected miles per gallon of gas? There is a specific oil needed based on the type of car we have, but gas mileage can vary wildly based on the options your car has, the type of gas used, and so on. This is a part of the reason that the oil requirements are printed in our owner's manual (because it is specific to our car) but the miles per gallon calculation is not.

This kind of separation requires us to separate the information that we want from how we get it. The data we are returning may come from different sources, but how we get it can be abstracted. If we own both a truck and a sports car, we would do the same thing to find the type of oil (pull out the owner's manual and find the page with the oil requirements). This level of separation which we see in the everyday world is the same separation that we should strive for in our applications.

Improving Entity Framework with Query Libraries

When we write software, there is a similar separation in queries and projections. Some queries are used by all of our entities, but in other cases, the query is so specific that it is tightly coupled to the type it queries on. We are confronted by a decision point here. We could put all of our queries in one place, but that would violate our single responsibility principle and separation of concern. The other option is to define query libraries that hold the queries in specific areas grouped by their level of abstraction.

Creating reusable queries

In this recipe, we will be working to create reusable queries that are defined outside of the data context and are specific to an object type.

Getting ready

We will be using the **NuGet** package manager to install the **Entity Framework 4.1** assemblies.

The package installer can be found at `http://nuget.org`.

We will also be using a database for connecting to and updating data.

Open the Improving **Reusable Queries** solution in the included source code examples.

How to do it...

Carry out the following steps in order to accomplish this recipe.

1. We will start by adding a new unit test named `QueryTests` to test the project. We will make a test that connects to the database and retrieves a couple of records with a reusable query using the following code:

   ```
   using System;
   using System.Linq;
   using BusinessLogic;
   using DataAccess;
   using DataAccess.Database;
   using DataAccess.Queries;
   using Microsoft.VisualStudio.TestTools.UnitTesting;
   using Test.Properties;

   namespace Test
   {
     [TestClass]
     public class QueryTests
     {
   ```

```
        [TestMethod]
        public void ShouldReturnRecordsFromTheDatabase()
        {
          //Arrange
          var init = new Initializer();
          var context = new
            BlogContext(Settings.Default.BlogConnection);
          init.InitializeDatabase(context);
          IBlogRepository repo = new BlogRepository(context);


          //Act
          var items = repo.Set<Blog>().FilterByBlogName("Test");

          //Assert
          Assert.AreEqual(2, items.Count());
        }
      }

  }
```

2. Add an initializer to the `DataAccess` project `Database` folder with the following code to set up data:

```
using System;
using System.Data.Entity;
using BusinessLogic;

namespace DataAccess.Database
{

  public class Initializer :
    DropCreateDatabaseAlways<BlogContext>
  {
    public Initializer()
    {

    }
    protected override void Seed(BlogContext context)
    {
      context.Set<Blog>().Add(new Blog()
        {
          Creationdate = DateTime.Now,
          ShortDescription = "Testing",
          Title = "Test Blog"
```

```
            });
         context.Set<Blog>().Add(new Blog()
            {
               Creationdate = DateTime.Now,
               ShortDescription = "Testing",
               Title = "Test Blog 2"
            });
         context.Set<Blog>().Add(new Blog()
            {
               Creationdate = DateTime.Now,
               ShortDescription = "Testing",
               Title = "not Blog"
            });
         context.SaveChanges();
      }
   }
}
```

3. In the `BusinessLogic` project, add a new C# class named `Blog` with the following code:

```
using System;
using System.ComponentModel.DataAnnotations;
using System.Text.RegularExpressions;

namespace BusinessLogic
{
   public class Blog
   {
      public int Id { get; set; }
      public DateTime Creationdate { get; set; }
      public string ShortDescription { get; set; }
      public string Title { get; set; }
      public double Rating { get; set; }
   }
}
```

4. Add a `Mapping` folder to the `DataAccess` project and then add a `BlogMapping` class to the folder with the following code:

```
using System.ComponentModel.DataAnnotations;
using System.Data.Entity.ModelConfiguration;
using BusinessLogic;

namespace DataAccess.Mappings
{
   public class BlogMapping : EntityTypeConfiguration<Blog>
   {
      public BlogMapping()
      {
         this.ToTable("Blogs");
```

```
            this.HasKey(x => x.Id);
            this.Property(x => x.Id).HasDatabaseGeneratedOption
               (DatabaseGeneratedOption.Identity)
                 .HasColumnName("BlogId");

            this.Property(x =>
               x.Title).IsRequired().HasMaxLength(250);
            this.Property(x => x.Creationdate)
               .HasColumnName("CreationDate").IsRequired();
            this.Property(x => x.ShortDescription)
               .HasColumnType("Text").IsMaxLength().IsOptional()
                  .HasColumnName("Description");
        }

    }
}
```

5. Modify the `BlogContext` class to contain the new mappings for `Blogs` with the following code:

```
using System;
using System.Data.Entity;
using System.Linq;
using BusinessLogic;
using DataAccess.Mappings;

namespace DataAccess
{
  public class BlogContext : DbContext, IUnitOfWork
  {
    public BlogContext(string connectionString)
    : base(connectionString)
    {

    }

    protected override void OnModelCreating
      (DbModelBuilder modelBuilder)
    {
      modelBuilder.Configurations.Add(new BlogMapping());
      base.OnModelCreating(modelBuilder);
    }

    public IQueryable<T> Find<T>() where T : class
    {
      return this.Set<T>();
    }

    public void Refresh()
    {
```

```
            this.ChangeTracker.Entries().ToList()
              .ForEach(x=>x.Reload());
        }

        public void Commit()
        {
          this.SaveChanges();
        }
      }
    }
```

6. Add a new folder named `Queries` to the `DataAccess` project and add a new C# class to it named `BlogQueries` with the following code:

```
using System.Linq;

namespace DataAccess.Queries
{
  public static class BlogQueries
  {
    public static IQueryable<Blog> FilterByBlogName
       (this IQueryable<Blog> items, string name)
    {
      return items.Where(x => x.Title.Contains(name));
    }
  }
}
```

7. Run our test and it will work.

How it works...

As we usually do, we start with a test that defines what we would like to accomplish. In this case, we want to seed a database with several records and then query those records for an expected return. The database initializer that we add inserts three records, two of which meet the requirements of our filter and one that does not.

We then set up our blog object, its mappings, and the object context, so we have a solid way to interact with the database. This will form the basis of the database communication and the framework for accessing the records that need to be filtered.

We then leverage a language feature of extension methods to layer on our queries without bloating our repository with every data query. This does two things, it lets us target a specific type, and it restricts the usage of that type. These queries will only be available on the types that use them and nowhere else.

Notice that we use an `IQueryable<T>` here. This is done to allow us to compose multiple statements together before translating it into an SQL statement that will be executed. If we want to limit this only to in memory objects, we can force it to be an array or a list.

There's more...

When using extension methods there are some things to keep in mind so you create a consistent and valuable library of queries.

Extension methods

Extension methods allow us to extend behavior onto a type without modifying that type or any of its inheritance chain. These methods are brought into scope at the namespace level. Therefore, we must add the `using` statement to have access to these.

Naming conflict

We can use extension methods to extend behavior to an existing type, but not to override it. The compiler gives priority to instance methods. Therefore, it will never call an extension method with the same signature as an instance method. It is also possible, though strongly discouraged, to have two extension methods with a same name, same parameters, and both in scope.

See also

In this chapter:

Improving entity and library reuse recipe

Improving entity and library reuse

In this recipe, we will decouple the query and entity definitions from the database communication to illustrate how they can be leveraged separately.

Getting ready

We will be using the NuGet package manager to install the Entity Framework 4.1 assemblies.

The package installer can be found at `http://nuget.org`.

We will also be using a database for connecting to and updating data.

Open the **Improving Entity and Library Reuse** solution in the included source code examples.

Improving Entity Framework with Query Libraries

How to do it...

Carry out the following steps in order to accomplish this recipe.

1. We will start by adding a new unit test named `QueryTests` to the test project. We will make a test that connects to the database and retrieves a couple of records with a reusable query using the following code:

```
using System;
using System.Linq;
using BusinessLogic;
using BusinessLogic.Queries;
using DataAccess;
using DataAccess.Database;
using Microsoft.VisualStudio.TestTools.UnitTesting;
using Test.Properties;

namespace Test
{
  [TestClass]
  public class QueryTests
  {

    [TestMethod]
    public void ShouldReturnRecordsFromTheDatabase()
    {
      //Arrange
      var init = new Initializer();
      var context = new
        BlogContext(Settings.Default.BlogConnection);
      init.InitializeDatabase(context);
      IBlogRepository repo = new BlogRepository(context);

      //Act
      var items = repo.Set<Blog>().FilterByBlogName("Test");

      //Assert
      Assert.AreEqual(2, items.Count());
    }

    [TestMethod]
    public void
      ShouldReturnRecordsFromAnotherSourceWithTheSameQuery()
    {
      //Arrange
```

```
          var anotherDatasource = new SomeOtherDataSource();

          //Act
          var items =
            anotherDatasource.Blogs.FilterByBlogName("Test");

          //Assert
          Assert.AreEqual(1,items.Count());
        }

    }
}
```

2. Add another C# class named `SomeOtherDataSource` to the test project with the following code:

```
using System;
using System.Collections.Generic;
using System.Linq;
using BusinessLogic;

namespace Test
{
  public class SomeOtherDataSource
  {
    public IQueryable<Blog> Blogs
    {
      get
      {
        return new List<Blog>()
        {
          new Blog()
          {
            Creationdate = DateTime.Now,
            Rating = 1,
            Id = 1,
            ShortDescription = "Test",
            Title = "Not This one"
          },
          new Blog()
          {
            Creationdate = DateTime.Now,
            Rating = 1,
            Id = 1,
            ShortDescription = "Test",
```

```
              Title = "Test"
            }

        }.AsQueryable();
      }

    }
  }
}
```

3. Add an initializer to the `DataAccess project Database` folder with the following code to set up data:

```
using System;
using System.Data.Entity;
using BusinessLogic;

namespace DataAccess.Database
{

  public class Initializer :
    DropCreateDatabaseAlways<BlogContext>
  {
    public Initializer()
    {

    }
    protected override void Seed(BlogContext context)
    {
      context.Set<Blog>().Add(new Blog()
      {
        Creationdate = DateTime.Now,
        ShortDescription = "Testing",
        Title = "Test Blog"
      });
      context.Set<Blog>().Add(new Blog()
      {
        Creationdate = DateTime.Now,
        ShortDescription = "Testing",
        Title = "Test Blog 2"
      });
      context.Set<Blog>().Add(new Blog()
      {
        Creationdate = DateTime.Now,
        ShortDescription = "Testing",
```

```
            Title = "not Blog"
         });
       context.SaveChanges();
      }
    }
}
```

4. In the `BusinessLogic` project, add a new C# class named `Blog` with the following code:

```
using System;
using System.ComponentModel.DataAnnotations;
using System.Text.RegularExpressions;

namespace BusinessLogic
{
  public class Blog
  {
    public int Id { get; set; }
    public DateTime Creationdate { get; set; }
    public string ShortDescription { get; set; }
    public string Title { get; set; }
    public double Rating { get; set; }
  }
}
```

5. Add a `Mapping` folder to the `DataAccess` project and then add a `BlogMapping` class to the folder with the following code:

```
using System.ComponentModel.DataAnnotations;
using System.Data.Entity.ModelConfiguration;
using BusinessLogic;

namespace DataAccess.Mappings
{
  public class BlogMapping : EntityTypeConfiguration<Blog>
  {
    public BlogMapping()
    {
      this.ToTable("Blogs");
      this.HasKey(x => x.Id);
      this.Property(x => x.Id).HasDatabaseGeneratedOption
         (DatabaseGeneratedOption.Identity)
            .HasColumnName("BlogId");

      this.Property(x => x.Title).IsRequired()
```

```csharp
            .HasMaxLength(250);
         this.Property(x => x.Creationdate)
            .HasColumnName("CreationDate").IsRequired();
         this.Property(x => x.ShortDescription)
            .HasColumnType("Text").IsMaxLength().IsOptional()
               .HasColumnName("Description");
      }

   }
}
```

6. Modify the `BlogContext` class to contain the new mappings for `Blogs` with the following code:

```csharp
using System;
using System.Data.Entity;
using System.Linq;
using BusinessLogic;
using DataAccess.Mappings;

namespace DataAccess
{
   public class BlogContext : DbContext, IUnitOfWork
   {
      public BlogContext(string connectionString)
       : base(connectionString)
      {

      }

      protected override void OnModelCreating
         (DbModelBuilder modelBuilder)
      {
         modelBuilder.Configurations.Add(new BlogMapping());
         base.OnModelCreating(modelBuilder);
      }

      public IQueryable<T> Find<T>() where T : class
      {
         return this.Set<T>();
      }

      public void Refresh()
      {
         this.ChangeTracker.Entries().ToList()
```

```
            .ForEach(x=>x.Reload());
      }

      public void Commit()
      {
        this.SaveChanges();
      }
    }
  }
```

7. Add a new folder named `Queries` to the `BusinessLogic` project, and add a new C# class to it named `BlogQueries` with the following code:

   ```
   using System.Linq;

   namespace BusinessLogic.Queries
   {
     public static class BlogQueries
     {
       public static IQueryable<Blog> FilterByBlogName
         (this IQueryable<Blog> items, string name)
       {
         return items.Where(x => x.Title.Contains(name));
       }
     }
   }
   ```

8. Modify the `Program.cs` of the project `ConsoleApp` with the following code:

   ```
   using System;
   using BusinessLogic.Queries;

   namespace ConsoleApp
   {
     class Program
     {
       static void Main(string[] args)
       {
         var repo = new InMemoryRepository();
         var items = repo.Blogs.FilterByBlogName("Test");

         foreach (var blog in items)
         {
           Console.WriteLine(blog.Title);
         }
   ```

```
            Console.ReadLine();
        }
    }
}
```

9. Add a new C# class to the `ConsoleApp` project named `InMemoryRepository` with the following code:

```
using System;
using System.Collections.Generic;
using System.Linq;
using BusinessLogic;

namespace ConsoleApp
{
    internal class InMemoryRepository
    {
        internal IQueryable<Blog> Blogs
        {
            get
            {
                return new List<Blog>()
                {
                    new Blog()
                    {
                        Creationdate = DateTime.Now,
                        Rating = 1,
                        Id = 1,
                        ShortDescription = "Test",
                        Title = "Not This one"
                    },
                    new Blog()
                    {
                        Creationdate = DateTime.Now,
                        Rating = 1,
                        Id = 1,
                        ShortDescription = "Test",
                        Title = "Test"
                    }
                }.AsQueryable();
            }
        }
    }
}
```

10. Run our test and it will work. Run the console application and it will work as well.

How it works...

We will start our solution by defining a test which encapsulates the functionality we are trying to complete. This will serve as our marker that we have accomplished the goal. The test, in this case, is that we can not only execute the defined queries on the database, but also use them against other collections of the proper type.

We initialized the database to seed records to filter, and we set up another data source that provides in memory lists of data to filter. We defined the blog entity, the mapping, and the `DbContext` so our test can function against the database. This will ensure that we have not broken the database communication by adding this level of reuse to the application.

The next piece that we move to is a console application that references the `BusinessLogic` project without referencing the `DataAccess`. This demonstrates that we have separated our functions correctly and that we can leverage it from multiple applications without any problems.

There's more...

This level of reuse should extend to applications that hit the same database but with different delivery mechanisms. There are several things to keep in mind here.

Schema and contract

This solution should only be used when we cannot define a service or we have tight control over the usage in both applications. The preferred way to share a database is to define a service that does the data access. We would then be sharing schema and contract details instead of sharing types and assemblies.

NuGet

If we need to share the assemblies between solutions directly, then there are some tools which will make this easier. One of those options is to define a NuGet package and host it internally in your company on a private NuGet repository. This will ensure updates are distributed and that everyone goes to the same place to get the reference instead of pulling and compiling their own updates, or even worse, changing and compiling them.

Implementing composed queries

Composed queries are an effective way to link separate but related pieces of filtering logic into reusable pieces. In this recipe, we will compose queries together to accomplish a certain filter without needing to write the code twice but still having it translated into a single SQL execution.

Improving Entity Framework with Query Libraries

Getting ready

We will be using the **NuGet Package Manager** to install the Entity Framework 4.1 assemblies.

The package installer can be found at http://nuget.org.

We will also be using a database for connecting to and updating data.

Open the **Improving Transaction Scope** solution in the included source code examples.

How to do it...

Carry out the following steps in order to accomplish this recipe.

1. We will start by adding a new unit test named `QueryTests` to the test project. We will make a test that connects to the database and retrieves a couple of records with a reusable query using the following code:

```
using System;
using System.Collections.Generic;
using System.Data.Entity.Validation;
using System.Linq;
using System.Text;
using System.Text.RegularExpressions;
using System.Transactions;
using BusinessLogic;
using BusinessLogic.Queries;
using DataAccess;
using DataAccess.Database;
using Microsoft.VisualStudio.TestTools.UnitTesting;
using Test.Properties;
using System.Data.Entity;

namespace Test
{
  [TestClass]
  public class QueryTests
  {
    [TestMethod]
    public void ShouldReturnRecordsFromTheDatabaseByName()
    {
      //Arrange
      var init = new Initializer();
      var context = new
        BlogContext(Settings.Default.BlogConnection);
```

```csharp
    init.InitializeDatabase(context);
    IBlogRepository repo = new BlogRepository(context);


    //Act
    var items = repo.Set<Blog>().FilterByBlogName("Test");

    //Assert
    Assert.AreEqual(2, items.Count());
}

[TestMethod]
public void ShouldReturnRecordsFromTheDatabaseByDescription()
{
    //Arrange
    var init = new Initializer();
    var context = new
      BlogContext(Settings.Default.BlogConnection);
    init.InitializeDatabase(context);
    IBlogRepository repo = new BlogRepository(context);


    //Act
    var items = repo.Set<Blog>().FilterByBlogName("es");

    //Assert
    Assert.AreEqual(2, items.Count());
}

[TestMethod]
public void ShouldReturnRecordsFromTheDatabaseByBoth()
{
    //Arrange
    var init = new Initializer();
    var context = new
      BlogContext(Settings.Default.BlogConnection);
    init.InitializeDatabase(context);
    IBlogRepository repo = new BlogRepository(context);


    //Act
    var items = repo.Set<Blog>()
      .FilterByNameAndDescription("Test","es");
```

```
        //Assert
        Assert.AreEqual(1, items.Count());
      }
    }

  }
```

2. Add an initializer to the `DataAccess project Database` folder with the following code to set up data:

```
using System;
using System.Data.Entity;
using BusinessLogic;

namespace DataAccess.Database
{

  public class Initializer : DropCreateDatabaseAlways<BlogContext>
  {
    public Initializer()
    {

    }
    protected override void Seed(BlogContext context)
    {
      context.Set<Blog>().Add(new Blog()
      {
        Creationdate = DateTime.Now,
        ShortDescription = "not this one",
        Title = "Test Blog"
      });
      context.Set<Blog>().Add(new Blog()
      {
        Creationdate = DateTime.Now,
        ShortDescription = "Testing",
        Title = "Test Blog 2"
            });
            context.Set<Blog>().Add(new Blog()
            {
              Creationdate = DateTime.Now,
              ShortDescription = "Testing",
              Title = "not Blog"
            });
          context.SaveChanges();
      }

    }
  }
```

3. In the `BusinessLogic` project, add a new C# class named `Blog` with the following code:

```csharp
using System;
using System.ComponentModel.DataAnnotations;
using System.Text.RegularExpressions;

namespace BusinessLogic
{
  public class Blog
  {
    public int Id { get; set; }
    public DateTime Creationdate { get; set; }
    public string ShortDescription { get; set; }
    public string Title { get; set; }
    public double Rating { get; set; }
  }
}
```

4. Add a `Mapping` folder to the `DataAccess` project and then add a `BlogMapping` class to the folder with the following code:

```csharp
using System.ComponentModel.DataAnnotations;
using System.Data.Entity.ModelConfiguration;
using BusinessLogic;

namespace DataAccess.Mappings
{
  public class BlogMapping : EntityTypeConfiguration<Blog>
  {
    public BlogMapping()
    {
      this.ToTable("Blogs");
      this.HasKey(x => x.Id);
      this.Property(x => x.Id).HasDatabaseGeneratedOption
        (DatabaseGeneratedOption.Identity)
          .HasColumnName("BlogId");

      this.Property(x => x.Title)
        .IsRequired().HasMaxLength(250);
      this.Property(x => x.Creationdate)
        .HasColumnName("CreationDate").IsRequired();
      this.Property(x => x.ShortDescription)
        .HasColumnType("Text").IsMaxLength().IsOptional()
          .HasColumnName("Description");
    }
  }
}
```

5. Modify the `BlogContext` class to contain the new mappings for `Blogs` with the following code:

```
using System;
using System.Data.Entity;
using System.Linq;
using BusinessLogic;
using DataAccess.Mappings;

namespace DataAccess
{
  public class BlogContext : DbContext, IUnitOfWork
  {
    public BlogContext(string connectionString)
      : base(connectionString)
    {

    }

    protected override void
      OnModelCreating(DbModelBuilder modelBuilder)
    {
      modelBuilder.Configurations.Add(new BlogMapping());
      base.OnModelCreating(modelBuilder);
    }

    public IQueryable<T> Find<T>() where T : class
    {
      return this.Set<T>();
    }

    public void Refresh()
    {
      this.ChangeTracker.Entries().ToList()
        .ForEach(x=>x.Reload());
    }

    public void Commit()
    {
      this.SaveChanges();
    }
  }
}
```

6. Add a new folder named `Queries` to the `BusinessLogic` project and add a new C# class to it named `BlogQueries` with the following code:

```csharp
using System;
using System.Linq;

namespace BusinessLogic.Queries
{
  public static class BlogQueries
  {
    public static IQueryable<Blog>
      FilterByBlogName(this IQueryable<Blog>
        items, string name)
  {
    return items.Where(x => x.Title.Contains(name));
  }

    public static IQueryable<Blog>
      FilterByDescription(this IQueryable<Blog>
        items, string description)
  {
    return items.Where(x=> x.ShortDescription
      .Contains(description));
  }

    public static IQueryable<Blog>
      FilterByNameAndDescription(this IQueryable<Blog> items,
        string name, string description)
    {
      return items.FilterByBlogName(name)
        .FilterByDescription(description);
    }

  }
}
```

7. Run our test and it will work.

How it works...

We begin our solution by defining a set of tests that apply filters one at a time and then in combination, and finally test the results. This ensures that we accomplish the functionality that we are aiming at without breaking any individual piece.

We initialize the database with a set of test data which we can assert against for the query filtering. This allows us to know the inputs and test if the outputs adhere to the expected results.

We then set up our blog entity, the mappings for it, and the `DbContext`, so we could communicate with the database and have our filters translated properly into SQL statements. This is the piece that allows us to ignore the database schema and worry only about the object filtering.

The next step is to define our three queries, so we can test them. Notice that the first two queries are the queries that specify a where statement. However, the third query merely composes the already defined behavior into a single execution without the developer being aware that it combines with the existing functionality. This allows us to adhere to the **DRY** principle.

There's more...

We leverage several principles here, which will help us in understanding how to implement this in a production environment.

Don't repeat yourself (DRY)

Each piece of functionality should not need to be typed more than once in an application. This is an ideal that if held to, will force us to abstract our code base into patterns that lend themselves to reuse. The effort is well worth it though, as it helps to ensure that each piece is doing just one thing, which helps us to adhere to single responsibility principle.

Single responsibility principle

This principle states that each method and class should have one and only one reason to change. This normally confuses some developers, but the confusion lies in how we define "one reason to change." At the method level, the reason to change should be very specific. For example, "The rules for this filter are now different." However, at a class level, this one reason should be more generalized. For example, "We have added another filter." This one reason to change is essential for our one reason for creating any class or method to begin with. This means that the consumers of the object will never be surprised by a change because it will be in line with what they would expect from your component.

Some people believe that **Object Relational Mappers** (**ORMs**), such as **Entity Framework**, intrinsically break this principle because an entity class might change because of the object or the database. However, as we have already learned, this is not the case. Entity Framework clearly separates mapping rules from the classes, thereby avoiding this conflict with the single responsibility principle.

Chapter 5

See also

In this chapter:

Improving query testing recipe

Increasing performance with code access

In this recipe, we will be creating a library which ensures that the queries which will be executed in the database are limited to the data access layer. It limits the queries by creating a clear boundary beyond which `IQueryable<T>` is not exposed, only allowing access to the business layer to an `IEnumerable<T>`. This ensures that the business layer cannot modify the queries in such a way as to make them non-performant, while still giving them complete access to the data.

Getting ready

We will be using the NuGet package manager to install the Entity Framework 4.1 assemblies.

The package installer can be found at `http://nuget.org`.

We will also be using a database for connecting to and updating data.

Open the Improving **Performance with Code Access** solution in the included source code examples.

How to do it...

Carry out the following steps in order to accomplish this recipe.

1. We will start by adding a new unit test named QueryTests to the test project. We will make a test that connects to the database and retrieves a couple of records with a reusable query using the following code:

```
using System.Linq;
using BusinessLogic.Queries;
using DataAccess;
using DataAccess.Database;
using Microsoft.VisualStudio.TestTools.UnitTesting;
using Test.Properties;

namespace Test
{
  [TestClass]
  public class QueryTests
  {
    [TestMethod]
```

```csharp
        public void ShouldReturnRecordsFromTheDatabaseByName()
        {
          //Arrange
          var init = new Initializer();
          var context = new
            BlogContext(Settings.Default.BlogConnection);
          init.InitializeDatabase(context);
          IBlogRepository repo = new BlogRepository(context);


          //Act
          var items = repo.GetBlogsByName("Test");

          //Assert
          Assert.AreEqual(2, items.Count());
        }
      }


}
```

2. Add an initializer to the `DataAccess project Database` folder with the following code to set up data:

```csharp
using System;
using System.Data.Entity;
using BusinessLogic;
namespace DataAccess.Database
{

  public class Initializer : DropCreateDatabaseAlways<BlogContext>
  {
    public Initializer()
    {

    }
    protected override void Seed(BlogContext context)
    {
      context.Set<Blog>().Add(new Blog()
      {
        Creationdate = DateTime.Now,
        ShortDescription = "not this one",
        Title = "Test Blog"
      });
      context.Set<Blog>().Add(new Blog()
      {
```

```
          Creationdate = DateTime.Now,
          ShortDescription = "Testing",
          Title = "Test Blog 2"
        });
        context.Set<Blog>().Add(new Blog()
        {
          Creationdate = DateTime.Now,
          ShortDescription = "Testing",
          Title = "not Blog"
        });
        context.SaveChanges();
      }

    }
  }
```

3. In the `BusinessLogic` project add a new C# class named `Blog` with the following code:

```
using System;
using System.ComponentModel.DataAnnotations;
using System.Text.RegularExpressions;

namespace BusinessLogic
{
  public class Blog
  {
    public int Id { get; set; }
    public DateTime Creationdate { get; set; }
    public string ShortDescription { get; set; }
    public string Title { get; set; }
    public double Rating { get; set; }
  }
}
```

4. Add a `Mapping` folder to the `DataAccess` project and then add a `BlogMapping` class to the folder with the following code:

```
using System.ComponentModel.DataAnnotations;
using System.Data.Entity.ModelConfiguration;
using BusinessLogic;

namespace DataAccess.Mappings
{
  public class BlogMapping : EntityTypeConfiguration<Blog>
  {
```

```
            public BlogMapping()
            {
            this.ToTable("Blogs");
            this.HasKey(x => x.Id);
            this.Property(x => x.Id).HasDatabaseGeneratedOption
               (DatabaseGeneratedOption.Identity)
                  .HasColumnName("BlogId");

             this.Property(x => x.Title).IsRequired()
                .HasMaxLength(250);
             this.Property(x => x.Creationdate)
                .HasColumnName("CreationDate").IsRequired();
             this.Property(x => x.ShortDescription)
                .HasColumnType("Text").IsMaxLength()
                   .IsOptional().HasColumnName("Description");
            }

        }
    }
```

5. Add a new interface in the `BusinessLogic` project named `IBlogRepository` with the following code:

```
namespace DataAccess
{
  public interface IBlogRepository
   {
     void RollbackChanges();
     void SaveChanges();
   }
}
```

6. Modify the `BlogContext` class to contain the new mappings for `Blogs` with the following code:

```
using System;
using System.Data.Entity;
using System.Linq;
using BusinessLogic;
using DataAccess.Mappings;

namespace DataAccess
{
   public class BlogContext : DbContext, IUnitOfWork
    {
       public BlogContext(string connectionString)
```

```
      : base(connectionString)
    {

    }

    protected override void OnModelCreating
      (DbModelBuilder modelBuilder)
    {
      modelBuilder.Configurations.Add(new BlogMapping());
      base.OnModelCreating(modelBuilder);
    }

    public IQueryable<T> Find<T>() where T : class
    {
      return this.Set<T>();
    }

    public void Refresh()
    {
      this.ChangeTracker.Entries().ToList()
        .ForEach(x=>x.Reload());
    }

    public void Commit()
    {
      this.SaveChanges();
    }
  }
}
```

7. Add a new folder named `Queries` to the `BusinessLogic` project and add a new C# class to it named `BlogQueries` with the following code:

```
using System.Collections.Generic;
using System.Linq;
using DataAccess;

namespace BusinessLogic.Queries
{
  public static class BlogQueries
  {
    public static IEnumerable<Blog> GetBlogsByName(this
IBlogRepository repo, string name)
    {
      return ((InternalBlogRepository)repo)
```

```
            .Set<Blog>().FilterByBlogName(name).ToArray();
      }

      public static IQueryable<Blog>
        FilterByBlogName(this IQueryable<Blog>
          items, string name )
      {
        return items.Where(x => x.Title.Contains(name));
      }
    }
  }
```

8. Add a new class to the `Queries` folder in `BusinessLogic` named `InternalBlogContext` with the following code:

   ```
   using System.Linq;

   namespace BusinessLogic.Queries
   {
     public abstract class InternalBlogRepository
     {
       public abstract IQueryable<T> Set<T>() where T : class;
     }
   }
   ```

9. Modify the `BlogRepository` class with the following code:

   ```
   using System;
   using System.Data.Entity;
   using System.Linq;
   using BusinessLogic;
   using BusinessLogic.Queries;

   namespace DataAccess
   {
     public class BlogRepository
       : InternalBlogRepository, IBlogRepository
     {
       private readonly IUnitOfWork _context;

       public BlogRepository(IUnitOfWork context)
       {
         _context = context;
       }

       public override IQueryable<T> Set<T>()
   ```

```
      {
        return _context.Find<T>();
      }

      public void RollbackChanges()
      {
        _context.Refresh();
          }

      public void SaveChanges()
        {
          try
          {
            _context.Commit();
      }
      catch (Exception)
      {
        RollbackChanges();
      throw;
      }

       }
     }
   }
```

10. Run our test and it will work.

How it works...

We start our solution by setting up a test which allows us to communicate with a database and return objects without having the ability to query directly. This test seeds the database with an initializer and then invokes a query that returns a set of data without surfacing how it does that.

We set up our blog entity, the database schema mapping, and the blog context as a basis for the database communication. These pieces allow us to translate our language integrated queries into SQL statements.

We then create a query that accepts an `IBlogRepository` and casts it to an `InternalBlogRepository` to get a set of items and return it. This cast allows us to grab a set of entities but not surface that into the interface that is widely used. We also limit the return type of the query to an `IEnumerable<>` instead of an `IQueryable<>`, so the returned enumerable cannot be used to modify the query in the other layers. This simple convention will indicate that data access is meant to be performed in the query libraries. If we need more control and want to tie this control more closely, then we can move our `InternalBlogRepository` and the queries to the data access project, and mark the `InternalBlogRepository` as internal. This will ensure that it cannot be used elsewhere.

Improving Entity Framework with Query Libraries

There's more...

When limiting access to code and trying to force certain programming behaviors, we should be sure of some things.

Developer discipline

As professional developers, we need to have a certain amount of discipline. There are ways around almost all code access restrictions with some being more complex than others. These pathways are there but we must avoid using them and try to adhere to the prescribed architecture. If we disagree with it, then there are ways to address that, but do not just start subverting it as that will only hurt you and the code base in the end.

Likewise, when we are serving as architects, we should always be mindful that we want our developers to "fall into the pit of success." That is to say we want the easiest way to do something to be the right way to do something. If it is not the easiest way, then we are subverting our own architecture from the outset because of how it is designed. One of the benefits brought to us by **test driven development** is that we always start by using the component that we will be writing, even before we write it. This keeps us focused on the consumer of our libraries. If the test is difficult to write, then the code will also be difficult.

Cost of architecture

When we start down the road of restricting the architecture, we need to be aware of the cost that it will incur. Making sure that all queries are defined in a testable and reusable fashion is a goal to strive for. However, do not think that it comes without cost. Productivity and learning curve are going to suffer slightly due to this, so be aware and do not make these choices lightly.

See also

In this chapter:

Improving entity and library reuse recipe

Improving query testing

One of the greatest benefits of well-defined abstractions in code is that we do not need to have an implementation before we begin to consume a component. The interface alone, in our case `IQueryable<>`, is sufficient to begin developing and testing the queries that we will use.

Chapter 5

Getting ready

We will be using the NuGet package manager to install the Entity Framework 4.1 assemblies.

The package installer can be found at http://nuget.org.

We will also be using a database for connecting to and updating data.

Open the **Improving Query Testing** solution in the included source code examples.

How to do it...

Carry out the following steps in order to accomplish this recipe.

1. We will start by adding a new unit test named QueryTests to the test project. We will make a test that connects to the database and retrieves a couple of records with a reusable query using the following code:

```
using System;
using System.Collections.Generic;
using System.Linq;
using BusinessLogic;
using BusinessLogic.Queries;
using Microsoft.VisualStudio.TestTools.UnitTesting;

namespace Test
{
  [TestClass]
  public class QueryTests
  {
    [TestMethod]
    public void ShouldFilterTestData()
    {
      //Arrange
      IQueryable<Blog> items = new List<Blog>
      {
        new Blog()
        {
          Creationdate = DateTime.Now,
          ShortDescription = "Test",
          Title = "Test"
        },
        new Blog()
        {
          Creationdate = DateTime.Now,
```

199

```csharp
                    ShortDescription = "not this one",
                    Title = "Blog"
                },
                new Blog()
                {
                    Creationdate = DateTime.Now,
                    ShortDescription = "not this",
                    Title = "TeBlog"
                },
                new Blog()
                {
                    Creationdate = DateTime.Now,
                    ShortDescription = "not this one",
                    Title = "TestBlog"
                }

            }.AsQueryable();
            //Act
            var returnedValues = items.FilterByBlogName("Test");

            //Assert
            Assert.AreEqual(2, returnedValues.Count());
        }

    }

}
```

2. In the `BusinessLogic` project add a new C# class named `Blog` with the following code:

```csharp
using System;
using System.ComponentModel.DataAnnotations;
using System.Text.RegularExpressions;

namespace BusinessLogic
{
    public class Blog
    {
        public int Id { get; set; }
        public DateTime Creationdate { get; set; }
        public string ShortDescription { get; set; }
        public string Title { get; set; }
        public double Rating { get; set; }
    }
}
```

3. Add a new folder named `Queries` to the `DataAccess` project and add a new C# class to it named `BlogQueries` with the following code:

```
using System.Linq;

namespace DataAccess.Queries
{
   public static class BlogQueries
    {
       public static IQueryable<Blog> FilterByBlogName(this IQueryable<Blog> items, string name)
       {
          return items.Where(x => x.Title.Contains(name));
       }
    }
}
```

4. Run our test and it will work.

How it works...

We start our solution, like we usually do, with a test that communicates the intended feature and serves to mark the completion point for us. In this case, the test is to check if we can exercise our queries without communicating with a database. The trick here is to create a list in the memory of `Blogs` and then use the `AsQueryable()` method to get that list into a queryable form to exercise the filters.

We will set up our blog object, so we have something that we can use our filters to test against. This allows us to use the same objects that would be stored to test the filters, instead of defining inherited mock objects.

We then define our query against an `IQueryable<T>` of `Blog`, the same as we would use against the database.

There's more...

By defining our queries and objects in this way, we have created a testable framework for database queries. However, there are a few things to keep in mind.

IQueryable<T>

`IQueryable` allows us to continue to add more statements before translating the expression into SQL. This is our explicit way of telling other developers that it is ok to continue to add filters and joins to this statement before it goes to the database. This will allow the building of large complex statements that do heavy lifting in the database server. However, this ability comes at the risk of a loss of control by introducing the possibility that a combination of filters and joins that are not at all performant might be created. Our previous recipe, *Improving performance with code access*, specifically addresses this risk.

`IQueryable` supports deferred execution, so we will not get records until they are required, and all of the statements are then translated to SQL and executed on the database server.

IEnumerable

`IEnumerable` does not allow further query composition to be translated into SQL. Basically, the SQL is frozen at that point but you can tack on further in memory processing. When we will be writing our query libraries, we will want to be sure that we use each of these libraries when they are called for. If we have an expensive projection, or a joined statement that we do not want to allow any further joins to be added to, then we need to return `IEnumerable`. This is our explicit way of communicating that we intended this code to come into memory in a certain way, and any further processing is to be done in the memory. This is especially handy if you need a SQL statement frozen at a certain point, so you can do something that does not translate to SQL such as type checking.

`IEnumerable` supports deferred execution, but it executes the SQL statement in the state that it was in when it became an `IEnumerable` and then proceeds to process all of the further composed tasks in memory on the objects loaded.

See also

In this chapter:

Increasing performance with code access recipe

6
Improving Complex Query Scenarios

In this chapter, we will cover:

- Improving dynamic sorting
- Grouping at runtime without Lambas
- Handling explicit loading
- Improving complex where clauses
- Implementing the specification pattern

Introduction

When we leverage Entity Framework, we gain a huge amount of flexibility and power. This power and flexibility make it easy to get data into and out of simple to moderately complex database structures in many ways. We can get a very nice API for simple queries. However, when our business problems get more complex, we need different patterns to handle this increasing complexity. These patterns range from minor adjustments to how we leverage code, to major refactoring of the data access layer. We will walk through these together, but each one will need to be weighed against the needs of our applications.

Improving dynamic sorting

In this recipe, we will be leveraging a string or set of strings to sort a list, much like you would sort a list based on a post back from an HTML page.

Improving Complex Query Scenarios

Getting ready

We will be using the NuGet package manager to install the Entity Framework 4.1 assemblies.

The package installer can be found at `http://nuget.org`.

We will also be using a database for connecting to and updating data.

Open the **Improving Dynamic Sorting** solution in the included source code examples.

How to do it...

Carry out the following steps in order to accomplish this recipe.

1. We will start by adding a new unit test named `SortingTests` to the test project. We will make a test that sorts some `TestObject` data in memory by property name and then returns the proper order with the following code:

```csharp
using System.Collections.Generic;
using System.Linq;
using BusinessLogic;
using BusinessLogic.Queries;
using Microsoft.VisualStudio.TestTools.UnitTesting;

namespace Test
{
  [TestClass]
  public class SortExtensionTest
  {
    [TestMethod]
    public void CanSortWithOnlyStrings()
    {
      IQueryable<TestObject> items = new List<TestObject>()
      {
        new TestObject(){id = 1, Test = "Test1"},
        new TestObject(){id = 3, Test = "Test3"},
        new TestObject(){id = 2, Test = "Test2"},

      }.AsQueryable();

      Assert.AreEqual(2, items.OrderBy("id", "ASC")
        .ToArray()[1].id);
    }

    [TestMethod]
    public void CanSortDescendingWithOnlyString()
```

204

```csharp
    {
      IQueryable<TestObject> items = new List<TestObject>()
      {
        new TestObject(){id = 1, Test = "Test1"},
        new TestObject(){id = 3, Test = "Test3"},
        new TestObject(){id = 2, Test = "Test2"},

      }.AsQueryable();

      Assert.AreEqual(1, items.OrderBy("id", "DSC")
        .ToArray()[2].id);

    }

    [TestMethod]
    public void CanSortMultipleTimesAscending()
    {
      IQueryable<TestObject> items = new List<TestObject>()
      {
        new TestObject(){id = 1, Test = "Test1"},
        new TestObject(){id = 3, Test = "Test3"},
        new TestObject(){id = 2, Test = "Test3"},
        new TestObject(){id = 2, Test = "Test2"},
        new TestObject(){id = 2, Test = "Test1"}

      }.AsQueryable();
      var item = items.OrderBy("id", "ASC")
        .ThenBy("Test", "ASC").ToArray()[3];
      Assert.AreEqual("Test3", item.Test);
    }

    [TestMethod]
    public void CanSortMultipleTimesWithMultipleDirrections()
    {
      IQueryable<TestObject> items = new List<TestObject>()
      {
        new TestObject(){id = 1, Test = "Test1"},
        new TestObject(){id = 3, Test = "Test3"},
        new TestObject(){id = 2, Test = "Test3"},
        new TestObject(){id = 2, Test = "Test2"},
        new TestObject(){id = 2, Test = "Test1"}

      }.AsQueryable();
      var item = items.OrderBy("id", "ASC")
```

Improving Complex Query Scenarios

```csharp
        .ThenBy("Test", "DSC").ToArray()[3];
      Assert.AreEqual("Test1", item.Test);

}

[TestMethod]
public void CanSortFromAListOfStrings()
{
  //Arrange
  IQueryable<TestObject> items = new List<TestObject>()
  {
    new TestObject(){id = 1, Test = "Test1",
      Test2 = "Test1"},
    new TestObject(){id = 2, Test = "Test3",
      Test2 = "Test1"},
    new TestObject(){id = 3, Test = "Test3",
      Test2 = "Test2"},
    new TestObject(){id = 4, Test = "Test3",
      Test2 = "Test3"},
    new TestObject(){id = 5, Test = "Test1",
      Test2 = "Test2"}

  }.AsQueryable();

  var strings = new[] { "Test", "Test2" };
  var dirrection = "ASC";
  //Act
  var orderedQuery = items.OrderBy("ASC", strings);

  //Assert
  var item = orderedQuery.FirstOrDefault();
  var thirdItem = orderedQuery.ToArray()[2];
  Assert.AreEqual(1, item.id);
  Assert.AreEqual(2, thirdItem.id);
}

[TestMethod]
public void CanEnumerableSortWithOnlyStrings()
{
  IEnumerable<TestObject> items = new List<TestObject>()
  {
    new TestObject(){id = 1, Test = "Test1"},
    new TestObject(){id = 3, Test = "Test3"},
    new TestObject(){id = 2, Test = "Test2"},
```

```csharp
      };

    Assert.AreEqual(2, items.OrderBy("id", "ASC")
      .ToArray()[1].id);
}

[TestMethod]
public void CanEnumerableSortDescendingWithOnlyString()
{
    IEnumerable<TestObject> items = new List<TestObject>()
    {
      new TestObject(){id = 1, Test = "Test1"},
      new TestObject(){id = 3, Test = "Test3"},
      new TestObject(){id = 2, Test = "Test2"},

    };

    Assert.AreEqual(1, items.OrderBy("id", "DSC")
      .ToArray()[2].id);

}

[TestMethod]
public void CanEnumerableSortMultipleTimesAscending()
{
    IEnumerable<TestObject> items = new List<TestObject>()
    {
      new TestObject(){id = 1, Test = "Test1"},
      new TestObject(){id = 3, Test = "Test3"},
      new TestObject(){id = 2, Test = "Test3"},
      new TestObject(){id = 2, Test = "Test2"},
      new TestObject(){id = 2, Test = "Test1"}

    };
    var item = items.OrderBy("id", "ASC")
      .ThenBy("Test", "ASC").ToArray()[3];
    Assert.AreEqual("Test3", item.Test);
}

[TestMethod]
public void
  CanEnumerableSortMultipleTimesWithMultipleDirrections()
{
    IEnumerable<TestObject> items = new List<TestObject>()
```

```csharp
        {
          new TestObject(){id = 1, Test = "Test1"},
          new TestObject(){id = 3, Test = "Test3"},
          new TestObject(){id = 2, Test = "Test3"},
          new TestObject(){id = 2, Test = "Test2"},
          new TestObject(){id = 2, Test = "Test1"}

        };
        var item = items.OrderBy("id", "ASC")
          .ThenBy("Test", "DSC").ToArray()[3];
            Assert.AreEqual("Test1", item.Test);

    }

    [TestMethod]
    public void CanEnumerableSortFromAListOfStrings()
    {
    //Arrange
    IEnumerable<TestObject> items = new List<TestObject>()
    {
      new TestObject(){id = 1, Test = "Test1",
        Test2 = "Test1"},
      new TestObject(){id = 2, Test = "Test3",
        Test2 = "Test1"},
      new TestObject(){id = 3, Test = "Test3",
        Test2 = "Test2"},
      new TestObject(){id = 4, Test = "Test3",
        Test2 = "Test3"},
      new TestObject(){id = 5, Test = "Test1",
        Test2 = "Test2"}

    };

    var strings = new[] { "Test", "Test2" };
    var dirrection = "ASC";
    //Act
    var orderedQuery = items.OrderBy("ASC", strings);

    //Assert
    var item = orderedQuery.FirstOrDefault();
    var thirdItem = orderedQuery.ToArray()[2];
    Assert.AreEqual(1, item.id);
    Assert.AreEqual(2, thirdItem.id);
    }
```

```
    }

      public class TestObject
      {
        public int id { get; set; }
        public string Test { get; set; }
        public string Test2 { get; set; }
        public string Test3 { get; set; }
        public string Test4 { get; set; }
      }
    }
```

2. In the `BusinessLogic` project, add a new C# class named `Blog` with the following code:

    ```
    using System;
    using System.ComponentModel.DataAnnotations;
    using System.Text.RegularExpressions;

    namespace BusinessLogic
    {
      public class Blog
      {
        public int Id { get; set; }
        public DateTime Creationdate { get; set; }
        public string ShortDescription { get; set; }
        public string Title { get; set; }
        public double Rating { get; set; }
      }
    }
    ```

3. Add a `Mapping` folder to the `DataAccess` project and then add a `BlogMapping` class to the folder with the following code:

    ```
    using System.ComponentModel.DataAnnotations;
    using System.Data.Entity.ModelConfiguration;
    using BusinessLogic;

    namespace DataAccess.Mappings
    {
      public class BlogMapping : EntityTypeConfiguration<Blog>
      {
        public BlogMapping()
        {
          this.ToTable("Blogs");
          this.HasKey(x => x.Id);
    ```

```
            this.Property(x => x.Id).HasDatabaseGeneratedOption
                (DatabaseGeneratedOption.Identity)
                  .HasColumnName("BlogId");

            this.Property(x => x.Title)
              .IsRequired().HasMaxLength(250);
            this.Property(x => x.Creationdate)
              .HasColumnName("CreationDate").IsRequired();
            this.Property(x => x.ShortDescription)
              .HasColumnType("Text").IsMaxLength()
                .IsOptional()  .HasColumnName("Description");
        }

    }
}
```

4. Modify the `BlogContext` class to contain the new mappings and a `DbSet` property for `Blogs` with the following code:

```
using System;
using System.Data.Entity;
using System.Linq;
using BusinessLogic;
using DataAccess.Mappings;

namespace DataAccess
{
  public class BlogContext : DbContext, IUnitOfWork
  {
    public BlogContext(string connectionString)
       : base(connectionString)
    {

    }

    protected override void OnModelCreating
    (DbModelBuilder modelBuilder)
    {
      modelBuilder.Configurations.Add(new BlogMapping());
      base.OnModelCreating(modelBuilder);
    }

    public IQueryable<T> Find<T>() where T : class
    {
      return this.Set<T>();
```

```csharp
    }

    public void Refresh()
    {
      this.ChangeTracker.Entries().ToList()
        .ForEach(x=>x.Reload());
    }

    public void Commit()
    {
      this.SaveChanges();
    }
  }
}
```

5. Add a new folder named Queries to the DataAccess project and add a new C# class to it named SortExtensions with the following code:

```csharp
using System;
using System.Collections.Generic;
using System.Linq;
using System.Linq.Expressions;
using System.Reflection;

namespace BusinessLogic.Queries
{
  public static class SortingExtension
  {
    private const string Ascending = "ASC";

    public static IOrderedQueryable<T> OrderBy<T>(this IQueryable<T> source, string property, string dirrection)
    {
      return dirrection == Ascending ? source.OrderBy(property) : source.OrderByDescending(property);
    }

    public static IOrderedQueryable<T> OrderBy<T>(this IQueryable<T> source, string property)
    {
      return ApplyOrder(source, property, "OrderBy");
    }

    public static IOrderedQueryable<T> OrderBy<T>(this IQueryable<T> source, OrderByParameter parameter)
    {
```

Improving Complex Query Scenarios

```csharp
    return ApplyOrder(source, parameter.Property,
      parameter.Dirrection == Ascending ? "OrderBy"
        : "OrderByDescending");
}

public static IOrderedQueryable<T> OrderBy<T>
  (this IQueryable<T> source, string dirrection,
    params string[] properties)
{
  if (properties.Length == 0)
    throw new InvalidOperationException
      ("Cannot Sort based on an Empty List of parameters");

  IOrderedQueryable<T> orderedQuery = null;
  for (int i = 0; i < properties.Count(); i++)
  {
    if (i == 0) orderedQuery =
       source.OrderBy(properties[i], dirrection);
    else orderedQuery.ThenBy(properties[i], dirrection);
  }
  return orderedQuery;
}

public static IOrderedQueryable<T> OrderBy<T>
  (this IQueryable<T> source,
    params OrderByParameter[] parameters)
{
  if (parameters.Length == 0)
    throw new InvalidOperationException("Cannot Sort based
      on an Empty List of parameters");

  IOrderedQueryable<T> orderedQuery = null;
  for (int i = 0; i < parameters.Count(); i++)
  {
    if (i == 0) orderedQuery =
       source.OrderBy(parameters[i]);
           else orderedQuery.ThenBy(parameters[i]);
  }
  return orderedQuery;
}

public static IOrderedQueryable<T>
  OrderByDescending<T>(this IQueryable<T> source,
    string property)
```

```csharp
{
  return ApplyOrder(source, property, "OrderByDescending");
}

public static IOrderedQueryable<T>
  OrderByDescending<T>(this IQueryable<T> source,
    params OrderByParameter[] parameters)
{
  if (parameters.Length == 0)
  throw new InvalidOperationException("Cannot Sort based
    on an Empty List of parameters");

  IOrderedQueryable<T> orderedQuery = null;
  for (int i = 0; i < parameters.Count(); i++)
  {
    if (i == 0) orderedQuery =
      source.OrderByDescending(parameters[i]);
    else orderedQuery.ThenByDescending(parameters[i]);
  }
  return orderedQuery;
}

public static IOrderedQueryable<T> ThenBy<T>
  (this IOrderedQueryable<T> source,
    OrderByParameter parameter)
{
  return ApplyOrder(source, parameter.Property,
  parameter.Dirrection == Ascending ? "OrderBy"
    : "OrderByDescending");
}

public static IOrderedQueryable<T> ThenBy<T>
  (this IOrderedQueryable<T> source, string property,
    string dirrection)
{
  return dirrection == Ascending ? source.ThenBy(property)
    : source.ThenByDescending(property);
}

public static IOrderedQueryable<T> ThenBy<T>
  (this IOrderedQueryable<T> source, string property)
{
  return ApplyOrder(source, property, "ThenBy");
}
```

Improving Complex Query Scenarios

```csharp
public static IOrderedQueryable<T> ThenByDescending<T>
  (this IOrderedQueryable<T> source, string property)
{
  return ApplyOrder(source, property, "ThenByDescending");
}

private static IOrderedQueryable<T>
  ApplyOrder<T>(IQueryable<T> source, string property,
    string methodName)
{
  string[] props = property.Split('.');
  Type type = typeof(T);
  ParameterExpression arg = Expression
    .Parameter(type, "x");
  Expression expr = arg;
  foreach (PropertyInfo pi in props.Select(prop =>
    type.GetProperty(prop)))
  {
    expr = Expression.Property(expr, pi);
    type = pi.PropertyType;
  }
  Type delegateType = typeof(Func<,>)
    .MakeGenericType(typeof(T), type);
  LambdaExpression lambda = Expression.Lambda
    (delegateType, expr, arg);

  object result = typeof(Queryable).GetMethods().Single(
  method => method.Name == methodName
    && method.IsGenericMethodDefinition
      && method.GetGenericArguments().Length == 2
        && method.GetParameters().Length == 2)
          .MakeGenericMethod(typeof(T), type)
            .Invoke(null, new object[] { source, lambda });
  return (IOrderedQueryable<T>)result;
}

public static IOrderedQueryable<T> OrderBy<T>
  (this IEnumerable<T> source, string property,
    string dirrection)
{
  return dirrection == Ascending ?
    source.AsQueryable().OrderBy(property)
      : source.AsQueryable().OrderByDescending(property);
}
```

```
public static IOrderedQueryable<T> OrderBy<T>
  (this IEnumerable<T> source, string property)
{
  return ApplyOrder(source.AsQueryable(),
    property, "OrderBy");
}

public static IOrderedQueryable<T> OrderBy<T>
  (this IEnumerable<T> source,
    OrderByParameter parameter)
{
  return ApplyOrder(source.AsQueryable(),
    parameter.Property,
   parameter.Dirrection == Ascending ? "OrderBy"
     : "OrderByDescending");
}

public static IOrderedQueryable<T> OrderBy<T>
  (this IEnumerable<T> source, string dirrection,
params string[] properties)
{
  if (properties.Length == 0)
  throw new InvalidOperationException("Cannot Sort
    based on an Empty List of parameters");

  IOrderedQueryable<T> orderedQuery = null;
  for (int i = 0; i < properties.Count(); i++)
  {
    if (i == 0) orderedQuery = source.AsQueryable()
      .OrderBy(properties[i], dirrection);
    else orderedQuery.ThenBy(properties[i], dirrection);
  }
  return orderedQuery;
}

public static IOrderedQueryable<T>
  OrderBy<T>(this IEnumerable<T> source,
    params OrderByParameter[] parameters)
{
  if (parameters.Length == 0)
  throw new InvalidOperationException("Cannot Sort
    based on an Empty List of parameters");

    IOrderedQueryable<T> orderedQuery = null;
```

Improving Complex Query Scenarios

```csharp
        for (int i = 0; i < parameters.Count(); i++)
        {
          if (i == 0) orderedQuery =
             source.AsQueryable().OrderBy(parameters[i]);
          else orderedQuery.ThenBy(parameters[i]);
        }
    return orderedQuery;
}

public static IOrderedQueryable<T>
  OrderByDescending<T>(this IEnumerable<T> source,
    string property)
{
  return ApplyOrder(source.AsQueryable(),
    property, "OrderByDescending");
}

public static IOrderedQueryable<T>
  OrderByDescending<T>(this IEnumerable<T> source,
    params OrderByParameter[] parameters)
{
  if (parameters.Length == 0)
  throw new InvalidOperationException("Cannot Sort
    based on an Empty List of parameters");

  IOrderedQueryable<T> orderedQuery = null;
  for (int i = 0; i < parameters.Count(); i++)
  {
    if (i == 0) orderedQuery =
      source.AsQueryable()
         .OrderByDescending(parameters[i]);
    else orderedQuery.ThenByDescending(parameters[i]);
  }
  return orderedQuery;
}

public static IOrderedQueryable<T> ThenBy<T>
  (this IOrderedEnumerable<T> source,
     OrderByParameter parameter)
{
  return ApplyOrder(source.AsQueryable(),
    parameter.Property,
      parameter.Dirrection == Ascending ?
        "OrderBy" : "OrderByDescending");
```

```
      }

      public static IOrderedQueryable<T> ThenBy<T>
        (this IOrderedEnumerable<T> source,
          string property,
      string dirrection)
      {
        return dirrection == Ascending ?
          source.ThenBy(property)
            : source.ThenByDescending(property);
      }

      public static IOrderedQueryable<T> ThenBy<T>
        (this IOrderedEnumerable<T> source,
          string property)
      {
        return ApplyOrder(source.AsQueryable(),
          property, "ThenBy");
      }

      public static IOrderedQueryable<T> ThenByDescending<T>
        (this IOrderedEnumerable<T> source, string property)
      {
        return ApplyOrder(source.AsQueryable(),
          property, "ThenByDescending");
      }


    }
  }
```

6. In the `Queries` folder, add a new C# class named `OrderByParameter` with the following code:

```
using System;

namespace BusinessLogic.Queries
{
  public class OrderByParameter
  {
    private const string Format = "{0}{1}";
    public string Dirrection { get; set; }
    public string Property { get; set; }

    private OrderByParameter()
```

Improving Complex Query Scenarios

```
      {

      }

      public static implicit operator string
         (OrderByParameter parameter)
      {
         return string.Format(Format, parameter.Property,
            parameter.Dirrection);
      }

      public static implicit operator OrderByParameter
         (string value)
      {
         if (value.Length < 4)
         throw new InvalidOperationException
            ("Cannot convert to OrderByParameter due to
               invalid string");
         return new OrderByParameter
         {
            Property = value.Substring(0, value.Length - 3),
            Dirrection = value.Substring(value.Length - 3)
         };
      }
   }
}
```

7. Run our test and it will work.

How it works...

We begin by setting up a suite of tests that will verify our sorting logic is full and complete without unintended side effects. This test serves as our safety net and our definition of done.

Once we have a test in place, we can move on to adding an object and mapping it to a context so we have a fully formed data access level. This will give us the ability to write integration tests to validate against a database if it is needed.

Once we have these structures in place, we can move on to adding the sorting extension methods which will make up the bulk of the logic in this recipe. These will be accepted in a queryable set of data, and apply a sort to it in the form of an expression. There are two big advantages to this, one is that we can compose these extension methods when needed and add them later. The second big advantage is the ability to have a deferred execution on something like dynamic sorting. We can create a sorting process, which not only accomplishes the goal but also has very few unintended side effects to the normal mode of execution.

After we have this logic in place, we need to add a parameter object in order to make the processing of string inputs easier. This wrapper will translate the incoming string into an actionable set of data. This ensures that the string parse logic is encapsulated and not a matter of concern for the sorting engine.

There's more...

There are several tools we can leverage in this recipe that are deep subjects. It will be a benefit to us if we can understand them thoroughly.

Expression Trees

Expression trees, at their most basic level, are a way of looking at executable code as data. We can use this to evaluate code, making decisions based on its parameters, or perform binary operations. This is tremendously helpful when translating executable code into SQL statements. This evaluation can be tedious and hard to learn, but once we understand, it gives unlimited cosmic power without the itty bitty living space.

When we are done with the code as data, we can simply compile the expression tree and execute it as code once again.

Deferred execution

When we leverage expression trees, we are in essence able to pass behavior around, and when it is finally needed it can be executed. This is a powerful concept that has built on years of delegate functions and pointers. Expression trees allow us to do this. We build and compose our statements, and then execute them at the last possible moment, or when we force them to execute. This is our choice and it gives us far greater control when data is accessed.

Encapsulation

Being able to separate the queries and the data allows us to gain a much higher level of encapsulation than we could previously achieve in standard data access. This encapsulation helps us gain more reusability without having to take on additional overhead.

See also

In this chapter:

- *Grouping at runtime without Lambdas*
- *Implementing the specification pattern* recipes

Improving Complex Query Scenarios

Grouping at runtime without Lambda

In this recipe, we will be composing dynamically grouped sets of data into a queryable set that is functional and generic enough that it can be used against most domains.

Getting ready

We will be using the NuGet package manager to install the Entity Framework 4.1 assemblies.

The package installer can be found at http://nuget.org.

We will also be using a database for connecting to and updating data.

Open the **Improving Transaction** Scope solution in the included source code examples.

How to do it...

Carry out the following steps in order to accomplish this recipe.

1. We will start by adding a new unit test named `QueryTests` to the test project. We will make a test that groups some in memory data by property name and returns the proper grouped set with the following code:

```
using System;
using System.Collections.Generic;
using System.Linq;
using BusinessLogic;
using BusinessLogic.Queries;
using Microsoft.VisualStudio.TestTools.UnitTesting;

namespace Test
{
  [TestClass]
  public class QueryTests
  {
    [TestMethod]
    public void ShouldFilterTestData()
    {
      //Arrange
      IQueryable<Blog> items = new List<Blog>
      {
        new Blog()
        {
          Creationdate = DateTime.Now,
```

```
              ShortDescription = "Test",
              Title = "Test"
            },
            new Blog()
            {
              Creationdate = DateTime.Now,
              ShortDescription = "not this one",
              Title = "Test"
            },
            new Blog()
            {
              Creationdate = DateTime.Now,
              ShortDescription = "not this",
              Title = "TeBlog"
            },
            new Blog()
            {
              Creationdate = DateTime.Now,
              ShortDescription = "not this one",
              Title = "TestBlog"
            }

        }.AsQueryable();
        //Act
        var returnedValues = items.GroupByBlogTitle("Title");

        //Assert
        Assert.AreEqual(2, returnedValues
           .First(x => x.Key.ToString() == "Test").Count);
      }

    }

}
```

2. In the `BusinessLogic` project, add a new C# class named `Blog` with the following code:

```
using System;
using System.ComponentModel.DataAnnotations;
using System.Text.RegularExpressions;

namespace BusinessLogic
{
  public class Blog
```

Improving Complex Query Scenarios

```
    {
        public int Id { get; set; }
        public DateTime Creationdate { get; set; }
        public string ShortDescription { get; set; }
        public string Title { get; set; }
        public double Rating { get; set; }
    }
}
```

3. Add a `Mapping` folder to the `DataAccess` project and then add a `BlogMapping` class to the folder with the following code:

```
using System.ComponentModel.DataAnnotations;
using System.Data.Entity.ModelConfiguration;
using BusinessLogic;

namespace DataAccess.Mappings
{
    public class BlogMapping : EntityTypeConfiguration<Blog>
    {
        public BlogMapping()
        {
            this.ToTable("Blogs");
            this.HasKey(x => x.Id);
            this.Property(x => x.Id)
                .HasDatabaseGeneratedOption
                    (DatabaseGeneratedOption.Identity)
                    .HasColumnName("BlogId");

            this.Property(x => x.Title)
                .IsRequired().HasMaxLength(250);
            this.Property(x => x.Creationdate)
                .HasColumnName("CreationDate").IsRequired();
            this.Property(x => x.ShortDescription)
                .HasColumnType("Text").IsMaxLength().IsOptional()
                    .HasColumnName("Description");
        }

    }
}
```

4. Modify the `BlogContext` class to contain the new mappings with the following code:

```
using System;
using System.Data.Entity;
using System.Linq;
```

```csharp
using BusinessLogic;
using DataAccess.Mappings;

namespace DataAccess
{
  public class BlogContext : DbContext, IUnitOfWork
  {
    public BlogContext(string connectionString)
      : base(connectionString)
    {

    }

    protected override void OnModelCreating
      (DbModelBuilder modelBuilder)
    {
      modelBuilder.Configurations.Add(new BlogMapping());
      base.OnModelCreating(modelBuilder);
    }

    public IQueryable<T> Find<T>() where T : class
    {
      return this.Set<T>();
    }

    public void Refresh()
    {
      this.ChangeTracker.Entries().ToList()
        .ForEach(x=>x.Reload());
    }

    public void Commit()
    {
      this.SaveChanges();
    }
  }
}
```

5. Add a new folder named `Queries` to the `DataAccess` project, and add a new C# class to it named `Extensions` with the following code:

```csharp
using System;
using System.Collections.Generic;
using System.Linq;
using System.Linq.Dynamic;
```

```csharp
using System.Linq.Expressions;
using DynamicExpression = System.Linq.Dynamic.DynamicExpression;

// These extensions are posted by Mitsu Furuta under the Micrsoft
Public License
// Found here -- http://blogs.msdn.com/b/mitsu/archive/2007/12/22/
playing-with-linq-grouping-groupbymany.aspx
// They are amazing work, and make any dynamic querying easier
namespace DataAccess.DyanmicQueries
{
  public static class Extensions
  {
    public static IEnumerable<GroupResult>
      GroupByMany<TElement>(this IEnumerable<TElement>
        elements, params string[] groupSelectors)
    {
      var selectors = new List<Func<TElement,
        object>>(groupSelectors.Length);
      foreach (var selector in groupSelectors)
      {
        LambdaExpression l = DynamicExpression
          .ParseLambda(typeof(TElement),
            typeof(object), selector);
        selectors.Add((Func<TElement, object>)l.Compile());
      }
      return elements.GroupByMany(selectors.ToArray());
    }

    public static IEnumerable<GroupResult> GroupByMany
      <TElement>(this IEnumerable<TElement> elements,
        params Func<TElement, object>[] groupSelectors)
    {
    if (groupSelectors.Length > 0)
    {
    var selector = groupSelectors.First();

    //reduce the list recursively until zero
    var nextSelectors = groupSelectors.Skip(1).ToArray();
    return elements.GroupBy(selector)
    .Select(g => new GroupResult
      {
        Key = g.Key,
        Count = g.Count(),
        Items = g,
```

```
            SubGroups = g.GroupByMany(nextSelectors)
        });
    }
    return null;
    }
    }
}
```

6. In the `Queries` folder add a new C# class named `GroupResult` with the following code:

```
using System.Collections;
using System.Collections.Generic;

namespace System.Linq.Dynamic
{
  public class GroupResult
  {
    public object Key { get; set; }
    public int Count { get; set; }
    public IEnumerable Items { get; set; }
    public IEnumerable<GroupResult> SubGroups { get; set; }
    public override string ToString()
    { return string.Format("{0} ({1})", Key, Count); }
  }
}
```

7. Run our tests and they will work.

How it works...

As always, we will start our solution with the definition of the problem, our tests. These will make sure we both accomplish the goal and don't over implement for features that were not requested.

Once we have our test, the next step for us is to set up the `Blog`, the mapping, and the context so we have a fully formed context to test with.

Our implementation of dynamic queries will be leveraging a couple of open source classes that we will find invaluable. These will allow us to focus on solving the problem instead of taking a deep dive into expression tree building. While it is a good technology to understand and use, it is not the focus of this recipe.

We will implement a couple of extension methods which will allow us to group queryable data into a set of grouped data. These groups can take in the name of the columns to group by. However, they can easily take in a business name and translate it to columns.

Improving Complex Query Scenarios

Dynamic grouping is difficult because we will not know the return type of the group key. This is shown by our implementation of the extensions. Notice that we have the extension methods returning `GroupResults`, and not just an `IGrouping<T>`. This is to allow for the scenario of not knowing the class at design time.

There's more...

With this recipe, we can leverage more than just Language Integrated Query, and can take a deeper look at those parts.

System.Linq.Dynamic

This namespace is part of a solution which allows developers the same level of flexibility with LINQ that we have with SQL. Dynamic SQL is nasty, but there are some problems that require it. Those same problems can now be solved using `System.Linq.Dynamic`. This is a powerful library that can be used to do many cool things, but should be used cautiously. We can quickly get into the nasty SQL land with it, and should be wary.

Separation of concern

As developers, one of the key things we need to focus on is **componentization** of an application. This means going through and trying to reuse things without coupling them together. We run into many struggles with this in pure object-oriented solutions, but when we start talking to database, this gets even more difficult. The data access layer has always been excused from this because it has to be coupled to the database, right? Wrong. We can overcome this by taking a few simple steps outlined here. Imagine a reusable data access layer that we can port into any application without fear, and without as much as one new line of code. If we implement our Entity Framework correctly, the core pieces will be portable and reusable in the extreme.

AsQueryable and AsEnumerable

`AsQueryable` and `AsEnumerable` are powerful methods that allow us to determine the amount of control we would like to give someone who is using our code. `AsQueryable` allows the return of a query that can be modified and changed before it is rendered into SQL. However, `AsEnumerable` takes that control and locks SQL in its current state. Further detail can be layered in and executions can be added, but the SQL will not change.

See also

In this chapter:

- *Implementing the specification pattern* recipe

Handling explicit loading

In this recipe, we will look at how we can explicitly load object graphs to avoid multiple calls to the database. We will also leverage Lambda statements and Language Integrated Query to bring these to bear on our queries.

Getting ready

We will be using the NuGet package manager to install the Entity Framework 4.1 assemblies.

The package installer can be found at http://nuget.org.

We will also be using a database for connecting to and updating data.

Open the **Improving Explicit Loading** solution in the included source code examples.

How to do it...

Carry out the following steps in order to accomplish this recipe.

1. We will start by writing a test which will query the database with a set of included objects and return the object graph. Use the following code:

    ```
    using System.Data.Entity;
    using BusinessLogic;
    using BusinessLogic.Queries;
    using DataAccess;
    using DataAccess.Database;
    using Microsoft.VisualStudio.TestTools.UnitTesting;
    using Test.Properties;

    namespace Test
    {
      [TestClass]
      public class QueryTests
      {
        [TestMethod]
        public void ShouldFilterTestData()
        {
          //Arrange
          Database.SetInitializer(new Initializer());
          var repository = new BlogRepository
            (new BlogContext(Settings.Default.BlogConnection));

          //Act
    ```

Improving Complex Query Scenarios

```csharp
            Blog item = repository.Set<Blog>().GetBlogById(1);

            //Assert
            Assert.IsNotNull(item);
            Assert.IsNotNull(item.Author);
            Assert.IsNotNull(item.Posts);
            Assert.IsTrue(item.Posts.Count != 0);
        }

    }

}
```

2. We will then add a folder to the `DataAccess` project named `Database` and a new C# file named `Initializer` with the following code:

```csharp
using System;
using System.Collections.Generic;
using System.Data.Entity;
using BusinessLogic;

namespace DataAccess.Database
{

  public class Initializer : DropCreateDatabaseAlways
     <BlogContext>
  {
    public Initializer()
    {

    }
    protected override void Seed(BlogContext context)
    {
      context.Set<Blog>().Add(new Blog()
      {
        Creationdate = DateTime.Now,
        ShortDescription = "Testing",
        Title = "Test Blog",
        Author = new Author() { Name = "Testing" },
        Posts = new List<Post>() { new Post() { Content =
           "Test content"} }
      });
      context.Set<Blog>().Add(new Blog()
      {
        Creationdate = DateTime.Now,
```

Chapter 6

```
            ShortDescription = "Testing",
            Title = "Test Blog 2",
            Author = new Author() { Name = "Testing" },
            Posts = new List<Post>() { new Post() { Content =
              "Test content" } }
        });
        context.Set<Blog>().Add(new Blog()
        {
          Creationdate = DateTime.Now,
          ShortDescription = "Testing",
          Title = "not Blog",
          Author = new Author() { Name = "Testing" },
          Posts = new List<Post>() { new Post() { Content =
            "Test content" } }
        });
        context.SaveChanges();
      }
    }
  }
```

3. In the `BusinessLogic` project, add a new C# class named `Blog` with the following code:

   ```
   using System;
   using System.ComponentModel.DataAnnotations;
   using System.Text.RegularExpressions;

   namespace BusinessLogic
   {
     public class Blog
     {
       public int Id { get; set; }
       public DateTime Creationdate { get; set; }
       public string ShortDescription { get; set; }
       public string Title { get; set; }
       public double Rating { get; set; }
     }
   }
   ```

4. Add a `Mapping` folder to the Data Access project and then add a `BlogMapping` class to the folder with the following code:

   ```
   using System.ComponentModel.DataAnnotations;
   using System.Data.Entity.ModelConfiguration;
   using BusinessLogic;
   ```

229

Improving Complex Query Scenarios

```
namespace DataAccess.Mappings
{
  public class BlogMapping : EntityTypeConfiguration<Blog>
  {
    public BlogMapping()
    {
      this.ToTable("Blogs");
      this.HasKey(x => x.Id);
      this.Property(x => x.Id)
        .HasDatabaseGeneratedOption
          (DatabaseGeneratedOption.Identity)
            .HasColumnName("BlogId");

      this.Property(x => x.Title)
        .IsRequired().HasMaxLength(250);
      this.Property(x => x.Creationdate)
        .HasColumnName("CreationDate").IsRequired();
      this.Property(x => x.ShortDescription)
        .HasColumnType("Text").IsMaxLength()
          .IsOptional().HasColumnName("Description");
    }

  }
}
```

5. Modify the `BlogContext` class to contain the new mappings for `Blogs` with the following code:

```
using System;
using System.Data.Entity;
using System.Linq;
using BusinessLogic;
using DataAccess.Mappings;

namespace DataAccess
{
  public class BlogContext : DbContext, IUnitOfWork
  {
    public BlogContext(string connectionString)
      : base(connectionString)
    {

    }

    protected override void OnModelCreating
```

```
        (DbModelBuilder modelBuilder)
    {
      modelBuilder.Configurations.Add(new BlogMapping());
      base.OnModelCreating(modelBuilder);
    }

    public IQueryable<T> Find<T>() where T : class
    {
      return this.Set<T>();
    }

    public void Refresh()
    {
     this.ChangeTracker.Entries().ToList()
        .ForEach(x=>x.Reload());
    }

    public void Commit()
    {
      this.SaveChanges();
    }
  }
}
```

6. We then want to add a `Queries` folder to the `DataAccess` project and a new C# class named `BlogQueries` with the following code:

```
using System;
using System.Collections.Generic;
using System.Data.Entity;
using System.Linq;
using System.Linq.Expressions;

namespace BusinessLogic.Queries
{
  public static class BlogQueries
  {
    static readonly List<Expression<Func<Blog,object>>>
      Includes = new List<Expression<Func<Blog, object>>>()
    {
      x=>x.Posts,
      x=>x.Author
    };

    public static Blog GetBlogById(this IQueryable<Blog>
```

Improving Complex Query Scenarios

```
            items, int id)
        {
            var query = Includes.Aggregate(items,
                (current, include) => current.Include(include));
            return query.FirstOrDefault(x => x.Id == id);
        }
    }
}
```

7. Run our test and everything will pass.

How it works...

We will start by defining our test so we have a definition of what success means, as well as a safety net for future refactoring. We would have a hard time with this kind of logic without a test that was repeatable to make these changes.

The next thing that we need to do is to set up our context, our objects, and our mappings. This gives us the structure needed to call the database for these explicit loading tests. We also need to set up an initializer to insert testable data into the database for us.

Once we have set up those things, we can write our query library. We will write this in the same way we normally would. The major difference is that in the query library we can set up a standard set of includes so we can apply these to each query. This will allow any query to include the object graph and give consistent expectations to the other developers leveraging our library. The other advantage of this is that we can define these includes in one place, and make them type safe.

There's more...

We can leverage some more Language Integrated Query features and Lambda statements here. For more details see the following sections.

Lambda statements

Lambda statements are simply the newest syntax for delegates. They give a standard language and syntax for short-lived and non-reusable methods. If we need to reuse these methods, we need to wrap them in a larger execution that will be named into a method or property.

LINQ aggregate

While the syntax is a bit difficult to read, the power of aggregation is difficult to ignore. We can take a list of anything and apply an accumulator function over every member of the sequence. For instance, taking a list of includable objects and accumulating them all in a query.

Expression of function of T

When we are building our application, it would be very easy to use functions instead of expressions and functions. However, this would not give us the power of deferred execution, or the ability to compose more to the expression tree before applying it. We want these benefits and therefore we will need to use **expression of function**.

Improving complex where clauses

In this recipe, we will be composing queries out of reusable chunks into larger business specific queries.

Getting ready

We will be using the NuGet package manager to install the Entity Framework 4.1 assemblies.

The package installer can be found at `http://nuget.org`.

We will also be using a database for connecting to and updating data.

Open the Improving **Complex Where Clauses** solution in the included source code examples.

How to do it...

Carry out the following steps in order to accomplish this recipe.

1. We will start by writing a test, which will query the database with a complex set of `where` clauses, which needs to be abstracted. Use the following code:

   ```
   using System;
   using System.Collections.Generic;
   using System.Linq;
   using BusinessLogic;
   using DataAccess.Queries;
   using Microsoft.VisualStudio.TestTools.UnitTesting;

   namespace Test
   {
     [TestClass]
     public class QueryTests
     {
         private static IQueryable<Blog> items;

         [ClassInitialize]
         public static void Setup(TestContext context)
   ```

Improving Complex Query Scenarios

```csharp
{
  //Arrange
  items = new List<Blog>
  {
    new Blog()
    {
      Creationdate = DateTime.Now,
      ShortDescription = "Test",
      Title = "Test"
    },
    new Blog()
    {
      Creationdate = DateTime.Now,
      ShortDescription = "not this one",
      Title = "Blog"
    },
    new Blog()
    {
      Creationdate = DateTime.Now,
      ShortDescription = "not this",
      Title = "TeBlog"
    },
    new Blog()
    {
      Creationdate = DateTime.Now,
      ShortDescription = "not this one",
      Title = "TestBlog"
    }

  }.AsQueryable();
}
[TestMethod]
public void ShouldApplyAllFilters()
{

  //Act
  var returnedValues = items.FilterByAll
    (x=>x.Title.Contains("e"), x=>x.Title.Contains("B"));

  //Assert
  Assert.AreEqual(2, returnedValues.Count());
}

[TestMethod]
```

```
      public void ShouldApplyAnyFilter()
      {

        //Act
        var returnedValues = items.FilterByAny
          (x => x.Title.Contains("e"),
            x => x.Title.Contains("B"));

        //Assert
        Assert.AreEqual(4, returnedValues.Count());
      }
    }

  }
```

2. In the `BusinessLogic` project, add a new C# class named `Blog` with the following code:

```
using System;
using System.ComponentModel.DataAnnotations;
using System.Text.RegularExpressions;

namespace BusinessLogic
{
  public class Blog
  {
    public int Id { get; set; }
    public DateTime Creationdate { get; set; }
    public string ShortDescription { get; set; }
    public string Title { get; set; }
    public double Rating { get; set; }
  }
}
```

3. Add a `Mapping` folder to the `DataAccess` project and then add a `BlogMapping` class to the folder with the following code:

```
using System.ComponentModel.DataAnnotations;
using System.Data.Entity.ModelConfiguration;
using BusinessLogic;

namespace DataAccess.Mappings
{
  public class BlogMapping : EntityTypeConfiguration<Blog>
  {
    public BlogMapping()
```

Improving Complex Query Scenarios

```
        {
           this.ToTable("Blogs");
           this.HasKey(x => x.Id);
           this.Property(x => x.Id)
              .HasDatabaseGeneratedOption
                 (DatabaseGeneratedOption.Identity)
                    .HasColumnName("BlogId");

           this.Property(x => x.Title)
              .IsRequired().HasMaxLength(250);
           this.Property(x => x.Creationdate)
              .HasColumnName("CreationDate").IsRequired();
           this.Property(x => x.ShortDescription)
              .HasColumnType("Text").IsMaxLength()
                 .IsOptional().HasColumnName("Description");
        }

    }
}
```

4. Modify the `BlogContext` class to contain the new mappings for `Blogs` with the following code:

```
using System;
using System.Data.Entity;
using System.Linq;
using BusinessLogic;
using DataAccess.Mappings;

namespace DataAccess
{
    public class BlogContext : DbContext, IUnitOfWork
    {
        public BlogContext(string connectionString)
            : base(connectionString)
        {

        }

        protected override void OnModelCreating
           (DbModelBuilder modelBuilder)
        {
            modelBuilder.Configurations.Add(new BlogMapping());
            base.OnModelCreating(modelBuilder);
        }
```

Chapter 6

```csharp
        public IQueryable<T> Find<T>() where T : class
        {
            return this.Set<T>();
        }

        public void Refresh()
        {
            this.ChangeTracker.Entries().ToList()
              .ForEach(x=>x.Reload());
        }

        public void Commit()
        {
            this.SaveChanges();
        }
    }
}
```

5. We then want to add a `Queries` folder to the `DataAccess` project and a new C# class named `BlogQueries` with the following code:

```csharp
using System;
using System.Linq;
using System.Linq.Expressions;
using BusinessLogic;

namespace DataAccess.Queries
{
  public static class BlogQueries
  {
    public static IQueryable<Blog>
      FilterByAll(this IQueryable<Blog> items,
        params Expression<Func<Blog,bool>>[] wheres)
    {
      return items.Where(ComplexWhereUtility.BuildAnd(wheres));
    }

    public static IQueryable<Blog>
      FilterByAny(this IQueryable<Blog> items,
        params Expression<Func<Blog,bool>>[] wheres)

      return items.Where(ComplexWhereUtility.BuildOr(wheres));
    }
  }
}
```

Improving Complex Query Scenarios

6. We want to add a new C# class to the `Queries` folder in the `DataAccess` project named `ComplexWhereUtility` with the following code:

```
using System;
using System.Linq;
using System.Linq.Expressions;
// Usage added to from
// http://blogs.msdn.com/b/meek/archive/2008/
//      05/02/linq-to-entities-combining-predicates.aspx
namespace DataAccess.Queries
{
  public static class ComplexWhereUtility
  {
    public static Expression<T> Compose<T>
      (this Expression<T> first, Expression<T> second,
        Func<Expression, Expression, Expression> merge)
    {
      // build parameter map (from parameters of
      //    second to parameters of first)
      var map = first.Parameters.Select((f, i) =>
        new {f, s = second.Parameters[i]})
          .ToDictionary(p => p.s, p => p.f);



      // replace parameters in the second lambda
      //   expression with parameters from the first

      var secondBody = ParameterRebinder
        .ReplaceParameters(map, second.Body);



      // apply composition of lambda expression
      //   bodies to parameters from the first expression

      return Expression.Lambda<T>(merge(first.Body,
        secondBody), first.Parameters);

    }

    public static Expression<Func<T, bool>> And<T>
      (this Expression<Func<T, bool>> first,
```

```csharp
      Expression<Func<T, bool>> second)
{

  return first.Compose(second, Expression.And);

}

public static Expression<Func<T, bool>> Or<T>
  (this Expression<Func<T, bool>> first,
    Expression<Func<T, bool>> second)
{

  return first.Compose(second, Expression.Or);

}

public static Expression<Func<T, bool>>
  OrElse<T>(this Expression<Func<T, bool>> first,
    Expression<Func<T, bool>> second)
{

  return first.Compose(second, Expression.Or);

}

public static Expression<Func<T, bool>>
  BuildAnd<T>(params Expression<Func<T,
    bool>>[] conditions)
{
  return conditions.Aggregate<Expression<Func<T,
    bool>>, Expression<Func<T, bool>>>(null,
      (current, expression) => current == null ?
        expression : current.And(expression));
}

public static Expression<Func<T, bool>>
  BuildOr<T>(params Expression<Func<T, bool>>[] conditions)
{
  return conditions.Aggregate<Expression<Func<T,
    bool>>, Expression<Func<T, bool>>>(null,
      (current, expression) => current == null ?
        expression : current.Or(expression));
}
```

Improving Complex Query Scenarios

```
    public static Expression<Func<T, bool>>
      BuildOrElse<T>(params Expression<Func<T,
        bool>>[] conditions)
    {
      return conditions.Aggregate<Expression<Func<T,
        bool>>, Expression<Func<T, bool>>>
          (null, (current, expression) => current == null ?
            expression : current.OrElse(expression));
    }

}
public class ParameterRebinder : ExpressionVisitor
{
    private readonly Dictionary<ParameterExpression,
      ParameterExpression> map;


    public ParameterRebinder(Dictionary<ParameterExpression,
      ParameterExpression> map)
    {
      this.map = map ?? new Dictionary<ParameterExpression,
        ParameterExpression>();
    }


    public static Expression ReplaceParameters
        (Dictionary<ParameterExpression,
          ParameterExpression> map, Expression exp)
    {
      return new ParameterRebinder(map).Visit(exp);
    }


    protected override Expression VisitParameter
        (ParameterExpression p)
    {
      ParameterExpression replacement;

      if (map.TryGetValue(p, out replacement))
      {
        p = replacement;
      }

      return base.VisitParameter(p);
```

                }
            }
        }

7. Run our test and everything will pass.

How it works...

As always, we start with a test that defines a set of data and a complex set of filters that we want to apply. We apply them and test the result against a known set of data. This allows us to define **done** and make sure we have accomplished the goal.

Once we have our test, we then need to set up the mapping and context to allow for a complete database and functional data access. Once this is done, we have a full database connection and a queryable repository.

We then create a query library, which leverages complex predicate builders that we can find in greater detail at http://blogs.msdn.com/b/meek/archive/2008/05/02/linq-to-entities-combining-predicates.aspx. This allows us to combine many predicates into an expression and then apply them in various configurations in order to easily adapt to the most complex business scenarios.

There's more...

We have leveraged several areas that can be handled in more detail and would give greater benefit with a deeper look.

Compose-able LINQ

When LINQ is referred to as **compose-able**, it means we can build a query and then add additional operators to that query before it is executed at runtime. This allows us to use smaller discreet queries, which can build on one another and be combined to handle even the most complex business scenarios. When we compose a LINQ statement it is iterated only one time to get the results into memory.

See also

In this chapter:

- *Implementing the specification pattern* recipe

Implementing the specification pattern

In this recipe, we will be implementing a specification pattern on top of **Entity Framework and Repository Pattern** to leverage maximum reuse without surfacing queryable objects to the consuming developers.

Getting ready

We will be using the NuGet package manager to install the Entity Framework 4.1 assemblies.

The package installer can be found at `http://nuget.org`.

We will also be using a database for connecting to and updating data.

Open the Improving **Complex Query Testing** solution in the included source code examples.

How to do it...

Carry out the following steps in order to accomplish this recipe.

1. We start by writing a test which will query the database with a predefined specification. Use the following code:

    ```
    using System;
    using System.Collections.Generic;
    using System.Linq;
    using BusinessLogic;
    using DataAccess.Queries;
    using Microsoft.VisualStudio.TestTools.UnitTesting;
    using Rhino.Mocks;
    using DataAccess;
    using BusinessLogic.QueryObjects;
    using Test.Properties;

    namespace Test
    {
      [TestClass]
      public class QueryTests
      {
        [TestMethod]
        public void ShouldFilterTestData()
        {
          //Arrange
          IQueryable<Blog> items = new List<Blog>
    ```

```csharp
            {
              new Blog()
              {
                Creationdate = DateTime.Now,
                ShortDescription = "Test",
                Title = "Test"
              },
              new Blog()
              {
                Creationdate = DateTime.Now,
                ShortDescription = "not this one",
                Title = "Blog"
              },
              new Blog()
              {
                Creationdate = DateTime.Now,
                ShortDescription = "not this",
                Title = "TeBlog"
              },
              new Blog()
              {
                Creationdate = DateTime.Now,
                ShortDescription = "not this one",
                Title = "TestBlog"
              }

            }.AsQueryable();

            var context = MockRepository
                .GenerateStrictMock<IDbContext>();
            context.Expect(x => x.AsQueryable<Blog>())
                .Return(items.AsQueryable());
            var repository = new BlogRepository(context);

            //Act
            var spec = new TitleNameQuery("Test");
            var returnedValues = repository.Find(spec);

            //Assert
            Assert.AreEqual(1, returnedValues.Count());
        }


        [TestMethod]
```

Improving Complex Query Scenarios

```csharp
    public void ShouldConnectToTheDatabase()
    {
      var repository = new BlogRepository
        (new BlogContext(Settings.Default.BlogConnection));
      var results = repository.Find(new TitleNameQuery("Test"));
    }
  }
}
```

2. In the `BusinessLogic` project, add a new C# class named `Blog` with the following code:

```csharp
using System;
using System.ComponentModel.DataAnnotations;
using System.Text.RegularExpressions;

namespace BusinessLogic
{
  public class Blog
  {
    public int Id { get; set; }
    public DateTime Creationdate { get; set; }
    public string ShortDescription { get; set; }
    public string Title { get; set; }
    public double Rating { get; set; }
  }
}
```

3. Add a `Mapping` folder to the `DataAccess` project and then add a `BlogMapping` class to the folder with the following code:

```csharp
using System.ComponentModel.DataAnnotations;
using System.Data.Entity.ModelConfiguration;
using BusinessLogic;

namespace DataAccess.Mappings
{
  public class BlogMapping : EntityTypeConfiguration<Blog>
  {
    public BlogMapping()
    {
      this.ToTable("Blogs");
      this.HasKey(x => x.Id);
      this.Property(x => x.Id)
        .HasDatabaseGeneratedOption
```

```
                    (DatabaseGeneratedOption.Identity)
                       .HasColumnName("BlogId");

            this.Property(x => x.Title).IsRequired()
               .HasMaxLength(250);
            this.Property(x => x.Creationdate)
               .HasColumnName("CreationDate").IsRequired();
            this.Property(x => x.ShortDescription)
               .HasColumnType("Text").IsMaxLength()
                 .IsOptional().HasColumnName("Description");
        }

    }
}
```

4. Modify the `BlogContext` class to contain the new mappings for `Blogs` with the following code:

```
using System;
using System.Data.Entity;
using System.Linq;
using BusinessLogic;
using DataAccess.Mappings;
using DataAccess.QueryObjects;
using BusinessLogic.QueryObjects;

namespace DataAccess
{
  public class BlogContext : DbContext, IDbContext
  {
      public BlogContext(string connectionString)
         : base(connectionString)
      {

      }

      protected override void OnModelCreating
         (DbModelBuilder modelBuilder)
      {
        modelBuilder.Configurations.Add(new BlogMapping());
        base.OnModelCreating(modelBuilder);
      }

      public void Refresh()
      {
```

Improving Complex Query Scenarios

```csharp
      this.ChangeTracker.Entries().ToList(
        .ForEach(x=>x.Reload());
    }

    public void Commit()
    {
      this.SaveChanges();
    }

    public IQueryable<T> AsQueryable<T>() where T : class
    {
    return this.Set<T>();
   }
  }
}
```

5. We want to add a new C# class to the `BusinessLogic` project named `QueryObject` with the following code:

```csharp
using System;
using System.Collections.Generic;
using System.Linq;
using BusinessLogic.QueryObjects;


namespace DataAccess.QueryObjects
{
  public class QueryObject : IQueryObject
  {
    public Func<IDbContext, int> ContextQuery { get; set; }

    protected void CheckContextAndQuery(IDbContext context)
    {
      if (context == null) throw new
        ArgumentNullException("context");
      if (this.ContextQuery == null) throw new
        InvalidOperationException("Null Query cannot
          be executed.");
    }

    #region IQueryObject<T> Members

    public virtual int Execute(IDbContext context)
    {
      CheckContextAndQuery(context);
```

```
      return this.ContextQuery(context);
    }

    #endregion
  }
}
```

6. We want to add a new C# class to the DataAccess project named QuerObjectOfT:

```
using System;
using System.Collections.Generic;
using System.Linq;
using System.Text;
using System.Collections.ObjectModel;
using System.Reflection;
using System.Linq.Expressions;


namespace DataAccess.QueryObjects
{
  public class QueryObject<T> : QueryObjectBase<T>
  {
    protected override IQueryable<T> ExtendQuery()
    {
      var source = base.ExtendQuery();
      source = this.AppendExpressions(source);
      return source;
    }

    public IQueryObject<T> Take(int count)
    {
      var generics = new Type[] { typeof(T) };
      var parameters = new Expression[]
        { Expression.Constant(count) };
      this.AddMethodExpression("Take", generics, parameters);
      return this;
    }

    public IQueryObject<T> Skip(int count)
    {
      var generics = new Type[] { typeof(T) };
      var parameters = new Expression[]
        { Expression.Constant(count) };
      this.AddMethodExpression("Skip", generics, parameters);
```

```csharp
      return this;
    }

    #region Helper methods

    static ReadOnlyCollection<MethodInfo> QueryableMethods;
    static QueryObject()
    {
      QueryableMethods = new ReadOnlyCollection<MethodInfo>
        (typeof(System.Linq.Queryable).GetMethods
          (BindingFlags.Public | BindingFlags.Static)
            .ToList());
    }

    List<Tuple<MethodInfo, Expression[]>>
      _expressionList = new List<Tuple<MethodInfo,
        Expression[]>>();
    private void AddMethodExpression(string methodName,
      Type[] generics, Expression[] parameters)
    {
      MethodInfo orderMethodInfo = QueryableMethods
        .Where(m => m.Name == methodName && m.GetParameters()
          .Length == parameters.Length + 1).First();

      orderMethodInfo = orderMethodInfo
        .MakeGenericMethod(generics);
      _expressionList.Add(new Tuple<MethodInfo,
        Expression[]>(orderMethodInfo, parameters));
    }

    private IQueryable<T> AppendExpressions(IQueryable<T> query)
    {
      var source = query;
      foreach (var exp in _expressionList)
      {
        var newParams = exp.Item2.ToList();
        newParams.Insert(0, source.Expression);
        source = source.Provider.CreateQuery<T>
          (Expression.Call(null, exp.Item1, newParams));
      }
      return source;
    }
    #endregion

  }
}
```

7. We want to add a new C# generic class to the DataAccess project named QueryObjectBase with the following code:

```
using System;
using System.Collections.Generic;
using System.Linq;
using System.Text;
using BusinessLogic.QueryObjects;


namespace DataAccess.QueryObjects
{
  public abstract class QueryObjectBase<T> : IQueryObject<T>
  {
    protected Func<IDbContext, IQueryable<T>> ContextQuery { get; set; }
    protected IDbContext Context { get; set; }

    protected void CheckContextAndQuery()
    {
      if (Context == null) throw new
        InvalidOperationException("Context cannot be null.");
      if (this.ContextQuery == null) throw new
        InvalidOperationException("Null Query cannot
          be executed.");
    }

    protected virtual IQueryable<T> ExtendQuery()
    {
      try
      {
        return this.ContextQuery(Context);
      }
      catch (Exception)
      {
        throw; //just here to catch while debugging
      }
    }

    #region IQueryObject<T> Members

    public virtual IEnumerable<T> Execute(IDbContext context)
    {
      Context = context;
      CheckContextAndQuery();
```

Improving Complex Query Scenarios

```csharp
            var query = this.ExtendQuery();
            return query.ToList();
        }

        #endregion
    }
}
```

8. We then want to add a new C# interface to the `BusinessLogic` project named `IQueryObject` with the following code:

```csharp
using System;
using System.Collections.Generic;
using System.Linq;
using System.Text;
using BusinessLogic.QueryObjects;

namespace DataAccess.QueryObjects
{
   public interface IQueryObject
   {
      int Execute(IDbContext context);
   }

   public interface IQueryObject<out T>
   {
      IEnumerable<T> Execute(IDbContext context);
   }
}
```

9. We want to modify the `IRepository` interface in the `BusinessLogic` project with the following code:

```csharp
using System.Collections.Generic;
using DataAccess.QueryObjects;

namespace BusinessLogic
{
   public interface IRepository
   {
      IEnumerable<T> Find<T>(IQueryObject<T> spec) where T : class;
   }
}
```

10. We also want to modify the `BlogRepository` class in Data Access with the following code:

```
using System;
using System.Collections.Generic;
using System.Data.Entity;
using System.Linq;
using BusinessLogic;
using DataAccess.QueryObjects;
using BusinessLogic.QueryObjects;

namespace DataAccess
{
  public class BlogRepository : IRepository, IDisposable
  {
    private readonly IDbContext _context;

    public void Dispose()
    {
      Dispose(true);
      GC.SuppressFinalize(this);
    }
    protected virtual void Dispose(bool disposing)
    {
      if (disposing)
      if (_context != null)
      _context.Dispose();
    }

    ~BlogRepository()
    {
      Dispose(false);
    }
    public BlogRepository(IDbContext context)
    {
      _context = context;
    }

    public IEnumerable<T> Find<T>(IQueryObject<T> spec)
      where T : class
    {
      return spec.Execute(_context);
    }
  }
}
```

Improving Complex Query Scenarios

11. We then want to add a `Queries` folder to the `DataAccess` project and a new C# class named `BlogQueries` with the following code:

    ```csharp
    using System.Linq;
    using DataAccess.QueryObjects;
    using BusinessLogic;

    namespace DataAccess.Queries
    {
      public class TitleNameQuery : QueryObject<Blog>
      {
        public TitleNameQuery(string title)
        {
          ContextQuery = (c) => c.AsQueryable<Blog>()
            .Where(x => x.Title == title);
        }

      }
    }
    ```

12. We run our test and everything passes.

How it works...

As always, we will start with a test that defines our scope. We want to be able to take a specification and limit a set with it. This will allow us to know when we have achieved the goal. We will then set up the blog object, the mapping, and the context.

Once those are in place, we will move to adding our abstract specification. This will serve as the base for all specifications we will use when moving forward. We will also add some extension methods and some generic specifications which will help us leverage the maximum amount of reuse from our efforts.

We will then need to modify the repository interface to accept in a specification of a certain type and return an enumerable collection of that type. These modifications will allow us to use the same repository interface no matter what we are querying against.

We will then need to modify our `BlogRepository` implementation to execute the specification chain. This could be as simple as our example of one specification, or many times it can be more complex. The beauty in a generic and simple implementation is its power and scalability.

Once this is accomplished, we then add our query library and will give prebuilt specifications back to anyone who needs to use it. We can then run our tests.

There's more...

There is one very important pattern that we should now discuss.

Specification pattern

Specification pattern is a pattern used which the developer outlines a business rule that is combinable with other rules. This allows for a highly customizable system of business rules that are at the same time incredibly testable. This fits perfectly for data access because there are certain reusable joins and filters that can be added to, combined, and used with almost infinite combinations.

See also

In *Chapter 7, Using Concurrent and Parallel Processing*:

- *Managing parallel contexts* recipe

7
Using Concurrent and Parallel Processing

In this chapter, we will cover the following recipes:

- Implementing optimistic concurrency
- Managing parallel contexts
- Handling data retrieval in highly-threaded environments
- Attaching objects with unit of work
- Improving multiple context performance

Introduction

When working with modern computers, there has been a transition on both the technology and the user experience that will drastically affect our applications. The technology has progressed to a point that microprocessor manufacturers can no longer make processors that are faster and smaller, but have shifted their focus to providing multiple cores on each chip. This shift does not automatically give performance increases to the applications running across the chip. Taking advantage of this takes some forethought and a different approach to the application development. We now want to focus on taking advantage of the time spent waiting on a processor. If we can reduce the amount of time that we spend waiting on something to complete, and use that time for other activities, then we will be able to create overall increase in the performance of the applications that we write.

Using Concurrent and Parallel Processing

The other major shift that we have to be aware of is that our users are becoming ever more technologically savvy. They are used to working with applications and websites that are fast, responsive, and user-friendly. This causes them to have higher expectations when they use our applications. We can help meet these expectations by making sure that all the work that will take an unacceptable amount of time is back grounded, and the application stays responsive during that work completion. We can also take advantage of the user's familiarity to the advanced systems, to show the notifications of this background work completion, without confusing most users.

Implementing optimistic concurrency

In this recipe, we are going to set up the Entity Framework to use a column for optimistic concurrency, so that multiple contexts do not over run each other without us knowing about it.

Getting ready

We will be using the `NuGet` Package Manager to install the Entity Framework 4.1 assemblies.

The package installer can be found at `http://nuget.org`.

We will also be using a database for connecting to the data and updating it.

Open the **Improving Optimistic Concurrency** solution in the included source code examples.

How to do it...

1. We start by defining a new C# Test class named `ConcurrencyTests` in the test project by which we will set up our scope of changes, and make sure that we get the expected results. We are going to set up one instance to which we want to throw a concurrency exception, and one to which we don't want to throw a concurrency exception, with the following code:

    ```csharp
    using System;
    using System.Collections.Generic;
    using System.Data;
    using System.Data.Entity;
    using System.Linq;
    using BusinessLogic;
    using DataAccess;
    using DataAccess.Database;
    using DataAccess.Queries;
    using Microsoft.VisualStudio.TestTools.UnitTesting;
    using Test.Properties;
    using System.Data.Entity.Infrastructure;
    ```

```csharp
namespace Test
{
  [TestClass]
  public class ConcurrencyTests
  {
    [TestMethod]
    [ExpectedException(typeof(DbUpdateConcurrencyException))]
    public void ShouldGiveConcurrencyErrorOnSecondUpdate()
    {
      //Arrange
      BlogContext blogContext = new
        BlogContext(Settings.Default.BlogConnection);
      Database.SetInitializer(new Initializer());
      blogContext.Database.Initialize(true);

      var repository = new BlogRepository(blogContext);
      var item = repository.Set<Blog>().First(b => b.Id ==1);
      item.Title = "Test Change";

      var repository2 = new BlogRepository(new
        BlogContext(Settings.Default.BlogConnection));
      varitem2 = repository2.Set<Blog>().First(b => b.Id == 1);
      item2.Title = "Testing Change";

      //Act
      repository2.SaveChanges();
      repository.SaveChanges();
    }

    [TestMethod]
    public void ShouldNotGiveConcurrencyErrorOnSecondUpdate()
    {
      //Arrange
      BlogContext blogContext = new
        BlogContext(Settings.Default.BlogConnection);
      Database.SetInitializer(new Initializer());
      blogContext.Database.Initialize(true);
      var repository = new BlogRepository(blogContext);
      var repository2 = new BlogRepository
        (new BlogContext(Settings.Default.BlogConnection));

      //Act Sequential Saves don't throw a concurency exception
      var item = repository.Set<Blog>().First();
      item.Title = "Test Change";
      repository.SaveChanges();
```

```
            var item2 = repository2.Set<Blog>().First();
            item2.Title = "Testing Change";
            repository2.SaveChanges();

        }
      }

    }
```

2. We then want to set up our blog object that will be used in this code base, by creating a new C# class in the `BusinessLogic` project, and name it `Blog`, using the following code:

    ```
    using System;
    using System.ComponentModel.DataAnnotations;
    using System.Text.RegularExpressions;

    namespace BusinessLogic
    {
      public class Blog
      {
        public int Id { get; set; }

        public DateTime Creationdate { get; set; }

        public string ShortDescription { get; set; }

        public string Title { get; set; }

        public double Rating { get; set; }

        public DateTime ModifiedDate { get; set; }

        [Timestamp]
        public Byte[] Timestamp { get; set; }
      }
    }
    ```

3. The next step is to set up our mappings, by adding a new C# class named `BlogMapping` to the `Mappings` folder in the `DataAccess` project, paying particular attention to the modified `date` field with the following code:

    ```
    using System.ComponentModel.DataAnnotations;
    using System.Data.Entity.ModelConfiguration;
    using BusinessLogic;
    ```

```csharp
namespace DataAccess.Mappings
{
  public class BlogMapping : EntityTypeConfiguration<Blog>
  {
    public BlogMapping()
    {
      ToTable("Blogs");
      HasKey(x => x.Id);
      Property(x => x.Id).HasDatabaseGeneratedOption(
        DatabaseGeneratedOption.Identity)
        .HasColumnName("BlogId");

      Property(x => x.Title).IsRequired().HasMaxLength(250);

      Property(x => x.Creationdate).HasColumnName
        ("CreationDate").IsRequired();

      Property(x => x.ShortDescription).HasColumnType("Text")
        .IsMaxLength().IsOptional().HasColumnName("Description");

      //Property(x => x.ModifiedDate).HasColumnType("DateTime")
        .IsConcurrencyToken(true).HasDatabaseGeneratedOption
        (DatabaseGeneratedOption.Computed);

      Property(x => x.Timestamp).IsConcurrencyToken(true)
        .HasDatabaseGeneratedOption(
        DatabaseGeneratedOption.Computed);
    }

  }
}
```

4. We now need to set up our `BlogContext` in the `DataAccess` project with the following code, to load the mappings for the objects:

```csharp
using System;
using System.Data.Entity;
using System.Linq;
using BusinessLogic;
using DataAccess.Mappings;

namespace DataAccess
{
  public class BlogContext : DbContext, IUnitOfWork
  {
```

Using Concurrent and Parallel Processing

```csharp
      public BlogContext(string connectionString) :
        base(connectionString)
      {

      }

      protected override void OnModelCreating(DbModelBuilder
        modelBuilder)
      {
        modelBuilder.Configurations.Add(new BlogMapping());
        base.OnModelCreating(modelBuilder);
      }

      public IQueryable<T> Find<T>() where T : class
      {
        return this.Set<T>();
      }

      public void Refresh()
      {
        this.ChangeTracker.Entries().ToList()
          .ForEach(x=>x.Reload());
      }

      public void Commit()
      {
        this.SaveChanges();
      }
    }
  }
```

5. Then, we run our tests and everything passes.

How it works...

The test is set up as a way of exercising our concurrent model as it would be in our application. The catch here gives us the ability of testing against the exception that was thrown. This would be where we would handle the concurrency issue, and probably notify the user that another person or system has updated the same record. The second test ensures that we can do a series of updates without causing concurrency issues. This will ensure that our concurrency is only truly applied when it is supposed to be, and not anywhere else.

The set up of our `Blog` object includes a few data points and a date field called `ModifiedDate`. This gives us a timestamp for changes that can then be used as our concurrency token. This column is updated when the `save changes` operation is called, and any stale data in other contexts will then throw a concurrency error if they try to update without refreshing from the database. We configure this by calling the `IsConcurrencyToken(true)` method on the property configuration on `Blog`.

There's more...

When we are dealing with concurrency in database communication, there are many things to keep in mind, and more details on several of those can be found in the following section. The Entity Framework handles these in a default way, but if we need to modify that default, then more depth of knowledge is needed.

Atomic execution

When dealing with concurrency in a database, we have to be even more aware of our executions. We need them to be atomic in all the applications, but if they are not, in non-concurrent applications, it is less likely to cause a data loss or corruption. In a concurrent system, the likelihood that this would cause trouble is much higher. We have to focus on each execution completely perfectly, or leaving no trace of the failure. This should appear to the rest of the users that either the changes are part of the data and do not violate any of the business rules, or that the changes never existed.

Leaving no mess behind

Every transaction to the database should leave the database in a stable state. No transaction should violate the integrity of the data in a way that is perceivable to other transactions. If we have to turn off identity insert, insert some data, and then turn it back on this should be done within one transaction so between those steps the data cannot be accessed in a non-complete state. It is our responsibility to make sure that the state in which we are trying to get the data into, with an update or transaction, is a valid and stable state. In a concurrently accessed database, this is massively important, because if we violate this, it is likely that our other threads of access will fail due to the state caused by our updates.

Isolation

Every transaction should not be visible to other transactions. This is to keep our dependencies in check, and make sure that if one failure occurs, then it doesn't cause a chain reaction. If we have two dependent executions, then we need to be sure to apply both of them within one transaction. This will ensure that if the first fails, then the second is not even attempted.

Using Concurrent and Parallel Processing

See also

In this chapter:

- *Improving data retrieval in highly-threaded environments*
- *Attaching objects with unit of work*

Managing parallel contexts

In this recipe, we will be setting up a management class that allows us to create and manage multiple contexts on a per thread basis.

Getting ready

We will be using `NuGet` Package Manager to install the Entity Framework 4.1 assemblies.

The package installer can be found at `http://nuget.org`.

We will also be using a database for connecting to the data and updating it.

Open the **Improving Parallel Context Management** solution in the included source code examples.

How to do it...

1. We start with a test that defines how the threads and the contexts should interact. This will let us control the scope, and make sure we have accomplished the goal of having a thread-specific context that can be reused with the following code:

```
using System.Threading;
using DataAccess;
using Microsoft.VisualStudio.TestTools.UnitTesting;

namespace Test
{
  [TestClass]
  public class MultiThreadedRepoManagementTests
  {
    private IBlogRepository repo1 = null;
    private IBlogRepository repo2 = null;
    private IBlogRepository repo3 = null;

    [TestMethod]
```

```csharp
      public void
        ShouldAllowCommitsToMultipleContextsWithoutConcernForThread()
      {
        //Arrange
        RepositoryFactory.Get("Test");

        //Act
        Thread thread = new Thread(GetRepositories);
        repo1 = RepositoryFactory.Get("Test");
        thread.Start();
        while (thread.ThreadState == ThreadState.Running)
        {
          Thread.Sleep(1);
        }

        //Assert
        Assert.IsNotNull(repo1);
        Assert.IsNotNull(repo2);
        Assert.IsNotNull(repo3);
        Assert.AreSame(repo2, repo3);
        Assert.AreNotSame(repo1, repo2);
        Assert.AreNotSame(repo1, repo3);
      }

      private void GetRepositories()
      {
        repo2 = RepositoryFactory.Get("Test");
        repo3 = RepositoryFactory.Get("Test");
      }
    }

}
```

2. We then want to add a new C# class named `Blog` to the `BusinessLogic` project with the following code:

```csharp
using System;

namespace BusinessLogic
{
  public class Blog
  {
    public int Id { get; set; }
    public DateTime Creationdate { get; set; }
    public string ShortDescription { get; set; }
```

```
        public string Title { get; set; }
        public double Rating { get; set; }
    }
}
```

3. Next up will be for us to add a new C# class named `BlogMapping` to the `DataAccess` project with the following code:

```
using System.ComponentModel.DataAnnotations;
using System.Data.Entity.ModelConfiguration;
using BusinessLogic;

namespace DataAccess.Mappings
{
   public class BlogMapping : EntityTypeConfiguration<Blog>
   {
     public BlogMapping()
     {
       this.ToTable("Blogs");
       this.HasKey(x => x.Id);
       this.Property(x => x.Id).HasDatabaseGeneratedOption(
          DatabaseGeneratedOption.Identity)
          .HasColumnName("BlogId");

       this.Property(x => x.Title).IsRequired().HasMaxLength(250);
       this.Property(x => x.Creationdate)
          .HasColumnName("CreationDate").IsRequired();

       this.Property(x => x.ShortDescription).HasColumnType("Text")
          .IsMaxLength().IsOptional().HasColumnName("Description");
     }

    }
}
```

4. We then want to add a new C# class named `BlogContext` to the `DataAccess` project with the following code:

```
using System;
using System.Data.Entity;
using System.Linq;
using BusinessLogic;
using DataAccess.Mappings;

namespace DataAccess
{
```

```csharp
public class BlogContext : DbContext, IUnitOfWork
{
  public BlogContext(string connectionString) :
    base(connectionString)
  {

  }

  protected override void OnModelCreating(DbModelBuilder
    modelBuilder)
  {
    modelBuilder.Configurations.Add(new BlogMapping());
    base.OnModelCreating(modelBuilder);
  }

  public IQueryable<T> Find<T>() where T : class
  {
    return this.Set<T>();
  }

  public void Refresh()
  {
    this.ChangeTracker.Entries().ToList()
      .ForEach(x=>x.Reload());
  }

  public void Commit()
  {
    this.SaveChanges();
  }
 }
}
```

5. We then want to add a new C# class named `RepositoryFactory` into the `DataAccess` project. The class will have another class defined in it that will handle identifying contexts with the following code:

```csharp
using System.Collections.Generic;
using System.Configuration;
using System.Threading;

namespace DataAccess
{
  public class RepositoryFactory
  {
    private static Dictionary<string, IBlogRepository>
```

Using Concurrent and Parallel Processing

```csharp
      repositories = new Dictionary<string, IBlogRepository>();

    public static IBlogRepository Get(string connectionString)
    {
      var id = new RepositoryIdentifier(Thread.CurrentThread,
        connectionString);

      if(!repositories.ContainsKey(id))
      {
        //This would more than likely not new up the blog
        //repository but supply it from an IoC implementation.
        repositories.Add(id, new BlogRepository(new
          BlogContext(connectionString)));
      }
      return repositories[id];
    }

    public static void Dispose(string connectionString)
    {
      var id = new RepositoryIdentifier(Thread.CurrentThread,
        connectionString);
      if (!repositories.ContainsKey(id))
      {
        repositories.Remove(id);
      }
    }

    private class RepositoryIdentifier
    {
      private readonly Thread _currentThread;
      private readonly string _connectionString;

      public RepositoryIdentifier(Thread currentThread, string
        connectionString)
      {
        _currentThread = currentThread;
        _connectionString = connectionString;
      }

      public override string ToString()
      {
        return _currentThread.ManagedThreadId + _connectionString;
      }
```

```
                public static implicit operator 
                  string(RepositoryIdentifier r)
                {
                    return r.ToString();
                }
            }
         }
     }
```

6. Run all of our tests, and they should pass.

How it works...

The test defines how the repository factory should be used to get a context per thread. It also ensures that the same thread will get a reusable context if it calls the factory with the same connection string. This definition of the problem that we are trying to solve gives us a clear model to solve.

The addition of the `Blog` object, the mappings, and the context will allow us to connect and communicate with a database, so that our example code is fully functional to the database. These pieces are essential for the full-testing of our solution.

The repository factory will act as a central creation point for all the repositories. This ensures that all repositories created this way are specific to the thread that they are in. The importance of this is that the `DbContext` is not thread-safe, and will cause problems if the same object is shared across many threads. We can avoid these problems by separating the context by thread and allowing for reuse without conflicts.

There's more...

When dealing with multi-threaded applications, there are several issues that we need to be aware of so that we can avoid them, and the following sections provide more details on some of those issues:

Race conditions

When we have two threads that have access to the shared data (such as a database), and one of them is somehow dependent on the execution happening in the right sequence, we have created a race condition. For example, when we have one thread adding a post to *blog 1*, and the second thread is selecting all posts from *blog 1*, and then modifying them to have a new title. If *thread 2* completes its select operation before the save operation of *thread 1*, then it will not achieve the goal, but if save operation of *thread 1* occurs first, then it will succeed. These two threads are now racing.

Using Concurrent and Parallel Processing

Locking

When resources are shared between threads, the resource may need to be locked. **Locking** ensures that only one thread can interact with the object at a time. This will allow shared resources to be used, without sacrificing the integrity of the system. This will enforce a serialization concurrency control.

See also

In this chapter:

- *Improving multiple context performance*

Handling data retrieval in highly-threaded environments

In this recipe, we will be retrieving data from the database in a threaded environment, making sure that it is the most current data possible.

Getting ready

We will be using the `NuGet` Package Manager to install the Entity Framework 4.1 assemblies.

The package installer can be found at http://nuget.org.

We will also be using a database for connecting to the data and updating it.

Open the **Improving Transaction Scope** solution in the included source code examples.

How to do it...

1. We start with a test that defines how threads and contexts should interact when pulling the most current data. This will let us control the scope and make sure we have accomplished the goal with the following code:

    ```
    using System.Data.Entity;
    using System.Linq;
    using System.Threading;
    using BusinessLogic;
    using DataAccess;
    using DataAccess.Database;
    using Microsoft.VisualStudio.TestTools.UnitTesting;
    using Test.Properties;

    namespace Test
    ```

```csharp
{
    [TestClass]
    public class MultiThreadedOjectsQueriesTests
    {
        private IBlogRepository repo1 = null;
        private IBlogRepository repo2 = null;
        private string _changedInThread;

        [TestMethod]
        public void
            ShouldGetMostRecentDataFromDatabaseAfter
            AnUpdateFromAnotherThread()
        {
            //Arrange
            Database.SetInitializer(new Initializer());
            repo1 = RepositoryFactory.Get(Settings.Default.Connection);

            //Act
            Thread thread = new Thread(UpdateFirstBlog);
            var item = repo1.Set<Blog>().First();
            Assert.IsNotNull(item);

            thread.Start();
            while (thread.ThreadState == ThreadState.Running)
            {
                Thread.Sleep(1);
            }

            item = repo1.CurrentSet<Blog>().First();
            //Assert
            Assert.AreEqual(_changedInThread, item.Title);
        }

        private void UpdateFirstBlog()
        {
            repo2 = RepositoryFactory.Get(Settings.Default.Connection);
            var item = repo2.Set<Blog>().First();
            _changedInThread = "Changed in Thread 2";
            item.Title = _changedInThread;
            repo2.SaveChanges();
        }
    }
}
```

2. We then want to add a new C# class named `Blog` to the `BusinessLogic` project with the following code:

```csharp
using System;

namespace BusinessLogic
{
  public class Blog
  {
    public int Id { get; set; }
    public DateTime Creationdate { get; set; }
    public string ShortDescription { get; set; }
    public string Title { get; set; }
    public double Rating { get; set; }
  }
}
```

3. Next up will be for us to add a new C# class named `BlogMapping` to the `DataAccess` project with the following code:

```csharp
using System.ComponentModel.DataAnnotations;
using System.Data.Entity.ModelConfiguration;
using BusinessLogic;

namespace DataAccess.Mappings
{
  public class BlogMapping : EntityTypeConfiguration<Blog>
  {
    public BlogMapping()
    {
      this.ToTable("Blogs");
      this.HasKey(x => x.Id);
      this.Property(x => x.Id).HasDatabaseGeneratedOption(
         DatabaseGeneratedOption.Identity)
        .HasColumnName("BlogId");

      this.Property(x => x.Title).IsRequired().HasMaxLength(250);
      this.Property(x => x.Creationdate)
         .HasColumnName("CreationDate").IsRequired();
      this.Property(x => x.ShortDescription).HasColumnType("Text")
         .IsMaxLength().IsOptional().HasColumnName("Description");
    }
  }
}
```

4. We then want to add a new C# class named `BlogContext` to the `DataAccess` project with the following code:

```
using System;
using System.Data.Entity;
using System.Data.Entity.Infrastructure;
using System.Data.Objects;
using System.Linq;
using BusinessLogic;
using DataAccess.Mappings;

namespace DataAccess
{
  public class BlogContext : DbContext, IUnitOfWork
  {
    public BlogContext(string connectionString) :
      base(connectionString)
    {

    }

    protected override void OnModelCreating(DbModelBuilder
      modelBuilder)
    {
      modelBuilder.Configurations.Add(new BlogMapping());
      base.OnModelCreating(modelBuilder);
    }

    public IQueryable<T> Find<T>() where T : class
    {
      return this.Set<T>();
    }

    public IQueryable<T> CurrentFind<T>() where T : class
    {
      var context = (IObjectContextAdapter) this;
      var query = context.ObjectContext.CreateObjectSet<T>();
      query.MergeOption = MergeOption.OverwriteChanges;
      return query;
    }

    public void Refresh()
    {
      this.ChangeTracker.Entries().ToList()
        .ForEach(x=>x.Reload());
```

```
      }

      public void Commit()
      {
        this.SaveChanges();
      }
    }
  }
```

5. We now want to add code to the repository, so that it can handle retrieving the current data with the code:

```
using System;
using System.Data.Entity;
using System.Linq;
using Logic;

namespace DataAccess
{
  public class BlogRepository : IBlogRepository
  {
    private readonly IUnitOfWork _context;

    public BlogRepository(IUnitOfWork context)
    {
      _context = context;
    }

    public IQueryable<T> Set<T>() where T : class
    {
      return _context.Find<T>();
    }

    public IQueryable<T> CurrentSet<T>() where T : class
    {
      return _context.CurrentFind<T>();
    }

    public void RollbackChanges()
    {
      _context.Refresh();
    }

    public void SaveChanges()
    {
```

```
          try
          {
            _context.Commit();
          }
          catch (Exception)
          {
            RollbackChanges();
            throw;
          }
        }
      }
    }
```

6. We then want to add the repository factory into the `DataAccess` project with the following code:

```
using System.Collections.Generic;
using System.Configuration;
using System.Threading;

namespace DataAccess
{
  public class RepositoryFactory
  {
    private static Dictionary<string, IBlogRepository>
      repositories = new Dictionary<string, IBlogRepository>();

    public static IBlogRepository Get(string connectionString)
    {
      var id = new RepositoryIdentifier(Thread.CurrentThread,
        connectionString);

      if(!repositories.ContainsKey(id))
        {
          //This would more than likely not new up the blog
          //repository but supply it from an IoC implementation.
          repositories.Add(id, new BlogRepository(new
            BlogContext(connectionString)));
        }
       return repositories[id];
    }

    public static void Dispose(string connectionString)
    {
```

Using Concurrent and Parallel Processing

```csharp
            var id = new RepositoryIdentifier(Thread.CurrentThread,
               connectionString);
            if (!repositories.ContainsKey(id))
            {
              repositories.Remove(id);
            }
         }

         private class RepositoryIdentifier
         {
            private readonly Thread _currentThread;
            private readonly string _connectionString;

            public RepositoryIdentifier(Thread currentThread, string
               connectionString)
            {
              _currentThread = currentThread;
              _connectionString = connectionString;
            }

            public override string ToString()
            {
               return _currentThread.ManagedThreadId + _connectionString;
            }

            public static implicit operator string
               (RepositoryIdentifier r)
            {
               return r.ToString();
            }
         }
      }
   }
```

7. Run all of our tests, and they should pass.

How it works...

Our test defines the problem that we are trying to solve as we retrieve an object from the database into the context. We then update it from another context, and retrieve it again. We want the most current values possible on the last retrieve.

We add our `Blog` object that we will be interacting with, the database-specific mappings, and the context, so we can retrieve and update data from the database.

We then add a current `Set` and `find` method to the context and the unit of work interface. These methods will allow us to explicitly bypass the entity cache and get the most current data from the database. This is essential for us to allow for the concurrent processing, without the data becoming stale.

There's more...

The validity of the data in the system is the key to making any system function correctly. There are many ways to handle concurrency issues, and the following sections give details on those solutions:

Client wins

The **Client wins concurrency conflict resolution** says that the data changed by the client application is the best version of the truth and overwrites the changes in the data store to match the data in the client. This can be useful for an administrative tool that needs to fix data problems, but is dangerous if set for all applications.

Store wins

The **Store wins concurrency conflict resolution** overwrites the data on the client entity with the data on the store. This not only ensures that the client entity is working on the most current data, but also requires the changes to the entity be made again. This may be a good solution for an application with a UI, where the user can redo changes or approve a programmatic redo, but doesn't work in automated service situations.

Custom determined

If neither of the previous two options fit your needs, then you can create your own custom solution. This would be hooked in at the point of the concurrency violation exception in Entity Framework, but you could then handle that in any way that you would like. This takes much more management, and more logic to be coded into the `DataAccess` layer, but is far less likely to have some of the fit issues of the previous two examples, because it can be tailored to your exact business needs.

See also

In this chapter:

- *Implementing optimistic concurrency*

Attaching objects with unit of work

In this recipe, we will be using multiple contexts to select the objects and update them, without having the knowledge of where they came from. This is a very common scenario when entities, or representations of entities, are being received by a web service or any other situation where the original context may have fallen out of scope.

Getting ready

We will be using the `NuGet` Package Manager to install the Entity Framework 4.1 assemblies.

The package installer can be found at `http://nuget.org`.

We will also be using a database for connecting to the data and updating it.

Open the **Improving Detached Objects** with **Unit Of Work** solution in the included source code examples.

How to do it...

1. We start with a test that defines how threads and contexts should interact when pulling data and then updating it from a different context. This will let us control the scope, and make sure that we have accomplished the goal with the following code:

```csharp
using System.Data.Entity;
using System.Linq;
using System.Threading;
using BusinessLogic;
using DataAccess;
using DataAccess.Database;
using Microsoft.VisualStudio.TestTools.UnitTesting;
using Test.Properties;

namespace Test
{
  [TestClass]
  public class MultiThreadedOjectsQueriesTests
  {
    private IBlogRepository repo1 = null;
    private IBlogRepository repo2 = null;
    private string _changedInThread;
    private Blog retreivedItem;

    [TestMethod]
```

```
    public void
       ShouldAllowUpdatesToAnObjectFromAContextOther
       ThanTheOneThatRetreivedIt()
    {
      //Arrange
      Database.SetInitializer(new Initializer());
      repo1 = RepositoryFactory.Get(Settings.Default.Connection);

      //Act
      Thread thread = new Thread(GetBlogFromSecondContext);

      thread.Start();
      while (thread.ThreadState == ThreadState.Running)
      {
        Thread.Sleep(1);
      }

      repo1.UnitOfWork.RegisterUnModified(retreivedItem);
      retreivedItem.Title = "Changed on context 1";

      //Assert
      Assert.AreEqual(repo1.SaveChanges(), 1);
    }

    private void GetBlogFromSecondContext()
    {
      repo2 = RepositoryFactory.Get(Settings.Default.Connection);
      retreivedItem = repo2.Set<Blog>().First();

    }
  }

}
```

2. We then want to add a new C# class named `Blog` to the `BusinessLogic` project with the following code:

```
using System;

namespace BusinessLogic
{
  public class Blog
  {
    public int Id { get; set; }
    public DateTime CreationDate { get; set; }
```

```
        public string ShortDescription { get; set; }
        public string Title { get; set; }
        public double Rating { get; set; }
    }
}
```

3. Next up will be for us to add a new C# class named `BlogMapping` to the data access project with the following code:

```
using System.ComponentModel.DataAnnotations;
using System.Data.Entity.ModelConfiguration;
using BusinessLogic;

namespace DataAccess.Mappings
{
  public class BlogMapping : EntityTypeConfiguration<Blog>
  {
    public BlogMapping()
    {
      this.ToTable("Blogs");
      this.HasKey(x => x.Id);

      this.Property(x => x.Id).HasDatabaseGeneratedOption(
        DatabaseGeneratedOption.Identity)
         .HasColumnName("BlogId");

      this.Property(x => x.Title).IsRequired().HasMaxLength(250);

      this.Property(x => x.Creationdate)
         .HasColumnName("CreationDate").IsRequired();

      this.Property(x => x.ShortDescription).HasColumnType("Text")
         .IsMaxLength().IsOptional().HasColumnName("Description");
    }

  }
}
```

4. We then want to add a new C# class named `BlogContext` to the `DataAccess` project with the following code:

```
using System.Data;
using System.Data.Entity;
using System.Data.Entity.Infrastructure;
using System.Linq;
using BusinessLogic;
using DataAccess.Mappings;
```

```csharp
namespace DataAccess
{
  public class BlogContext : DbContext, IUnitOfWork
  {
    public BlogContext(string connectionString) :
      base(connectionString)
    {

    }

    public int Commit()
    {
      return SaveChanges();
    }

    public IQueryable<T> Find<T>() where T : class
    {
      return Set<T>();
    }

    public void Refresh()
    {
      ChangeTracker.Entries().ToList().ForEach(x => x.Reload());
    }

    public void RegisterAdded<T>(T item) where T : class
    {
      AttachObjectInState(item, EntityState.Added);
    }

    public void RegisterDeleted<T>(T item) where T : class
    {
      AttachObjectInState(item, EntityState.Deleted);
    }

    public void RegisterModified<T>(T item) where T : class
    {
      AttachObjectInState(item, EntityState.Modified);
    }

    public void RegisterUnModified<T>(T item) where T : class
    {
      AttachObjectInState(item, EntityState.Unchanged);
    }
```

```
            private void AttachObjectInState<T>(T item, EntityState state)
              where T : class
            {
              DbEntityEntry<T> entry = Entry(item);
              if (entry == null)
              {
                Set<T>().Attach(item);
                entry = Entry(item);
              }
              entry.State = state;
            }

            protected override void OnModelCreating(DbModelBuilder
              modelBuilder)
            {
              modelBuilder.Configurations.Add(new BlogMapping());
              base.OnModelCreating(modelBuilder);
            }
          }
        }
```

5. We now add the `IUnitOfWork` methods for registering objects with the following code:

```
using System.Linq;

namespace BusinessLogic
{
    public interface IUnitOfWork
    {
        IQueryable<T> Find<T>() where T : class;
        void Refresh();
        int Commit();
        void RegisterModified<T>(T item) where T : class;
        void RegisterUnModified<T>(T item) where T : class;
        void RegisterAdded<T>(T item) where T : class;
        void RegisterDeleted<T>(T item) where T : class;
    }
}
```

6. We also need to change the interface for `IBlogRepository` to surface the unit of work with the following code:

```
using System.Linq;

namespace BusinessLogic
{
  public interface IBlogRepository
```

```
    {
      void RollbackChanges();
      int SaveChanges();
      IQueryable<T> Set<T>() where T : class;
      IUnitOfWork UnitOfWork { get; }
    }
  }
```

7. We now want to add code to the `BlogRepository` so it can handle surfacing the new interface member with the following code:

```
using System;
using System.Data.Entity;
using System.Linq;
using BusinessLogic;

namespace DataAccess
{
  public class BlogRepository : IBlogRepository
  {
    private readonly IUnitOfWork _context;

    public BlogRepository(IUnitOfWork context)
    {
      _context = context;
    }

    public IQueryable<T> Set<T>() where T : class
    {
      return _context.Find<T>();
    }

    public IUnitOfWork UnitOfWork
    {
      get { return _context; }
    }

    public void RollbackChanges()
    {
      _context.Refresh();
    }

    public int SaveChanges()
    {
      try
```

Using Concurrent and Parallel Processing

```csharp
        {
            return _context.Commit();
        }
        catch (Exception)
        {
            RollbackChanges();
            throw;
        }
    }
  }
}
```

8. We then want to add the repository factory into the `DataAccess` project with the following code:

```csharp
using System.Collections.Generic;
using System.Configuration;
using System.Threading;

namespace DataAccess
{
  public class RepositoryFactory
  {
    private static Dictionary<string, IBlogRepository>
       repositories = new Dictionary<string, IBlogRepository>();

    public static IBlogRepository Get(string connectionString)
    {
      var id = new RepositoryIdentifier(Thread.CurrentThread,
         connectionString);

      if(!repositories.ContainsKey(id))
      {
        //This would more than likely not new up the blog
        //repository but supply it from an IoC implementation.
        repositories.Add(id, new BlogRepository(new
           BlogContext(connectionString)));
      }
      return repositories[id];
    }

    public static void Dispose(string connectionString)
    {
      var id = new RepositoryIdentifier(Thread.CurrentThread,
         connectionString);
```

```csharp
          if (!repositories.ContainsKey(id))
          {
            repositories.Remove(id);
          }
        }

        private class RepositoryIdentifier
        {
          private readonly Thread _currentThread;
          private readonly string _connectionString;

          public RepositoryIdentifier(Thread currentThread, string
            connectionString)
          {
            _currentThread = currentThread;
            _connectionString = connectionString;
          }

          public override string ToString()
          {
            return _currentThread.ManagedThreadId + _connectionString;
          }

          public static implicit operator string
            (RepositoryIdentifier r)
          {
            return r.ToString();
          }
        }
      }
    }
```

9. Run all of our tests, and they should pass.

How it works...

The test defines that the problem we are trying to solve is selecting an object from one context, and then committing an update to it in another context. This definition gives us the bounds of our scope.

We then add our `Blog` entity to interact with from the database, our mappings to which we specify the tables and the columns, and finally our context to finish the database interactions. This gives us the basis for the communication to the database.

Using Concurrent and Parallel Processing

We then add our repository factory on to this, to allow for the creation of contexts per thread for our selection and updates of data. This gives us the means to get more than one context involved in multiple threads.

We can then leverage our unit of work pattern to attach objects, and set up the pattern by which objects can be moved from one context to another without friction. This allows us to select our object from one context, dispose off that context, and update the objects that are selected from another context, once they are attached to it.

There's more...

Attaching and detaching objects from a context brings on some overhead and patterns that warrant deeper understanding, and so we have outlined them in the following sections:

Attaching related objects

Related objects are not attached by default, and will have to be attached manually. This is to keep an `Attach` method call from creating duplicate entries for objects already being tracked in the context. This is just something that we have to be aware of, and handle inside our implementation of the `attach` command.

Detaching objects

When an object is detached, it is set to the `detached` state in the object tracker, and is no longer change-tracked. You can attach the object to another context to allow it to be change-tracked. It can also be attached back to the original context. Any changes made during the detached time, however, are not tracked, and will need to be manually set by editing the entry state in the change tracker.

See also

In this chapter:

- *Handling data retrieval in highly-threaded environments*

Improving multiple context performance

In this recipe, we will look at performance timings for multi-threaded environments so as to keep from making the mistake of thinking that multi-threading is always faster, without having the proof of the performance increases.

Getting ready

We will be using the `NuGet` Package Manager to install the Entity Framework 4.1 assemblies.

The package installer can be found at `http://nuget.org`.

We will also be using a database for connecting to the data and updating it.

Open the **Improving Multiple Context Performance** solution in the included source code examples.

How to do it...

1. This integration test will insert 100 entries into the database twice, one using a single thread, the second using four threads. It then asserts that the multiple thread option should have taken less time.

```
using System;
using System.Collections.Generic;
using System.Data.Entity;
using System.Diagnostics;
using System.Linq;
using System.Threading;
using BusinessLogic;
using DataAccess;
using DataAccess.Database;
using Microsoft.VisualStudio.TestTools.UnitTesting;
using Test.Properties;
using ThreadState = System.Threading.ThreadState;

namespace Test
{
  [TestClass]
  public class MultiThreadedOjectsQueriesTests
  {

    public TimeSpan ElapsedTime = new TimeSpan(0);

    [TestMethod]
    public void ShouldGetMostRecentDataFromDatabase
      AfterAnUpdateFromAnotherThread()
    {
      //Arrange
      Database.SetInitializer(new Initializer());
```

```csharp
          var repo = RepositoryFactory
            .Get(Settings.Default.Connection);

          //Act
          Stopwatch sw = Stopwatch.StartNew();
          for (int i = 0; i < 100; i++)
          {
            repo.Add(new Blog()
            {
              Creationdate = DateTime.Now,
              Title = string.Format("Test {0}", i),
              Rating = 4,
              ShortDescription = "Test"
            });
          }
          repo.SaveChanges();
          sw.Stop();

          List<Thread> threads = new List<Thread>
          {
            new Thread(InsertTwentyFiveBlogs),
            new Thread(InsertTwentyFiveBlogs),
            new Thread(InsertTwentyFiveBlogs),
            new Thread(InsertTwentyFiveBlogs)
          };

          Stopwatch sw2 = Stopwatch.StartNew();
          threads.ForEach(x=>x.Start());

          while (threads.Any(x=>x.ThreadState == ThreadState.Running))
          {
            Thread.Sleep(1);
          }

          sw2.Stop();

          //Assert
          Console.WriteLine("Singled Threaded took {0} ms",
            sw.ElapsedMilliseconds);
          Console.WriteLine("Multithreaded took {0} ms",
            sw2.ElapsedMilliseconds);
          Assert.IsTrue(sw2.Elapsed < sw.Elapsed);

        }
```

```
      private void InsertTwentyFiveBlogs()
      {
        var repo = RepositoryFactory
          .Get(Settings.Default.Connection);
        for (int i = 0; i < 25; i++)
        {
          repo.Add(new Blog()
          {
            Creationdate = DateTime.Now,
            Title = string.Format("Test {0}", i),
            Rating = 4,
            ShortDescription = "Test"
          });
        }

        repo.SaveChanges();
      }
    }
```

2. We then want to add our `Blog` object to the `BusinessLogic` project with the following code:

```
using System;

namespace BusinessLogic
{
  public class Blog
  {
    public int Id { get; set; }
    public DateTime Creationdate { get; set; }
    public string ShortDescription { get; set; }
    public string Title { get; set; }
    public double Rating { get; set; }
  }
}
```

3. Next up will be for us to add `BlogMapping` to the `DataAccess` project with the following code:

```
using System.ComponentModel.DataAnnotations;
using System.Data.Entity.ModelConfiguration;
using BusinessLogic;

namespace DataAccess.Mappings
```

```csharp
{
  public class BlogMapping : EntityTypeConfiguration<Blog>
  {
    public BlogMapping()
    {
      this.ToTable("Blogs");
      this.HasKey(x => x.Id);
      this.Property(x => x.Id).HasDatabaseGeneratedOption(
          DatabaseGeneratedOption.Identity)
        .HasColumnName("BlogId");

      this.Property(x => x.Title).IsRequired().HasMaxLength(250);

      this.Property(x => x.Creationdate).
        HasColumnName("CreationDate").IsRequired();

      this.Property(x => x.ShortDescription).HasColumnType("Text")
        .IsMaxLength().IsOptional().HasColumnName("Description");
    }

  }
}
```

4. We now add the `IUnitOfWork` methods for adding objects with the following code:

```csharp
using System.Linq;

namespace DataAccess
{
  public interface IUnitOfWork
  {
    IQueryable<T> Find<T>() where T : class;
    void Refresh();
    void Commit();
    IQueryable<T> CurrentFind<T>() where T : class;
    void Add<T>(T item) where T : class;
  }
}
```

5. We then want to update the `Blogcontext` with the following code:

```csharp
using System;
using System.Data.Entity;
using System.Data.Entity.Infrastructure;
using System.Data.Objects;
using System.Linq;
using BusinessLogic;
```

```csharp
using DataAccess.Mappings;

namespace DataAccess
{
  public class BlogContext : DbContext, IUnitOfWork
  {
    public BlogContext(string connectionString) :
      base(connectionString)
    {

    }

    protected override void OnModelCreating(DbModelBuilder
      modelBuilder)
    {
      modelBuilder.Configurations.Add(new BlogMapping());
      base.OnModelCreating(modelBuilder);
    }

    public IQueryable<T> Find<T>() where T : class
    {
      return this.Set<T>();
    }

    public IQueryable<T> CurrentFind<T>() where T : class
    {
      var context = (IObjectContextAdapter) this;
      var query = context.ObjectContext.CreateObjectSet<T>();
      query.MergeOption = MergeOption.OverwriteChanges;
      return query;
    }

    public void Add<T>(T item) where T : class
    {
      this.Set<T>().Add(item);
    }

    public void Refresh()
    {
      this.ChangeTracker.Entries().ToList()
        .ForEach(x=>x.Reload());
    }

    public void Commit()
```

```
        {
            this.SaveChanges();
        }
    }
}
```

6. We also need to change the interface for `IBlogRepository` with the following code:

```
using System.Linq;
using BusinessLogic;

namespace DataAccess
{
    public interface IBlogRepository
    {
        void RollbackChanges();
        void SaveChanges();
        IQueryable<T> Set<T>() where T : class;
        IQueryable<T> CurrentSet<T>() where T : class;
        IUnitOfWork UnitOfWork { get; }
        void Add<T>(T item) where T : class;
    }
}
```

7. We now want to update the repository `BlogRepository` with the following code:

```
using System;
using System.Data.Entity;
using System.Linq;
using BusinessLogic;

namespace DataAccess
{
    public class BlogRepository : IBlogRepository
    {
        private readonly IUnitOfWork _context;

        public BlogRepository(IUnitOfWork context)
        {
            _context = context;
        }

        public IQueryable<T> Set<T>() where T : class
        {
            return _context.Find<T>();
        }
```

```
            public IQueryable<T> CurrentSet<T>() where T : class
            {
              return _context.CurrentFind<T>();
            }

            public IUnitOfWork UnitOfWork
            {
              get { return _context; }
            }

            public void Add<T>(T item) where T : class
            {
              _context.Add(item);
            }

            public void RollbackChanges()
            {
              _context.Refresh();
            }

            public void SaveChanges()
            {
              try
              {
                _context.Commit();
              }
              catch (Exception)
              {
                RollbackChanges();
                throw;
              }

            }
        }
    }
```

8. We then want to add the repository factory into the `DataAccess` project with the following code:

```
using System.Collections.Generic;
using System.Configuration;
using System.Threading;

namespace DataAccess
{
```

Using Concurrent and Parallel Processing

```csharp
public class RepositoryFactory
{
  private static Dictionary<string, IBlogRepository>
    repositories = new Dictionary<string, IBlogRepository>();

  public static IBlogRepository Get(string connectionString)
  {
    var id = new RepositoryIdentifier(Thread.CurrentThread,
      connectionString);
    if(!repositories.ContainsKey(id))
    {
      //This would more than likely not new up the blog
      //repository but supply it from an IoC implementation.
      repositories.Add(id, new BlogRepository(new
        BlogContext(connectionString)));
    }
    return repositories[id];
  }

  public static void Dispose(string connectionString)
  {
    var id = new RepositoryIdentifier(Thread.CurrentThread,
      connectionString);

    if (!repositories.ContainsKey(id))
    {
      repositories.Remove(id);
    }
  }

  private class RepositoryIdentifier
  {
    private readonly Thread _currentThread;
    private readonly string _connectionString;

    public RepositoryIdentifier(Thread currentThread, string
      connectionString)
    {
      _currentThread = currentThread;
      _connectionString = connectionString;
    }

    public override string ToString()
    {
```

```csharp
            return _currentThread.ManagedThreadId + _connectionString;
          }

          public static implicit operator string(
            RepositoryIdentifier r)
          {
            return r.ToString();
          }
        }
      }
    }
```

9. Run all of our tests, and they should pass.

How it works...

We start by using a test that compares the update timings from a single thread and multiple background threads. This test gives us the scope by which we implement our multi-threaded solution.

We add our `Blog` to interact with the mappings and the context that talk to the database. This gives us the communication link that we need to test our threading solution.

We then leverage our repository factory to create multiple contexts to test against, and insert 25 records on each background thread. This will give us a comparison to the main thread.

This recipe is all about the timings of inserting 100 records into the database. We have set up the `insert` to run both on a single thread, and on four background threads. This will compare the timings of both the runs.

Notice that the threads doing the update are much faster than the single thread doing the same work. This is due to the wait time of the database doing the work, and waiting for a response.

There's more...

When timing and testing multi-threaded applications, we have to make sure to use more than just the code coverage as a metric, as this will not test race conditions and locking scenarios. The following sections show some techniques that can help testing multi-threaded code:

Thread interleaving

Each thread that is spun up can be halted for random amounts of time to test execution locks, data race conditions, and create tests around this. Normally, this includes creating manual harnesses throughout the multi-threaded code so as to insert random blocks to create these scenarios. This can be very time-consuming, but valuable testing.

Data race conditions

Randomly pausing threads to create completion patterns that are not normally seen will surface data race conditions in the multi-threaded code, or optimistic concurrency, and allow them to be reproduced (with the proper amount of logging). This is essential for multi-threading a `DataAccess` layer, as these bugs are often dismissed as loss data, bad data, flukes, or non-reproducible.

Chess

Microsoft research has developed a tool for automatically testing thread interleaving and data race conditions in multi-threaded applications. You can refer to the following URL for the same:

http://research.microsoft.com/en-us/projects/chess/

8
Improving Entity Framework with Complex Business Scenarios

In this chapter, we will cover the following recipes:

- Handling soft delete
- Implementing refreshing data on save
- Capturing the audit data
- Improving MVC 3 applications

Introduction

Sometimes, we walk a fine line when learning a new technology. We need an example set to be simple enough to grasp the issue, but we still need an understanding of more complex scenarios. We are going to be walking through these kinds of scenarios together.

There are many ways to solve problems in programming, and we all know that there are pros and cons to each way. We will cover the ways that experience and production failures have taught us, so we can benefit from the shared experience. This objective will be covered in this chapter.

Improving Entity Framework with Complex Business Scenarios

No project has a perfect domain, design, or implementation. We have all the written legacy code that we don't like, or have seen things that we would like to do better. This is where you get into some of the more complex business scenarios. How do we handle soft delete? How do we maximize data freshness? How do we seamlessly add auditable data to our objects? How does it all fit together? Let us move forward, and answer these questions together with the Entity Framework.

Handling soft delete

In this recipe, we will cover how to implement a soft delete solution with the Entity Framework, leveraging an open source library of interceptors.

Getting ready

We will be using the `NuGet` Package Manager to install the Entity Framework 4.2 assemblies, and the Entity Framework Interceptors assemblies.

The package installer can be found at `http://nuget.codeplex.com/`.

We will also be using a database for connecting to the data and updating it.

We then the following command:

`Install-Package Isg.EntityFramework.Interceptors.SoftDelete`

Open the **Improving Soft Delete** solution in the included source code examples.

How to do it...

1. We start by writing out a test that will allow us to define the scope of our problem. In this case, we want to deal with soft deletable objects in the same way as we deal with other objects in our context. We define it with the following code:

```
using System;
using System.Data.Entity;
using System.Linq;
using BusinessLogic;
using DataAccess;
using Isg.EntityFramework.Interceptors;
using Isg.EntityFramework.Interceptors.SoftDelete;
using Microsoft.VisualStudio.TestTools.UnitTesting;

namespace Test
{
    [TestClass]
```

```csharp
public class QueryTests
{
  [TestMethod]
  public void DeleteShouldSetIsDeleted()
  {
    var title = Guid.NewGuid().ToString();
    InterceptorProvider.SetInterceptorProvider(
      new DefaultInterceptorProvider(
      new SoftDeleteChangeInterceptor()));
    Database.SetInitializer(new
      DropCreateDatabaseAlways<BlogContext>());

    using (var db = new BlogRepository(new BlogContext()))
    {
      var customer = new Blog {IsDeleted = false, Title =
        title};
      db.Add(customer);
      db.SaveChanges();
    }

    using (var db = new BlogRepository(new BlogContext()))
    {
      var customer = db.Set<Blog>()
        .SingleOrDefault(i => i.Title == title);
      db.Remove(customer);
      db.SaveChanges();
    }

    using (var db = new BlogRepository(new BlogContext()))
    {
      var customer = db.Set<Blog>()
        .SingleOrDefault(i => i.Title == title);
      Assert.IsNotNull(customer);
      Assert.AreEqual(true, customer.IsDeleted);
    }
  }
}
```

2. We then add our `Blog` object as a new C# file named `Blog.cs` to our `BusinessLogic` project, so that we have an example object to connect to, with the following code:

```csharp
using System;
using Isg.EntityFramework.Interceptors.SoftDelete;

namespace BusinessLogic
{
  public class Blog : ISoftDelete
  {
    public Blog()
    {
      CreationDate = DateTime.UtcNow;
      ArchiveDate = DateTime.UtcNow;
    }
    public int Id { get; set; }
    public DateTime CreationDate { get; set; }
    public string ShortDescription { get; set; }
    public string Title { get; set; }
    public double Rating { get; set; }
    public DateTime ArchiveDate { get; set; }
    public bool IsDeleted { get; set; }
  }
}
```

3. We then add our `Mapping` as a new C# file named `BlogMapping` to the `DataAccess` project, with the following code:

```csharp
using System.ComponentModel.DataAnnotations;
using System.Data.Entity.ModelConfiguration;
using BusinessLogic;

namespace DataAccess.Mappings
{
  public class BlogMapping : EntityTypeConfiguration<Blog>
  {
    public BlogMapping()
    {
      this.ToTable("Blogs");
      this.HasKey(x => x.Id);

      this.Property(x => x.Id).HasDatabaseGeneratedOption
        (DatabaseGeneratedOption.Identity)
        .HasColumnName("BlogId");
```

```
          this.Property(x => x.Title).IsRequired().HasMaxLength(250);

          this.Property(x => x.CreationDate)
            .HasColumnName("CreationDate").IsRequired();

          this.Property(x => x.ShortDescription).HasColumnType("Text")
            .IsMaxLength().IsOptional().HasColumnName("Description");

          this.Property(x => x.IsDeleted)
            .HasColumnName("DeletedFlag");
      }

    }
}
```

4. The next step is to add the mapping to the context and make the context inherit from our `Interceptors` base class with the following code:

```
using System.Data.Entity;
using System.Linq;
using DataAccess.Mappings;
using Isg.EntityFramework.Interceptors;

namespace DataAccess
{
  public class BlogContext : InterceptorDbContext, IUnitOfWork
  {
    public void Add<T>(T entity) where T : class
    {
      this.Set<T>().Add(entity);
    }

    public void Commit()
    {
      SaveChanges();
    }

    public IQueryable<T> Find<T>() where T : class
    {
      return this.Set<T>();
    }

    public void Refresh()
    {
      this.ChangeTracker.Entries().ToList()
        .ForEach(x => x.Reload());
```

```csharp
        }

        public void Remove<T>(T entity) where T : class
        {
            this.Set<T>().Remove(entity);
        }

        protected override void
            OnModelCreating(DbModelBuilder modelBuilder)
        {
            modelBuilder.Configurations.Add(new BlogMapping());
            base.OnModelCreating(modelBuilder);
        }
    }
}
```

5. Then, we modify the `IUnitOFWork` interface with the following code:

```csharp
using System.Linq;

namespace DataAccess
{
    public interface IUnitOfWork
    {
        IQueryable<T> Find<T>() where T : class;
        void Refresh();
        void Commit();
        void Remove<T>(T entity) where T : class;
        void Add<T>(T entity) where T : class;
    }
}
```

6. Then, we modify the `IBlogRepository` interface with the following code:

```csharp
using System.Linq;

namespace BusinessLogic
{
    public interface IRepository
    {
        void RollbackChanges();
        void SaveChanges();
        IQueryable<T> Set<T>() where T : class;
        void Add<T>(T entity) where T : class;
        void Remove<T>(T entity) where T : class;
    }
}
```

7. We then modify `BlogRepository` to implement the interface with the following code:

```
using System;
using System.Collections.Generic;
using System.Data.Entity;
using System.Linq;
using BusinessLogic;
using BusinessLogic.Queries;
using DataAccess.Queries;

namespace DataAccess
{
  public class BlogRepository : IRepository, IDisposable
  {
    private readonly IUnitOfWork _context;

    public BlogRepository(IUnitOfWork context)
    {
      _context = context;
    }

    public IQueryable<T> Set<T>() where T : class
    {
      return _context.Find<T>();
    }

    public void RollbackChanges()
    {
      _context.Refresh();
    }

    public void SaveChanges()
    {
      try
      {
        _context.Commit();
      }
      catch (Exception)
      {
        RollbackChanges();
        throw;
      }

    }
```

```csharp
            public void Dispose()
            {

            }

            public void Add<T>(T entity) where T : class
            {
                _context.Add(entity);
            }

            public void Remove<T>(T entity) where T : class
            {
                _context.Remove(entity);
            }
        }
    }
```

8. All of our tests pass.

How it works...

Our test defines that we want to be able to add an object, delete it, and the object still exists, but in a deleted state (soft deleted). This defines the scope of the problem, and makes sure that we don't over engineer the solution. This is one of those problems where it is easy to provide too many solutions. We don't want some giant profiling solution that modifies everything to and from the database, or anything that extreme, and our test will help us limit ourselves to solving the problem that we have defined.

We define our `Blog` object which we will use to exercise the interceptors. Notice that we implement the `ISoftDelete` interface. This allows the interceptor to catch the saves of deletes for this object, and mark the flag instead of committing a true delete.

We then define our context, and inherit from the interceptor context. This gives us the hooks to intercept the save changes call and modify the behavior as we need. In this case, the soft delete.

The repository is implemented to give us a clean interface to interact with and hide some of the implementation details from our consuming code.

There's more...

There are a couple of details that will help us understand the problem in more depth, and enhance our solution.

Entity framework interceptors

This is an open source project by *Chris McKenzie* that gives a standard implementation to the common extension points for the Entity Framework. It is well written and will save time, if you are considering rolling your own interception.

`http://nuget.org/packages/Isg.EntityFramework.Interceptors`

Soft delete pattern

The **soft delete pattern** (or **anti-pattern**, as the case may be argued) is the pattern by which the data is put into an inactive state, and is no longer displayed or interacted with by the system. This normally comes in the form of additional properties on the object that mark it as deleted with a date time, or active date ranges. This pattern ensures that no data is ever truly lost. There are many blogs and discussions on this pattern being good or bad. They are all based on opinion at this point, but this one is for certain. This is in production in a lot of places, and you have to deal with it for the foreseeable future.

See also

In this chapter:

- *Capturing the Audit Data*

Implementing refreshing data on save

In this recipe, we are going to look at how to get your application on a change to get the most current data it can, so that when you are modifying objects, you get the most current one back.

Getting ready

We will be using the `Nuget` Package Manager to install the Entity Framework 4.1 assemblies.

The package installer can be found at `http://nuget.codeplex.com/`.

We will also be using a database for connecting to the data and updating it.

Open the **Improving Refreshing Data on Save** solution in the included source code examples.

How to do it...

1. We start be writing out a test that will allow us to define the scope of our problem. In this case, we want our context to refresh any object that it commits after the commit is final. We define it with the following code:

```
using System;
using System.Linq;
using BusinessLogic;
using DataAccess;
using Microsoft.VisualStudio.TestTools.UnitTesting;

namespace Test
{
  [TestClass]
  public class QueryTests
  {
    [TestMethod]
    public void ShouldRefreshDataOnSave()
    {
      var blogContext = new BlogContext();
      Database.SetInitializer(new Initializer());
      blogContext.Database.Initialize(true);

      var repo = new BlogRepository(new BlogContext());
      var repo2 = new BlogRepository(new BlogContext());

      var blog = repo.Set<Blog>().FirstOrDefault();

      var blog2 = repo2.Set<Blog>().FirstOrDefault();

      blog.Title = "Something new";
      blog2.Rating = 3;

      repo2.SaveChanges();
      repo.SaveChanges();

      Assert.AreEqual(blog.Rating, blog2.Rating);

    }

  }

}
```

2. We then add our `Blog` object as a new C# file named `Blog.cs` to our `BusinessLogic` project, so that we have an example object to connect to, with the following code:

```csharp
using System;

namespace BusinessLogic
{
  public class Blog
  {
    public int Id { get; set; }
    public DateTime Creationdate { get; set; }
    public string ShortDescription { get; set; }
    public string Title { get; set; }
    public double Rating { get; set; }
    public bool IsDeleted { get; set; }
  }
}
```

3. We then add our mapping as a new C# file named `BlogMapping` to the `DataAccess` project with the following code:

```csharp
using System.ComponentModel.DataAnnotations;
using System.Data.Entity.ModelConfiguration;
using BusinessLogic;

namespace DataAccess.Mappings
{
  public class BlogMapping : EntityTypeConfiguration<Blog>
  {
    public BlogMapping()
    {
      this.ToTable("Blogs");
      this.HasKey(x => x.Id);
      this.Property(x => x.Id).HasDatabaseGeneratedOption
        (DatabaseGeneratedOption.Identity)
        .HasColumnName("BlogId");

      this.Property(x => x.Title).IsRequired().HasMaxLength(250);

      this.Property(x => x.Creationdate)
        .HasColumnName("CreationDate").IsRequired();

      this.Property(x => x.ShortDescription).HasColumnType("Text")
        .IsMaxLength().IsOptional().HasColumnName("Description");
```

```
            this.Property(x => x.IsDeleted)
                .HasColumnName("DeletedFlag");
        }

    }
}
```

4. The next step is for us to add the mapping to the `BlogContext` and make the context change the `commit` behavior with the following code:

```
using System.Data;
using System.Data.Entity;
using System.Linq;
using DataAccess.Mappings;

namespace DataAccess
{
    public class BlogContext : DbContext, IUnitOfWork
    {
        public void Add<T>(T entity) where T : class
        {
            this.Set<T>().Add(entity);
        }

        public void Commit()
        {
            var itemsToBeSaved = this.ChangeTracker.Entries()
                .Where(x => x.State == EntityState.Modified).ToList();

            SaveChanges();
            foreach (var dbEntityEntry in itemsToBeSaved)
            {
                dbEntityEntry.Reload();
            }
        }

        public IQueryable<T> Find<T>() where T : class
        {
            return this.Set<T>();
        }

        public void Refresh()
        {
            this.ChangeTracker.Entries().ToList()
                .ForEach(x => x.Rload());
        }
```

```
            public void Remove<T>(T entity) where T : class
            {
                this.Set<T>().Remove(entity);
            }

            protected override void
                OnModelCreating(DbModelBuilder modelBuilder)
            {
                modelBuilder.Configurations.Add(new BlogMapping());
                base.OnModelCreating(modelBuilder);
            }
        }
    }
```

5. All of our tests pass.

How it works...

We start with a test that explicitly defines our goals. In this case, we want the data on a save operation to be the most current version possible. We define a test where we select an object back from two contexts. We update the objects differently, and call a save operation on both. The second object should get saved, and then updated.

We then create our `Blog` object that we want to update, and the mapping that will tie it into the database context. This will give us the ability to interact with the database, and make sure that the object is truly refreshed.

We then get to the `SaveChange` method in the context that will allow us to save the objects as we would normally do, but we also want to store the change tracking entries from before we save, so that we know which objects to refresh. This allows us to leverage the change tracker to reload the object from the database.

There's more...

The change tracker in Entity Framework code first is complex and worth understanding a bit more.

EntityState

The `EntityState` is what the change tracker uses to know if it cares about the object and how it has been modified. When we add, delete, or modify a tracked object, the state is changed to reflect this operation. We are given access to this by passing in the `EntityKey`, or the entity itself to the `Entry` method, and getting back the object that represents the entity to the change tracker.

EntityKey

`EntityKey` is an immutable object that uniquely identifies the entity in the context. This is used for updates, edits, change tracking, and constraint checking. This is the main identifier for the object. It is derived from how the object is mapped to a database table.

DbEntityEntry

This is the object which will hold the original values from the selection, the current values, and the state information that the Entity Framework needs to operate on. This gives a powerful API for managing the state of the object in reference to how the framework sees it.

See also

Chapter 7, *Using Concurrent and Parallel Processing*

- Handling data retrieval in highly-threaded environments

Capturing the audit data

In this recipe, we will be walking through how to add a seamless audit data to your objects with minimal effort.

Getting ready

We will be using the `NuGet` Package Manager to install the Entity Framework 4.1 assemblies.

The package installer can be found at http://nuget.codeplex.com/.

We will also be using a database for connecting to the data, and updating it.

Open the **Improving Audit Data** solution in the included source code examples.

How to do it...

1. We start be writing out a test that will allow us to define the scope of our problem. In this case, we want our context to handle the data for auditable objects without the user input. We define it with the following code:

   ```
   using System;
   using System.Linq;
   using BusinessLogic;
   ```

```csharp
using DataAccess;
using Microsoft.VisualStudio.TestTools.UnitTesting;

namespace Test
{
  [TestClass]
  public class QueryTests
  {
    [TestMethod]
    public void ShouldAddAuditDataWithoutUserInteraction()
    {
      var blog = new Blog()
      {
        Title = "Test",
        Rating = 4,
        ShortDescription = "Testing"
      };
      var repo = new BlogRepository(new BlogContext());

      repo.Add(blog);

      repo.SaveChanges();

      Assert.IsNotNull(blog.ModifiedDate);
      Assert.IsNotNull(blog.ModifiedBy);
      Assert.IsNotNull(blog.Creationdate);
      Assert.IsNotNull(blog.CreatedBy);

    }

  }

}
```

2. We then add our `Blog` object and it's inheritance chain as a new C# file named `Blog.cs` to our `BusinessLogic` project, so we have an example object to connect to, with the following code:

```csharp
using System;

namespace BusinessLogic
{
  public class Blog : AuditableEntity
  {
    public string ShortDescription { get; set; }
```

```csharp
        public string Title { get; set; }
        public double Rating { get; set; }
    }

    public class AuditableEntity : Entity
    {
        public string ModifiedBy { get; set; }
        public DateTime ModifiedDate { get; set; }
        public string CreatedBy { get; set; }
        public DateTime Creationdate { get; set; }

    }

    public class Entity
    {
        public int Id { get; set; }
    }
}
```

3. We then add our mapping as a new C# file named `BlogMapping` to the `DataAccess` project, with the following code:

```csharp
using System.ComponentModel.DataAnnotations;
using System.Data.Entity.ModelConfiguration;
using BusinessLogic;

namespace DataAccess.Mappings
{
    public class BlogMapping : EntityTypeConfiguration<Blog>
    {
        public BlogMapping()
        {
            this.ToTable("Blogs");
            this.HasKey(x => x.Id);
            this.Property(x => x.Id).HasDatabaseGeneratedOption
                (DatabaseGeneratedOption.Identity)
                .HasColumnName("BlogId");

            this.Property(x => x.Title).IsRequired().HasMaxLength(250);

            this.Property(x => x.Creationdate)
                .HasColumnName("CreationDate").IsRequired();

            this.Property(x => x.ShortDescription).HasColumnType("Text")
                .IsMaxLength().IsOptional().HasColumnName("Description");
        }

    }
}
```

4. The next step is for us to add the mapping to the context and make the context change the commit behavior with the following code:

```csharp
using System;
using System.Collections.Generic;
using System.Data;
using System.Data.Entity;
using System.Data.Entity.Infrastructure;
using System.Linq;
using BusinessLogic;
using DataAccess.Mappings;
using Isg.EntityFramework.Interceptors;

namespace DataAccess
{
  public class BlogContext : InterceptorDbContext, IUnitOfWork
  {
    public void Add<T>(T entity) where T : class
    {
      this.Set<T>().Add(entity);
    }

    public void Commit()
    {
      var addedItems = this.ChangeTracker.Entries()
        .Where(x => x.State == EntityState.Added
        && x.Entity is AuditableEntity);

      var modifiedItems = this.ChangeTracker.Entries()
        .Where(x => x.State == EntityState.Modified
        && x.Entity is AuditableEntity);

      AttachAuditDataForInserts(addedItems);
      AttachAuditDataForModifications(modifiedItems);
      SaveChanges();
    }

    private void AttachAuditDataForModifications
      (IEnumerable<DbEntityEntry> modifiedItems)
    {
      modifiedItems.Each(x =>
      {
        var auditableEntity = (AuditableEntity) x.Entity;
        auditableEntity.ModifiedBy = "UserName";
        auditableEntity.ModifiedDate = DateTime.Today;
```

```csharp
        });
      }

      private void AttachAuditDataForInserts
        (IEnumerable<DbEntityEntry> addedItems)
      {
        addedItems.Each(x =>
        {
          var auditableEntity = (AuditableEntity) x.Entity;
          auditableEntity.CreatedBy = "UserName";
          auditableEntity.Creationdate = DateTime.Today;
          auditableEntity.ModifiedBy = "UserName";
          auditableEntity.ModifiedDate = DateTime.Today;
        });
      }

      public IQueryable<T> Find<T>() where T : class
      {
        return this.Set<T>();
      }

      public void Refresh()
      {
        this.ChangeTracker.Entries().ToList()
          .ForEach(x => x.Reload());
      }

      public void Remove<T>(T entity) where T : class
      {
        this.Set<T>().Remove(entity);
      }

      protected override void
        OnModelCreating(DbModelBuilder modelBuilder)
      {
        modelBuilder.Configurations.Add(new BlogMapping());
        base.OnModelCreating(modelBuilder);
      }
    }
  }
```

5. All of our tests pass.

How it works...

We start with a test that defines how we want the audit data to get attached to the object. We want the objects to get saved, and the data to be supplied automatically, so users are ignorant of the interaction.

We define our `Blog` object as an `AuditableEntity`, so that the properties we need are defined in one spot, and we can leverage them in any object we need. We could do this in an interface if we wanted to avoid inheritance.

The mapping doesn't change drastically for this, as the fields are mapped within the standard. We then attached the object and it's mapping to the context.

The context is where we override the `SaveChanges` method and use the change tracker to find objects that were added or modified. We then modify those objects with the audit data just before saving them to the database. This gives us the accurate modification times, and also allows us to separate our object modification from the audit data attachment.

There's more...

When we look at most of the databases, there are several pieces of data that we want to collect, but want the user to have very little interaction with.

Created date and created by, modified date and modified by

These fields are fairly standard and allow us to see what is happening at a high-level in the database, without having to parse application logs and look for errors. This gives us the answer to *Who is creating/modifying the objects* view.

Action taken

If we need more data, we can leverage the **change tracker** to pull what properties on the entity were modified and what their current value versus original value is, so that we can log this data off, or save it to the database. This will give the **Recreation** or a **point in time** view of the data. This is value for fault-tolerant systems, and systems where a single change in the middle of a change may need to be rolled back, and the rest reapplied.

See also

In this chapter:

- *Handling soft delete*

Improving MVC 3 applications

In this recipe, we will work through a full MVC 3 application, using patterns and the Entity Framework to give a solid basis for any enterprise application.

Getting ready

We will be using the `NuGet` Package Manager to install the Entity Framework 4.1 assemblies.

The package installer can be found at http://nuget.codeplex.com/.

We will also be using a database for connecting to the data, and updating.

Open the **Improving MVC 3 Applications** solution in the included source code examples.

How to do it...

1. We start off with a couple of tests that will make sure that our controller and our repository work the way that we intend. We need to add a new C# test class named `ControllerTests` with the following code:

```csharp
using System.Collections.Generic;
using System.Web.Mvc;
using BusinessLogic;
using BusinessLogic.Interfaces;
using DataAccess.Queries;
using Microsoft.VisualStudio.TestTools.UnitTesting;
using Rhino.Mocks;
using UI.Controllers;

namespace Test
{
    [TestClass]
    public class ControllerTests
    {
        [TestMethod]
        public void ShouldQueryRepository()
        {
            //Arrange
            var repo = MockRepository.GenerateStrictMock<IRepository>();
            repo
              .Stub(x => x.Find(Arg<BlogByTitleQuery>.Is.Anything))
              .Return(new Blog()
              {
```

```csharp
            Title = "Test",
            ShortDescription = "This is a test description",
            Posts = new List<Post>()
            {
              new Post()
              {
                Title = "Test Post 1",
                Content = "Test Content 1"
              },
              new Post()
              {
                Title = "Test Post 1",
                Content = "Test Content 1"
              }
            }
          });
          var controller = new HomeController(repo);

          //Act
          var result = controller.Index();

          //Assert
          Assert.IsInstanceOfType(result, typeof(ViewResult));
          var viewResult = result as ViewResult;
          Assert.IsNotNull(viewResult.Model);
          Assert.IsInstanceOfType(viewResult.Model, typeof(Blog));
          Assert.AreEqual("Test", ((Blog)viewResult.Model).Title);
        }
      }
    }
```

2. We then want to add a new C# test class named `RepositoryTests` with the following code, which will define our problem scope:

```csharp
using System.Collections.Generic;
using System.Linq;
using BusinessLogic;
using BusinessLogic.Interfaces;
using DataAccess;
using DataAccess.Queries;
using Microsoft.VisualStudio.TestTools.UnitTesting;
using Rhino.Mocks;

namespace Test
{
```

Improving Entity Framework with Complex Business Scenarios

```csharp
[TestClass]
public class RepositoryTests
{
  [TestMethod]
  public void ShouldQueryBlogs()
  {
    //Arrange
    var context =
      MockRepository.GenerateStrictMock<IDbContext>();
    context
      .Stub(x => x.AsQueryable<Blog>())
      .Return(new List<Blog>
    {
      new Blog()
      {
        Title = "Test",
        ShortDescription = "This is a test description",
        Posts = new List<Post>()
        {
          new Post()
          {
            Title = "Test Post 1",
            Content = "Test Content 1"
          },
          new Post()
          {
            Title = "Test Post 1",
            Content = "Test Content 1"
          }
        }
      },
      new Blog(){Title = "Not Test"}
    }.AsQueryable());
    var repository = new BlogRepository(context);

    //Act
    var blog = repository.Find(new BlogByTitleQuery("Test"));

    //Assert
    Assert.IsNotNull(blog);
    Assert.IsNotNull(blog.Posts);
    Assert.AreEqual(2, blog.Posts.Count());
  }
}
```

3. We then will add our Blog and Post objects as new C# classes to the BusinessLogic project, and the audit objects that will back it with the following code:

```csharp
using System;
using System.Collections;
using System.Collections.Generic;

namespace BusinessLogic
{
  public class Blog : AuditableEntity
  {
    public Blog()
    {
      Posts = new List<Post>();
    }
    public string ShortDescription { get; set; }
    public string Title { get; set; }
    public double Rating { get; set; }

    public ICollection<Post> Posts { get; set; }
  }

  public class AuditableEntity : Entity
  {
    public DateTime Created { get; set; }
    public string CreatedBy { get; set; }
    public DateTime Modified { get; set; }
    public string ModifiedBy { get; set; }
  }

  public class Entity
  {
    public int Id { get; set; }
  }

  public class Post : Entity
  {
    public string Title { get; set; }
    public string Content { get; set; }
  }
}
```

Improving Entity Framework with Complex Business Scenarios

4. We will then add our mapping for `Blog` and `Post` to the `DataAccess` project as new C# classes with the following code:

```csharp
using System.ComponentModel.DataAnnotations;
using System.Data.Entity.ModelConfiguration;
using BusinessLogic;

namespace DataAccess.Mappings
{
  public class BlogMapping : EntityTypeConfiguration<Blog>
  {
    public BlogMapping()
    {
      this.ToTable("Blogs");
      this.HasKey(x => x.Id);

      this.Property(x => x.Id).HasDatabaseGeneratedOption
         (DatabaseGeneratedOption.Identity)
         .HasColumnName("BlogId");

      this.Property(x => x.Title).IsRequired().HasMaxLength(250);

      this.Property(x => x.Created)
         .HasColumnName("CreationDate").IsRequired();

      this.Property(x => x.ShortDescription).HasColumnType("Text")
         .IsMaxLength().IsOptional().HasColumnName("Description");

      this.HasMany(x => x.Posts).WithRequired();
    }

  }

  public class PostMapping : EntityTypeConfiguration<Post>
  {
    public PostMapping()
    {
      this.ToTable("Posts");
      this.HasKey(x => x.Id);

      this.Property(x => x.Id).HasDatabaseGeneratedOption(
         DatabaseGeneratedOption.Identity).HasColumnName("PostId");

      this.Property(x => x.Title).IsRequired().HasMaxLength(250);
```

```
            this.Property(x => x.Content).IsRequired()
              .HasMaxLength(5000);

        }
      }
    }
```

5. We now want to add a new interface to the `BusinessLogic` project named `IDbContext` with the following code:

```
using System;
using System.Linq;

namespace BusinessLogic.Interfaces
{
  public interface IDbContext : IDisposable
  {
    IQueryable<T> AsQueryable<T>() where T : class;
    T Add<T>(T item) where T : class;
    T Remove<T>(T item) where T : class;
    T Update<T>(T item) where T : class;
    T Attach<T>(T item) where T : class;
    T Detach<T>(T item) where T : class;
    int SaveChanges();
  }
}
```

6. We then want to modify the `BlogContext` to use the mappings, and implement the `IDbContext` interface with the following code:

```
public class BlogContext : BaseDbContext, IDbContext
  {
    static BlogContext()
    {
      System.Data.Entity.Database.SetInitializer(new
        Initializer());
    }

    public BlogContext(string connection) : base(connection) { }

    protected override void
      OnModelCreating(DbModelBuilder modelBuilder)
    {
      modelBuilder.Configurations.Add(new BlogMapping());
      modelBuilder.Configurations.Add(new PostMapping());
      base.OnModelCreating(modelBuilder);
```

```csharp
        }
    }

    public class BaseDbContext : DbContext
    {
        protected BaseDbContext(string connection) : base(connection)
        {

        }

        public override int SaveChanges()
        {
            var auditableCreates =this.ChangeTracker.Entries()
                .Where(x => x.State == EntityState.Added
                && x.Entity is AuditableEntity);

            foreach (var item in auditableCreates
                .Select(auditableCreate => auditableCreate
                .Entity as AuditableEntity))
            {
                item.Created = item.Modified = DateTime.Now;
                item.CreatedBy = item.ModifiedBy = "UserName";
            }

            var auditableModifies = this.ChangeTracker.
                Entries().Where(x => x.State == EntityState.Modified
                && x.Entity is AuditableEntity);

            foreach (var item in auditableModifies.Select
                (auditableModify => auditableModify.Entity as
                AuditableEntity))
            {
                item.Modified = DateTime.Now;
                item.ModifiedBy = "UserName";
            }
            return base.SaveChanges();
        }

        public IQueryable<T> AsQueryable<T>() where T : class
        {
            return this.Set<T>();
        }

        public T Add<T>(T item) where T : class
        {
```

```
      this.Set<T>().Add(item);
      return item;
    }

    public T Remove<T>(T item) where T : class
    {
      this.Set<T>().Remove(item);
      return item;
    }

    public T Update<T>(T item) where T : class
    {
      var entry = this.Entry(item);

      if (entry != null)
      {
        entry.CurrentValues.SetValues(item);
      }
      else
      {
        this.Attach(item);
      }

      return item;
    }

    public T Attach<T>(T item) where T : class
    {
      this.Set<T>().Attach(item);
      return item;
    }

    public T Detach<T>(T item) where T : class
    {
      this.Entry(item).State = EntityState.Detached;
      return item;
    }
  }
}
```

7. We now want to create the interfaces for the query specifications and the related objects, with the following interfaces:

```
using System.Collections.Generic;

namespace BusinessLogic.Interfaces
{
  public interface IQueryObject
  {
    int Execute(IDbContext context);
  }

  public interface ICommandObject
  {
    void Execute(IDbContext context);
  }

  public interface IScalarObject<out T>
  {
    T Execute(IDbContext context);
  }

  public interface IQueryObject<out T>
  {
    IEnumerable<T> Execute(IDbContext context);
  }
}
```

8. Now, we want to create the classes that implement these interfaces in the `BusinessLogic` project with the following code:

```
using System;
using System.Collections.Generic;
using System.Collections.ObjectModel;
using System.Linq;
using System.Linq.Expressions;
using System.Reflection;
using BusinessLogic.Interfaces;

namespace BusinessLogic.Domain
{
  public class QueryObject : IQueryObject
  {
    public Func<IDbContext, int> ContextQuery { get; set; }

    protected void CheckContextAndQuery(IDbContext context)
```

```csharp
        {
          if (context == null) throw new
            ArgumentNullException("context");

          if (this.ContextQuery == null) throw new
            InvalidOperationException("Null Query
            cannot be executed.");

        }

        #region IQueryObject<T> Members

        public virtual int Execute(IDbContext context)
        {
          CheckContextAndQuery(context);
         return this.ContextQuery(context);
        }

        #endregion
    }

    public abstract class QueryObjectBase<T> : IQueryObject<T>
    {
      //if this func returns IQueryable then we can add
      //functionaltly, such as Where, OrderBy, Take, and so on, to
      //the QueryOjbect and inject that into the expression before
      //is it is executed
      protected Func<IDbContext, IQueryable<T>>
          ContextQuery { get; set; }
      protected IDbContext Context { get; set; }

      protected void CheckContextAndQuery()
      {
        if (Context == null) throw new InvalidOperationException
          ("Context cannot be null.");

        if (this.ContextQuery == null) throw new
          InvalidOperationException("Null Query
          cannot be executed.");
      }

      protected virtual IQueryable<T> ExtendQuery()
      {
        return this.ContextQuery(Context);
      }
```

```csharp
    #region IQueryObject<T> Members

    public virtual IEnumerable<T> Execute(IDbContext context)
    {
      Context = context;
      CheckContextAndQuery();
      var query = this.ExtendQuery();
      return query.AsEnumerable() ?? Enumerable.Empty<T>();
    }

    #endregion
}

public class QueryObject<T> : QueryObjectBase<T>
{
  protected override IQueryable<T> ExtendQuery()
  {
    var source = base.ExtendQuery();
    source = this.AppendExpressions(source);
    return source;
  }

  public IQueryObject<T> Take(int count)
  {
    var generics = new Type[] { typeof(T) };
    var parameters = new Expression[] {
      Expression.Constant(count) };

    this.AddMethodExpression("Take", generics, parameters);
    return this;
  }

  public IQueryObject<T> Skip(int count)
  {
    var generics = new Type[] { typeof(T) };
    var parameters = new Expression[] {
      Expression.Constant(count) };

    this.AddMethodExpression("Skip", generics, parameters);
    return this;
  }

  #region Helper methods
```

```csharp
    static ReadOnlyCollection<MethodInfo> QueryableMethods;
    static QueryObject()
    {
      QueryableMethods = new ReadOnlyCollection<MethodInfo>
        (typeof(System.Linq.Queryable)
        .GetMethods(BindingFlags.Public |
        BindingFlags.Static).ToList());
    }

    List<Tuple<MethodInfo, Expression[]>> _expressionList = new
      List<Tuple<MethodInfo, Expression[]>>();

    private void AddMethodExpression(string methodName, Type[]
      generics, Expression[] parameters)
    {
      MethodInfo orderMethodInfo = QueryableMethods
        .Where(m => m.Name == methodName &&
        m.GetParameters().Length ==
        parameters.Length + 1).First();

      orderMethodInfo = orderMethodInfo
        .MakeGenericMethod(generics);

      _expressionList.Add(new Tuple<MethodInfo,
        Expression[]>(orderMethodInfo, parameters));
    }

    private IQueryable<T> AppendExpressions(IQueryable<T> query)
    {
      var source = query;
      foreach (var exp in _expressionList)
      {
        var newParams = exp.Item2.ToList();
        newParams.Insert(0, source.Expression);
        source = source.Provider.CreateQuery<T>
          (Expression.Call(null, exp.Item1, newParams));
      }
      return source;
    }
    #endregion

}

public class ScalarObject<T> : IScalarObject<T>
{
```

```csharp
    public Func<IDbContext, T> ContextQuery { get; set; }

    protected void CheckContextAndQuery(IDbContext context)
    {
      if (context == null) throw new
        ArgumentNullException("context");

      if (this.ContextQuery == null) throw new
        InvalidOperationException("Null Query
        cannot be executed.");
    }

    #region IQueryObject<T> Members

    public virtual T Execute(IDbContext context)
    {
      CheckContextAndQuery(context);
      return this.ContextQuery(context);
    }

    #endregion
  }
}
```

9. We now want to modify the `IRepository` interface to accept the query objects on `Find` with the following code:

```csharp
using System.Collections.Generic;

namespace BusinessLogic.Interfaces
{
  public interface IRepository
  {
    T Find<T>(IScalarObject<T> query);
    IEnumerable<T> Find<T>(IQueryObject<T> query);
    T Add<T>(T item) where T: class;
    T Remove<T>(T item) where T : class;
    T Update<T>(T item) where T : class;
    T Attach<T>(T item) where T : class;
    T Detach<T>(T item) where T : class;
     void SaveChanges();
  }
}
```

10. We then modify the `BlogRepository` to implement this interface with the following code:

```
using System;
using System.Collections.Generic;
using System.Data.Entity;
using System.Linq;
using BusinessLogic;
using BusinessLogic.Interfaces;

namespace DataAccess
{
  public class BlogRepository : IRepository, IDisposable
  {
    private readonly IDbContext _context;

    public BlogRepository(IDbContext context)
    {
      _context = context;
    }

    public T Detach<T>(T item) where T : class
    {
      return _context.Detach(item);
    }

    public void SaveChanges()
    {
      _context.SaveChanges();
    }

    public void Dispose()
    {

    }

    public T Find<T>(IScalarObject<T> query)
    {
      return query.Execute(_context);
    }

    public IEnumerable<T> Find<T>(IQueryObject<T> query)
    {
      return query.Execute(_context);
    }
```

```csharp
      public T Add<T>(T entity) where T : class
      {
        return _context.Add(entity);
      }

      public T Remove<T>(T entity) where T : class
      {
        return _context.Remove(entity);
      }

      public T Update<T>(T item) where T : class
      {
        throw new NotImplementedException();
      }

      public T Attach<T>(T item) where T : class
      {
        throw new NotImplementedException();
      }
    }
  }
```

11. The last step is to modify the `HomeController` to supply the correct data to the view with the following code:

```csharp
using System.Web.Mvc;
using BusinessLogic.Interfaces;
using DataAccess.Queries;

namespace UI.Controllers
{
  public class HomeController : Controller
  {
    private readonly IRepository _repository;

    public HomeController(IRepository repo)
    {
      _repository = repo;
    }

    public ActionResult Index()
    {
      var blog = _repository.Find(new BlogByTitleQuery("Test"));
      return View(blog);
    }
```

Chapter 8

```
      public ActionResult About()
      {
        return View();
      }
    }
  }
}
```

12. All of our tests pass.

How it works...

We start with a set of tests, one to define the behavior we want from our controller, and the other to define the behavior we want from the repository. The controller should send a query to the repository but have no control over how the predefined query is executed, and the repository should execute the query with no knowledge of what is in it. This gives us clear lines of separation, and allows us to plug in new queries at will.

We then need to define our object graph, in this case, a `Blog` with many `Post` objects. These are mapped conventionally to focus our attention on the problem domain.

We then add our interface to the `DbContext` that will allow interaction with the database in an abstract fashion. We implement this interface on the `DbContext`, and abstract the reusable chunks into a base repository that will allow us to reuse this behavior at will.

We then define the `IQueryObject`, `ICommandObject`, `IScalarObject`, `IQueryObject<out T>` interfaces to our `Query` objects. This will give us a contract definition that can be implemented for new queries. The objects that implement this will store the query and a function on `IDbContext` to give us a deferred execution and compose-ability. These interfaces will also give some extension points, through the `Extend` query, which will allow us to implement behaviors such as paging or ordering.

We define the repository interface to accept the query objects as parameters for the `Find` methods. The implementation of these `Find` methods invoke the `execute` method of the query, and pass in the `DbContext`. This gives the repository a layer of separation from the implementation of queries, and keeps the repository interface simple and incredibly powerful.

There's more...

This leverages the specification pattern, expression trees, and strategy pattern that are well worth understanding and we are using them extensively.

Specification pattern

The **specification pattern** is a pattern that allows the business rules, or, in our case, queries to be chained together and reused by simply adhering to a standard contract. We specified that all `Query` objects had to have an `execute` method that is overrideable and is a `ContextQuery`. This allows us to chain them together and define ever more complex query paths without sacrificing the elegance and simplicity of the solution.

Expression trees

Expression trees are a data representation of code, and are traversable as such. They allow us to build large and complex code chunks, store them until needed, and supply the parameters required for them to be compiled and executed. This gives us a fairly flexible framework for defining queries and database interactions without needing to focus on when the call will be made.

Strategy pattern

The **Strategy pattern** simply allows the functionality being executed to vary without the code exercising it being changed. This is to say that we pass in new derived types with new `ContextQueries`, without the code that uses it ever having to know that is is dealing with a different object. No `if` statements, no `switch` statements, just exercising the behavior we have pre-loaded.

See also

Chapter 5, Improving Entity Framework with Query Libraries:

- *Increasing Performance with Code Access*

Index

A

ACID principles
   Atomic 148
   Consistent 148
   Durability 148
   Isolation 148
Act 14
Application Programming Interface (API) 10, 46
Arrange 14
AsQueryable method 226, 226
AsQueryable() method 201
Assert 14
atomic execution 261
AuditableEntity 313
audit data
   capturing 308-312
   working 313
AuthorDetailValidatorAttribute 119

B

behavior 46
BlogContext class 173
blog entity 9
BlogMapping class 157, 172, 179, 180, 193, 209
BlogQueries class 181
BusinessLogic project 172, 179

C

caching 18
call per change, unit of work pattern 27
change tracker 313
chess
   URL 294
Client wins concurrency conflict resolution 275
code
   databases, creating from 33-36
Code First 131
code-first approach
   used, for improving Entity Framework 7-9
collection properties
   validating 109-114
collection properties validation
   internal structure, validating 115
   reusability, limiting 115
   working 115
column mapping 159
complex key maps
   handling 87-91
complex properties
   validating 102-107
complex properties validation
   about 108
   all at once validation, performing 108
   base class logic, reusing 108
   working 108
complex query scenarios
   complex where clauses, improving 233-240
   dynamic sorting, improving 203-218
   explicit loading, handling 227-231
   improving 203
   runtime, grouping without Lambda 220-225
   specification pattern, implementing 242-252
complex where clauses
   improving 233-241
   working 241

componentization 226
compose-able LINQ 241
composed queries
  implementing 183-189
  working 189
ConcurrencyTests 256
ConsoleApp project 182
content validation 93
ControllerTests 314
convention, over configuration 10
cost of architecture 198
created by field 313
created date field 313
custom property validation
  complexity, avoiding 122
  coupling 122
  creating 116-121
  working 122

D

DataAccess project 172, 174
DataBase Administrators (DBAs) 28
database-first approach 6
databases
  configuring 36
  creating 36
  creating, from code 33-36
  load testing, performing against 40-44
data race conditions 294
data retrieval
  Client wins concurrency conflict resolution 275
  custom determined 275
  handling, in highly-threaded environments 268-273
  Store Wins concurrency conflict resolution 275
  working 274
Data Transfer Object (DTO) 159
DbContext 329
DbEntityEntry 308
deferred execution 219
dependency inversion principle 18
developer discipline 198
Display method 8
DRY principle 190

dynamic sorting
  deferred execution 219
  encapsulation 219
  expression trees 219
  functioning 218
  improving 203-217

E

eager load
  versus lazy load 58
entities
  retrieving, with stored procedures 154-158
  updating, with stored procedures 160-166
entity and library reuse
  improving 175-182
Entity Framework
  about 6, 46
  audit data, capturing 308-312
  collection properties, validating 109-114
  complex properties, validating 102-107
  complex query scenarios, improving 203
  composed queries, implementing 183-189
  content validation 93
  convention, over configuration 10
  custom property validation, creating 116-121
  databases, creating from code 33-36
  data retrieval, handling in highly-threaded environments 268-274
  DbEntityEntry 308
  entities, retrieving with stored procedures 154-158
  entities, updating with stored procedures 160-166
  entity and library reuse, improving 175-182
  EntityKey 308
  EntityState 307
  improving, code-first approach used 7-9
  load testing, performing against database 40-44
  mock database connections, creating 11-13
  multiple context performance, improving 284-293
  multiple context transactions, handling 142-147
  MVC 3 applications, improving 314-328

MVC UI, improving with entity framework validation 123-130
objects, attaching with unit of work 276-283
optimistic concurrency, implementing 256-260
parallel contexts, managing 262-267
performance, increasing with code access 191-196
queries, testing 28, 31
queries, testing for performance 37-39
query testing, improving 198-201
refreshing data on save, implementing 303-306
repository pattern, implementing 15-18
reusable queries, creating 170-174
simple properties, validating 94-99
soft delete, handling 296-301
stored procedures, executing 148-153
structure validation 93
transaction scopes, using 134-139
unit of work pattern, implementing 19-26

Entity Framework 4.1 assemblies
installing 7

Entity Framework Code First Power Toys 52

Entity framework interceptors 303

Entity Framework profiler 32

EntityKey 308

EntityState 307

explicit loading
functioning 232
handling 227-231

expression of function 233

expression trees 219, 330

extension methods 175

F

Fluent Configuration API
complex key maps, handling 87-91
HasColumnOrder() 51
HasForeignKey() 63
HasOptional() 57
inheritance handling, based on database values 81-86
IsConcurrencyToken() 51
IsUnicode() 51
many-to-many maps, creating 64-70

Map() 57, 63, 70
multiple tables, mapping to single object 76-80
one-to-many maps, creating 58-63
one-to-one maps, creating 52-57
property maps, improving 46-51
single table, mapping to multiple objects 71-75
ToTable(tableName,schemaName) 51
WithOptional() 63
WithRequiredDependant() 57
WithRequiredPrinciple() 57

G

grouped sets of data
composing, into queryable set 220-225

H

HasColumnlOrder() method 91
HasColumnType() method 51
HasDatabaseGeneratedOption() method 50
HasKey() method 50, 91
HasMany() method 62, 70
HasMaxLength method 51
HasRequired() method 57
HomeController 328
Html helper 131

I

IBlogRepository 194
ICommandObject 329
IDbContext 319
IEnumerable 202
Include() method 58
inheritance
handling, based on database values 81-86
InMemoryRepository class 182
integration tests 14
IntelliTrace 32
interface segregation principle 27
InternalBlogContext class 196
IQueryable<T> 202
IQueryObject 329
IQueryObject<out T> 329

IRepository interface 27
IScalarObject 329
IsConcurrencyToken(true) method 261
IsMaxLength() method 51
isolation 261
IsOptional method 51
IUnitOfWork interface 27

L

Lambda statements 232
lazy load
   versus eager load 58
LINQ aggregate 232
LINQ statement 28
load testing
   performing, against database 40-44
locking 268

M

Manual tracing 32
many-to-many maps
   creating 64-70
Map() method 80
mapping storage 51
Microsoft ASP.NET 10
mock database connections
   creating 11-13
   one object, under test 13
mocking 18
mocks 18
Model-View-Controller (MVC) 10
modified by field 313
ModifiedDate 261
modified date field 313
multiple context performance
   improving 284-293
multiple context transactions
   ACID principles 148
   handling 142-146
   working 147
multiple objects
   single table, mapping to 71-75
multiple tables
   mapping, to single object 76-80
MVC 3 applications
   improving 314-328

working 329
MVC 3 Framework 10
MVC UI
   improving, with entity framework validation 123-130
   working 131

N

naming conflict 175
NuGet 183
NuGet package manager
   about 7, 47, 170
   URL 170

O

object graphs 57
Object Relational Mappers (ORMs) 46, 190
objects
   about 46
   attaching, with unit of work 276-283
   detaching 284
   related objects, attaching 284
one-to-many maps
   creating 58-63
one-to-one maps
   creating 52-57
optimistic concurrency
   implementing 256-260
   working 260
OrderByParameter 217

P

parallel contexts
   locking 268
   managing 262-266
   race conditions 267
   working 267
payload
   on many-to-many relationships 70
performance
   increasing, code access used 191-197
   queries, testing for 37-39
performance testing
   need for 39
POCOs (Plain Old CLR Objects) 6, 52

Properties() method 80
property maps
  improving 46-51

Q

queries
  testing 28, 31
  testing, for performance 37-39
query execution plan 32
query performance 32
query testing
  improving 198-201
QueryTests 199

R

race conditions 267
Razor view engine 10
real-world simulation 44
record 46
refactor, unit of work pattern 27
refreshing data on save solution
  implementing 303-306
  working 307
repository 18
repository pattern
  about 14
  dependency inversion principle 18
  implementing 15-18
reusable queries
  creating 170-174
RhinoMocks 13

S

SaveChange method 307
SaveChanges method 313
schema and contract 183
shared primary key association 76
ShortDescription property 51
simple properties
  configuration and attributes, deciding between 101
  validating 94-99
simple properties validation
  delaying 101
  error messages, displaying 101
  sharing 101
  working 100
single object
  multiple tables, mapping to 76-80
single responsibility principle 10, 190
single table
  mapping, to multiple objects 71-75
soft delete
  handling 296-301
  working 302
soft delete pattern 303
SortingTests 204
specification pattern
  about 253, 330
  implementing 242-252
  working 252
SQL 32
SQL statements 28
state 46
stored procedures
  about 148
  abstract usage 168
  access rules 154
  executing 148-153
  return type mapping, handling 154
  states, changing manually 168
  working 153, 159
stored procedure support
  extensions 168
Store Wins concurrency conflict resolution 275
strategy pattern 330
stress testing 44
structure validation 93
System.Linq.Dynamic 226

T

table 46
table per concrete type 86
table per hierarchy pattern 86
table per type pattern 86
TestObject data 204
thread interleaving 293
Title property 51
ToTable() method 50, 80

transaction scopes
   controlling 141
   read/update separation, ensuring 141
   triggering 141
   using 134-139
   working 140

U

unified field theory 46
unit of work pattern
   call per change 27
   implementing 19-26
   interface segregation principle 27
   refactor 27
unit test 13

V

ValidationTests 116

W

where constraint 19
WillCascadeOnDelete() method 57, 63
WithMany() method 70
WithOptional() method 57
WithRequired() method 63

[PACKT] enterprise
PUBLISHING
professional expertise distilled

Thank you for buying
Entity Framework 4.1: Expert's Cookbook

About Packt Publishing

Packt, pronounced 'packed', published its first book "*Mastering phpMyAdmin for Effective MySQL Management*" in April 2004 and subsequently continued to specialize in publishing highly focused books on specific technologies and solutions.

Our books and publications share the experiences of your fellow IT professionals in adapting and customizing today's systems, applications, and frameworks. Our solution-based books give you the knowledge and power to customize the software and technologies you're using to get the job done. Packt books are more specific and less general than the IT books you have seen in the past. Our unique business model allows us to bring you more focused information, giving you more of what you need to know, and less of what you don't.

Packt is a modern, yet unique publishing company, which focuses on producing quality, cutting-edge books for communities of developers, administrators, and newbies alike. For more information, please visit our website: www.PacktPub.com.

About Packt Enterprise

In 2010, Packt launched two new brands, Packt Enterprise and Packt Open Source, in order to continue its focus on specialization. This book is part of the Packt Enterprise brand, home to books published on enterprise software – software created by major vendors, including (but not limited to) IBM, Microsoft and Oracle, often for use in other corporations. Its titles will offer information relevant to a range of users of this software, including administrators, developers, architects, and end users.

Writing for Packt

We welcome all inquiries from people who are interested in authoring. Book proposals should be sent to author@packtpub.com. If your book idea is still at an early stage and you would like to discuss it first before writing a formal book proposal, contact us; one of our commissioning editors will get in touch with you.

We're not just looking for published authors; if you have strong technical skills but no writing experience, our experienced editors can help you develop a writing career, or simply get some additional reward for your expertise.

MVVM Survival Guide for Enterprise Architectures in Silverlight and WPF

ISBN: 978-1-84968-342-5 Paperback: 412 pages

Eliminate unnecessary code by taking advantage of the MVVM pattern—less code means less bugs

1. Build an enterprise application using Silverlight and WPF, taking advantage of the powerful MVVM pattern
2. Discover the evolution of presentation patterns—by example—and see the benefits of MVVM in the context of the larger picture of presentation patterns
3. Customize the MVVM pattern for your projects' needs by comparing the various implementation styles

WCF 4.0 Multi-tier Services Development with LINQ to Entities

ISBN: 978-1-849681-14-8 Paperback: 348 pages

Build SOA applications on the Microsoft platform with this hands-on guide updated for VS2010

1. Master WCF and LINQ to Entities concepts by completing practical examples and applying them to your real-world assignments
2. The first and only book to combine WCF and LINQ to Entities in a multi-tier real-world WCF service
3. Ideal for beginners who want to build scalable, powerful, easy-to-maintain WCF services

Please check www.PacktPub.com for information on our titles

Managing Data and Media in Silverlight 4: A mashup of chapters from Packt's bestselling Silverlight books

ISBN: 978-1-84968-564-1   Paperback: 530 pages

Manage data in Silverlight, build and maintain rich dashboards, integrate SharePoint with Silverlight, and more

1. A mashup book from expert Silverlight professionals, from 6 Packt donor titles - professional expertise distilled in a true sense starting at just $19.99

2. Packed with practical, hands-on examples, illustrating techniques to solve particular data problems effectively within your Silverlight business applications

3. Manage data in Silverlight, build and maintain rich dashboards, integrate Sharepoint with Silverlight and more

Entity Framework Tutorial

ISBN: 978-1-847195-22-7   Paperback: 228 pages

Learn to build a better data access layer with the ADO. NET Entity Framework and ADO.NET Data Services

1. Clear and concise guide to the ADO.NET Entity Framework with plentiful code examples

2. Create Entity Data Models from your database and use them in your applications

3. Learn about the Entity Client data provider and create statements in Entity SQL

4. Learn about ADO.NET Data Services and how they work with the Entity Framework

Please check **www.PacktPub.com** for information on our titles

Made in the USA
Lexington, KY
29 June 2012